Clear Grammar 2

2nd Edition

Clear Grammar 2

2nd Edition

Keys to Grammar for English Language Learners

Keith S. Folse

Ann Arbor
University of Michigan Press

Thanks to the readers and contributors of exercises—Elan Azuz, Robert Bushong, Melanie Gonzalez, Ekaterina Goussakova, Laura Monroe, Shawn Pollgreen, and Alison Youngblood. Contributions from Dorothy Zemach are acknowledged.

I am also grateful to graduate students who gave suggestions that improved this text: Devon Bazata, Abdelhay Belfakir, Jean Bubriski, Bruno Castagnetto, Brandon Harris, Stephanie Lancaster, Natalia Reilly, Monica Sebastiani, and Robyn Socha.

ISBN-13: 978-0-472-03242-6

2015   2014   2013   4   3   2

Contents

To the Teacher

The purpose of a grammar book for English language learners (ELLs) is to help our students acquire the patterns of English. Simply put, grammar is nothing more than patterns. Some of these patterns are relatively easy (e.g., adjectives precede nouns), while others are more difficult (e.g., prepositions or articles). To help our students acquire these patterns, the four books in the *Clear Grammar* series feature a unique combination of useful grammar information written in simple language with activities that promote more accurate and fluent writing, speaking, reading, and vocabulary.

Clear Grammar 2 offers students and teachers solid presentations of grammar information and useful practice activities for lower-intermediate students. It is part of a four-volume series of grammar books for all levels of students of English as a second or foreign language. Book 2 covers grammar points for lower-intermediate non-native speakers of English, including articles, irregular past tense verbs, present perfect tense, and modals.

Clear Grammar 1 begins the series with basic grammar points, such as simple present and simple past tenses, count and non-count nouns, and prepositions. *Clear Grammar 3* continues with grammar points such as present perfect, infinitives vs. gerunds, and relative clauses. *Clear Grammar 4* concludes the series with advanced topics such as reductions of clauses, past modals, and the past perfect.

Clear Grammar 2 contains exercises that provide relevant practice in basic grammar points for ELLs at the lower-intermediate level. It assumes that students have knowledge of basic English grammar, including simple sentence structure and verb tenses (simple present, simple past, and present progressive). It is designed to be used by adult learners—high school age and up. It is suitable for either intensive or non-intensive programs.

Important features of all four new editions of *Clear Grammar* include:

1. clear grammar explanations with user-friendly charts
2. a grammar discovery task using students' inductive learning skills
3. a large number of activities (more than 235 in this book), as well as a wide variety of activities (fill in the blank, sentence completion, scrambled sentences, matching, error ID, editing, original writing, reading, and vocabulary)
4. many more grammar activities at the longer discourse level
5. corpus-informed vocabulary items connected to a unit's target grammar
6. reading skills: each unit includes a critical reading activity and a sentence-reading exercise in which the target grammar is featured
7. writing skills: each unit concludes with two writing activities, one on editing student writing and the other for original student writing
8. vocabulary quizzes: each unit includes at least two vocabulary reviews, one of which focuses on collocations
9. communication skills: each unit includes one to five speaking activities that require students to speak and listen to each other while using the target grammar
10. online extra practice activities that are indicated within each unit

The books in the *Clear Grammar* series have eight main goals:

1. to teach the basic grammar points necessary for ELL students
2. to expose students to a substantial amount of useful, high-frequency, corpus-informed vocabulary that is related to the grammar point being studied, including words, phrases, and idioms
3. to provide ample written practice in these structures at the multi-sentence and dialogue levels
4. to provide practice at varying cognitive levels (i.e., not just rote grammar knowledge and comprehension but also synthesis and evaluation)
5. to engage ELLs through a variety of activities and games
6. to improve students' writing, speaking, reading, and listening
7. to provide ample opportunities for students to check their progress while studying these structures
8. to serve as a grammar reference that is written with language and terms that an ELL at the lower-intermediate level can understand without teacher assistance

The units may be done in any order. However, it is recommended that the general sequencing of the units be followed whenever possible. An attempt has been made to recycle material from one unit into following units where appropriate. For example, once past tense for irregular verbs has been covered, many of the sentences in subsequent exercises in other units include irregular past tense for further reinforcement.

Although a great deal of variety of material exists in the book, there is a general pattern within each unit.

If you see a key in the right margin in a grammar lesson, it means that this grammar point is featured as one of the 15 keys in *Keys to Teaching Grammar to English Language Learners* by Keith Folse (2009).

Unit Organization

1. **Discover Grammar Task**. In many grammar classes, the teacher simply presents the grammar lesson to the students. Another effective technique is to involve the students in a grammar discovery task that begins each unit.

   Students work together to read a short passage or conversation of one to two paragraphs that are rich in examples of the target grammar and then answer a series of questions about the structures in the text. These questions focus on grammar and meaning.

   Students may or may not be able to actually figure out the grammar issue, but this creates a teachable moment in response to the learners' need to know. Your goal is to pique the students' curiosity about the lesson's grammar. After completing the task in their books, students should discuss their answers as a class before beginning the actual lesson. Some students are better able to remember information that they themselves have worked with, so involving students in this kind of discovery task may ultimately benefit their learning.

2. **Grammar Presentation Charts.** Simple, easy-to-follow charts explain the target grammar, which often features corpus-based vocabulary connected to the grammar point.

3. **List of Potential Errors with Corrections.** This section of the unit includes a list of several of the most common errors made by learners. Following each error is the corrected form so that students can see not only what they should avoid but how it should be corrected. Our students represent a wide range of linguistic groups, and every effort has been made to take this into account in selecting which kinds of errors to include here.

4. **Written (as opposed to Speaking) Exercises.** Teachers and students want a large number of written exercises to allow for ample practice of the newly learned structure. The exercises have been sequenced so that the early exercises require only passive knowledge of the grammar point. For example, students circle one of two answers or put a check mark by the correct word. These exercises are followed by others that are more cognitively demanding and require active production of the language structure. In this way, students can comfortably move from passive knowledge to active production of a structure.

   The written exercises in this book are short enough to be done in a small amount of time, yet they are thorough enough to provide sufficient practice for the structure in question. These exercises may be done in class or as homework. Furthermore, they may be checked quickly either by individual students or by the class.

5. **Grammar at the Discourse Level.** As often as possible, the written exercises in this book consist of connected sentences related to a single topic, with the title of the material indicated just before the grammar activity. This connected discourse helps ELLs improve their overall English fluency while focusing on the target grammar items.

6. **Extra Online Practice.** After students have practiced a structure, they are directed to do corresponding interactive activities on the website that accompanies this series (**www.press.umich.edu/esl/compsite/cleargrammar/**). Students record their scores for these activities in their books, which gives teachers who so desire an opportunity to see how students are doing on a particular grammar item.

7. **Mini-Conversations.** Instead of unconnected single-sentence exercises, this written exercise consists of dialogues that require students to recognize or use the target grammar in a broader context than single sentences.

8. **Editing.** Students need to become proficient at editing their own grammar. To that end, a special activity in each unit allows ELLs to be the judge of whether or not a given sentence does or does not contain an error with the target grammar items.

9. **Sentence Study for Critical Reading.** In this activity, students read a sentence that contains the target grammar and then must choose which of three sentences that follow are true based on the information in the original sentence. To improve critical-thinking skills, one, two, or all three of the statements may be true, so students must read all three and carefully consider their veracity.

10. **Speaking Exercises.** Each unit has at least one interactive speaking activity that provides an opportunity for students to practice the grammar and build fluency.

11. **Two Review Tests.** Equally as important as the teaching of a given grammar point is the measurement of the learning that has taken place. Near the end of every unit are two review tests. These review tests have various kinds of questions to assess learners' ability in different ways.

    Review Test 1 contains multiple choice questions. It is important to discuss not only why the correct answers are correct but also why the distractors are not correct. Review Test 2 is Production and Evaluation. Part 1 of this review test requires production of the grammar, usually through a fill-in-the-blank activity. Because editing grammar is such an important student skill, Part 2 requires students to edit material that contains typical ELL errors.

12. **Reading Practice.** This longer reading activity generally consists of 200–400 words of text followed by several comprehension questions. The target grammar has been underlined to reinforce students' knowledge and awareness of the grammar.

13. **Two Vocabulary Practices.** Grammar knowledge without expanding vocabulary knowledge is useless, so vocabulary must be practiced and learned. The units overtly present new vocabulary to help students increase their vocabulary as much as possible. To this end, two vocabulary practice activities help solidify students' knowledge of vocabulary.

    Word Knowledge features 25–35 key words from the unit and two answer options. Students should select the one word that is clearly related to the target vocabulary word.

    Collocations features 25–40 key phrases or word combinations that are used frequently. Here students choose the one word that best completes the phrase. Examples include *a* _____ *menu* with *sauce* and *special* as answer choices, and *in* _____ with *fact* and *menu*.

14. **Writing Practice.** The writing practice at the end of each unit has two parts. Part 1 provides additional editing practice as students must edit a student writing sample according to a list of errors that have been identified. These errors represent the most typical ELL errors for this proficiency level and grammar point. In Part 2, students are to write a short assignment based on something similar to the passage written for Part 1. Teachers may elect to have their students write sentences or paragraphs depending on the curriculum in their program.

15. **One-Minute Lesson Notes.** A unique feature of this series is the inclusion of numerous student notes, which appear as small shaded boxes throughout the chapters. These notes contain important information on an array of language areas, including grammar, vocabulary, pronunciation, capitalization, punctuation, and learning strategies, which teachers may discuss with the whole class or just point out to students for additional information.

Keys to Using This Book for Students

 Grammar Lesson

These charts have useful grammar information. Learn this information. If you do not understand something, ask your teacher.

 BE CAREFUL!

These mistakes are common. Do you make these same mistakes? Study these mistakes and the corrections very carefully.

 Editing Practice

Editing practice is offered in several places within a unit. This exercise practices the grammar by asking students to recognize errors.

 Connecting Grammar and Vocabulary

This symbol indicates a box explaining how vocabulary is tied to a specific grammar text. Content is based on corpus research.

 One-Minute Lesson

These boxes have important information about grammar, vocabulary, spelling, or language usage.

 Online Exercise

This symbol means that there is an extra practice activity online. Be sure to write your score in your book.

 Speaking Practice

Doing exercises on paper is not enough. In these conversations and speaking activities, you must try to use your new grammar as much as possible. Listen to other students' grammar.

 Review Tests

Each unit has two review tests. The first one has multiple choice questions, and the second has other kinds of questions.

 Reading Practice

As you do this practice, be sure to notice the underlined grammar examples in the reading.

 Vocabulary Practice

Grammar is important, but you need to have a large vocabulary. Pay careful attention to the two vocabulary practices.

 Writing Practice

Part 1 works on editing. You need to be able to write correctly, so this part is very useful. In Part 2, you can write original work.

Unit 1

Review of Verb Tenses

Discover the Grammar

An English teacher is talking about his job. Read his story, and then answer the seven questions.

Line	
1	My name is Rob Taylor, and I am an English teacher. I teach at Williams
2	Adult Learning Center. I got my Master's degree in teaching English in 2005,
3	and I have taught here since 2009. Before coming here, I taught in New York.
4	I like my current school, and I really like the students here.
5	Our students come from all over. Our three biggest countries are Mexico,
6	El Salvador, and Colombia, so many students in my classes speak Spanish. We
7	also have students from Asia, and most of those students speak Chinese or
8	Japanese. My students attend school five days a week. The first class starts at 9
9	AM, and the last class finishes at 2 PM. My
10	students study grammar, reading, writing,
11	vocabulary, and conversation.
12	The photo shows the students in my
13	Level 2 class. In this photo, they look serious
14	because they are taking their first big exam. No one is talking. Everyone is
15	trying to think of the correct answers. What great students!

16	Although I enjoy teaching at Williams Adult Learning Center, I am sorry to
17	say that this year is my last year here. Next year I am going to teach English in
18	Korea. Last week I signed a contract with a language school in Pusan, which is
19	the second largest city in Korea. I don't have all the details about my new job,
20	but I am going to talk to the director of the school tomorrow, and she is going
21	to explain more about my new job. I'm very excited about this new change in
22	my career.

1. Circle these verbs in Lines 1–3: *teach, have taught, taught.* Can you explain why three verb tenses are used here for the same verb (*teach*)?

   _____

   _____

   _____

   _____

2. Underline these verbs in Lines 6–9: *speak* (2 times), *attend, starts, finishes.* Can you explain why simple present tense is used here?

   _____

   _____

3. Look at the verbs in Lines 6–9. Why does *starts* (but not *speak* and *attend*) end in –*s*? Why does *finish* end in –*es* but *start* has only –*s*?

   _____

   _____

4. Underline these verbs in Lines 14–15: *are taking, is talking, is trying.* Can you explain why these verbs are in the present progressive tense, which consists of *is/are* + VERB + –*ing*?

   _____

   _____

5. Circle the verb *look* in Line 13. Other verbs in this paragraph use *is/are* and VERB + –*ing*. Why is *look* (not *are looking*) correct?

   _____

   _____

6. Look at the verbs in Lines 17–21. Can you explain the use of *going to* in *am going to teach*, *am going to talk*, and *is going to explain*?

_____

_____

7. Circle the verb *signed* in Line 18. Why does this verb end in *–ed*? Are these verbs possible here: *are signing*? *sign*? *are going to sign*? *have signed*? Why or why not?

_____

_____

 ## Grammar Lesson

Simple Present Tense of Verbs: Affirmative

I, you, we, they + VERB	*he, she, it* + VERB + *–s*
I get up at 7:30 AM.	She gets up at 6:45 AM.
I eat a big breakfast.	She eats a light breakfast.
I walk to work.	She walks to work.
I work from 8 to 4.	She works from 7:45 to 2.
I get home at 4:30.	She gets home at 2:30.

<u>Rule 1</u>. In the simple present tense, a verb has two forms: **VERB** or **VERB** + **–s.**

<u>Rule 2</u>. **VERB** is used with *I, you, we,* and *they.*

<u>Rule 3</u>. **VERB** + **–s** used with *he, she,* and *it.*

<u>Rule 4</u>. Use simple present tense for actions that are always true or that happen repeatedly. Common time expressions for simple present include *always, sometimes, never,* and *every* _____ (*every week*).

<u>Rule 5</u>. For verbs that end in **consonant** + **–y,** change the **–y** to **–i** and then add **–es:** *fly → flies* but *play → plays.*

<u>Rule 6</u>. For verbs that end in o, sh, ch, s, z, and x, add **–es:** *do → does.*

Other examples:

	work	eat	take	try	go	have
I	I work	I eat	I take	I try	I go	I have
you	you work	you eat	you take	you try	you go	you have
we	we work	we eat	we take	we try	we go	we have
they	they work	they eat	they take	they try	they go	they have
he	he works	he eats	he takes	he tries	he goes	he has
she	she works	she eats	she takes	she tries	she goes	she has
it	it works	it eats	it takes	it tries	it goes	it has

 BE CAREFUL!

Common Learner Errors	Explanation
1. Laura ~~cook~~ cooks scrambled eggs for breakfast every day.	Remember to use a VERB + –s when the subject is he, she, or it.
2. Canada ~~have~~ has two official languages.	The –s form of have is has.
3. My baby sister ~~crys~~ cries when she is hungry.	If a verb ends in consonant + –y, remember to change –y to –i and add –es. Do not change y to i if the letter before y is a vowel (a, e, i, o, u): s<u>ay</u>, says; enj<u>oy</u>, enjoys; b<u>uy</u>, buys.
4. Zeke always ~~dos~~ does the dishes after dinner.	Remember to add –es after o, sh, ch, s, x, and z.
5. Colin and Laura ~~cooks~~ cook scrambled eggs for breakfast every day.	Use only a VERB (no –s) when the subject is I, you, we, or they.
6. I ~~am walk~~ walk to school every day.	Do not use be with other verbs in simple present tense.

Simple Present Tense: Negative

Making a negative statement with verbs is easy. Study these two steps:		
Step 1	Check for a **verb** (not be).	Colombia and Brazil **have** kings. Colombia **has** a king.
Step 2	a. If the verb does not end in –s, put **do not** (OR **don't**) before the verb.	Colombia and Brazil **do not have** kings.
	b. If the verb ends in –s, remove the –s and put **does not** (OR **doesn't**) before the base (simple) verb. (The –s moves from the verb to the word **does**.)	Colombia **does not have** a king.

Other examples:

Affirmative	Negative
I have a car. We get off work at 6 PM. Pierre speaks French. The class lasts for four months.	I **do not** have a bicycle. We **don't** work after 6 PM. He **does not** speak Spanish. The class **does not** last for a year.

<u>Rule 1</u>. To make a negative statement with a verb, add **do not** OR **does not** before the base (simple) form of the verb.

<u>Rule 2</u>. It is also possible to use contractions for **do not** and **does not**: **don't, doesn't**.

 # BE CAREFUL!

Common Learner Errors	Explanation
1. The U.S. ~~no have~~ doesn't have 100 states.	Remember to use **don't** (do not) or **doesn't** (does not) with a verb (except *be*).
2. Nell and Vic ~~aren't eat~~ don't eat lunch together every day.	Do not use **am not, isn't,** or **aren't** with a verb. Use **don't** or **doesn't** only.
3. The coffee doesn't ~~smells~~ smell good to him.	If you use **does**, don't use –s with the verb. You need only one –s for **he/she/it**.

Simple Present Tense: Making a Question

Making a question with a verb (not *be*) is easy. Study these four steps:		
Step 1	Check for a **verb** (not **be**).	Colombia and Brazil **have** kings. Colombia **has** a king.
Step 2	Put **do** or **does** at the beginning of the sentence.	**do** Colombia and Brazil **have** kings. **does** Colombia **has** a king.
Step 3	Make sure the verb is in the base (simple) form.	do Colombia and Brazil **have** kings. does Colombia **have** a king.
Step 4	Use a capital letter for the first word of the question, and change the period (.) to a question mark (?).	**Do** Colombia and Brazil have kings? **Does** Colombia have a king?

Other examples:

Statement	Question
I **talk** fast. You **like** black coffee. We **have** two classes together They **live** on Green Street.	**Do** I **talk** fast? **Do** you **like** black coffee? **Do** we **have** two classes together? **Do** they **live** on Green Street?
He **takes** a bus to work. She **has** a new car. It **rains** a lot in the summer.	**Does** he **take** a bus to work? **Does** she **have** a new car? **Does** it **rain** a lot in the summer?

<u>Rule 1.</u> To make a question with a verb (not *be*), add **do OR does** before the subject.

<u>Rule 2.</u> Be sure to use only the base (simple) form of the verb.

 # BE CAREFUL!

Common Learner Errors	Explanation
1. ~~Are~~ **Do** you speak English?	Do not use **be** (**am, is, are**) with other verbs in simple present tense.
2. Does your car ~~has~~ **have** a good radio?	Do not put −s on the verb in *yes-no* questions. Use only the base (simple) form of the verb. For **he/she/it,** you need only one −s in the question. If you have **does**, the verb doesn't have −s.
3. ~~Do~~ **Does** China export wheat?	Remember to use **does** with **he/she/it.** Use **do** with other subjects.

EXERCISE 1. Simple Present Tense: Affirmative

Fill in the blanks with the correct forms of the verbs. Follow the examples.

speak	watch	do	try
I _speak_	I _____	I _____	I _____
you _speak_	you _____	you _____	you _____
he _speaks_	he _____	he _____	he _____
she _speaks_	she _____	she _____	she _____
it _speaks_	it _____	it _____	it _____
we _speak_	we _____	we _____	we _____
they _speak_	they _____	they _____	they _____
Jo _speaks_	Jo _____	Jo _____	Jo _____
Jo and I _speak_	Jo and I _____	Jo and I _____	Jo and I _____
you and I _speak_	you and I _____	you and I _____	you and I _____

take	play	have	be
I _____	I _____	I _____	I _____
you _____	you _____	you _____	you _____
he _____	he _____	he _____	he _____
she _____	she _____	she _____	she _____
it _____	it _____	it _____	it _____
we _____	we _____	we _____	we _____
they _____	they _____	they _____	they _____
Jo _____	Jo _____	Jo _____	Jo _____
Jo and I _____	Jo and I _____	Jo and I _____	Jo and I _____
you and I _____	you and I _____	you and I _____	you and I _____

Do Online Exercise 1.1. My score: ____ /10. ____ % correct.

EXERCISE 2. Simple Present Tense: Negative

Fill in the blanks with the correct negative forms of the verbs. Follow the examples. Use the short forms **don't** and **doesn't**.

like	go	study	do
I _don't like_	I _____	I _____	I _____
you _don't like_	you _____	you _____	you _____
he _doesn't like_	he _____	he _____	he _____
she _doesn't like_	she _____	she _____	she _____
it _doesn't like_	it _____	it _____	it _____
we _don't like_	we _____	we _____	we _____
they _don't like_	they _____	they _____	they _____
Jo _doesn't like_	Jo _____	Jo _____	Jo _____
Jo and Sue _don't like_	Jo and Sue _____	Jo and Sue _____	Jo and Sue _____

know	get	have	be
I _____	I _____	I _____	I _____
you _____	you _____	you _____	you _____
he _____	he _____	he _____	he _____
she _____	she _____	she _____	she _____
it _____	it _____	it _____	it _____
we _____	we _____	we _____	we _____
they _____	they _____	they _____	they _____
Jo _____	Jo _____	Jo _____	Jo _____
Jo and Sue _____	Jo and Sue _____	Jo and Sue _____	Jo and Sue _____

ONE-MINUTE LESSON

Do you do your homework at night? The word **do** occurs two times in this question. **The first do** is a helping verb, and **the second do** is the main verb. At the beginning of a yes-no question, **do** is a helping verb. The verb after the subject is the main verb. Do not be confused by a question that begins *Do you do . . . ?*

EXERCISE 3. Simple Present Tense: Questions

Fill in the blanks with the correct question forms of the verbs. Be sure to include the subjects. Follow the example.

have	do	work
I _Do I have . . . ?_	I _____	I _____
you _____	you _____	you _____
he _____	he _____	he _____
she _____	she _____	she _____
it _____	it _____	it _____
we _____	we _____	we _____
they _____	they _____	they _____
Jo _____	Jo _____	Jo _____
Jo and I _____	Jo and I _____	Jo and I _____
you and I _____	you and I _____	you and I _____

need	know	be
I _____	I _____	I _____
you _____	you _____	you _____
he _____	he _____	he _____
she _____	she _____	she _____
it _____	it _____	it _____
we _____	we _____	we _____
they _____	they _____	they _____
Jo _____	Jo _____	Jo _____
Jo and I _____	Jo and I _____	Jo and I _____
you and I _____	you and I _____	you and I _____

Do Online Exercise 1.2. My score: ____ /10. ____ % correct.

EXERCISE 4. Practicing Simple Present Tense in Context

Write the correct form of the verb on the line in the conversation. Remember to add **do** in negative and question forms.

Fun Hobbies

Max: (you, have) **❶** _____ any hobbies?

Ahmad: Yes, I (like) **❷** _____ sports, especially soccer. My friends and I (play) **❸** _____ soccer together every Saturday. What about you?

Max: Actually, I (like, not) **❹** _____ sports. My brother (play) **❺** _____ soccer almost every day, but I (prefer) **❻** _____ reading.

Ahmad: (you, read) **❼** _____ a lot?

Max: Yes. In fact, my entire family (read) **❽** _____ a lot.

Ahmad: What (you, like) **❾** _____ to read?

Max: I (love) **❿** _____ biographies, but my sister (like) **⓫** _____ fiction. She and I (compete) **⓬** _____ with each other. The faster reader (win) **⓭** _____! Honestly, I (win, not) **⓮** _____ most of the time.

Ahmad: Your competition (sound) **⓯** _____ like a sport.

ONE-MINUTE LESSON

The verb **like** is difficult for some students. If you use this verb, be sure to put a noun or pronoun after this verb. For example, we say *I* **like** *soccer* or *We* **like** *spaghetti*. Some students say *I* **like** or *We* **like**—without a noun or pronoun after. This is a common mistake.

EXERCISE 5. Practicing Simple Present Tense in a Paragraph

Circle the correct form of the verb.

TV in the United States

How much ❶ (do, does) Americans love watching TV? Approximately 99 percent of Americans ❷ (own, owns) at least one TV, and Americans ❸ (watch, watches) 250 billion hours of TV a year. The average American ❹ (watch, watches) nearly 5 hours of TV each day. The average American child ❺ (watch, watches) about 1,680 minutes of TV per week, or 1,500 hours per year. The same child ❻ (spend, spends) only about 900 hours in school a year. Over a 65-year lifetime, the number of hours of TV ❼ (total, totals) 9 years! Clearly, the average American ❽ (have, has) a serious love affair with TV.

Source: www.csun.edu/science/health/docs/tv&health.html

Grammar Lesson

Simple Past Tense of Regular Verbs: Affirmative

KEY
3

Past   *Now*   *Future*

All Subjects	VERB + –ed
I/you/he/she/it/we/they start**ed** at noon yesterday.	

Rule 1. In the simple past tense, a regular verb has one form: VERB + –ed.

Rule 2. Use simple past tense for actions that happened in the past and are completely finished. Common time expressions for simple past tense include *yesterday*, *last _____ (last week)*, and *_____ ago (two weeks ago)*.

Spelling Rule 3. For verbs that end in **consonant** + **–y**, change the –y to –i and then add –ed: *try → tried* and *worry → worried*. However, for verbs that end in vowel + –y, just add –ed: *stay → stayed* and *enjoy → enjoyed*.

Spelling Rule 4. For one-syllable verbs that end in **consonant + vowel + consonant** (c-v-c), double the final consonant: *stop* → *stopped* and *plan* → *planned*. However, do not double final letters for verbs that end in –*w* (*snowed*), –*x* (*taxed*), or –*y* (*played*).

Spelling Rule 5. For two-syllable verbs that end in **consonant + vowel + consonant** (c-v-c) with stress on the second syllable, double the final consonant: ocCUR → *occurred* and perMIT → *permitted*. However, if the stress is on the first syllable, just add –ed: HAPpen → *happened* and LISten → *listened*.

Other examples:

	want	**need**	**add**	**subtract**	**play**	**pass**
I, you, he, she, it, we, they	I wanted	you needed	he added	she subtracted	we played	they passed

 BE CAREFUL!

Common Learner Errors	**Explanation**
1. My great-grandparents ~~live~~ **lived** in Chicago long ago.	Remember to use simple past tense. Don't use **VERB** or **VERB + –s** for a past action.
2. Carlos ~~was worked~~ **worked** in Miami last month.	Do not use **was** or **were** with simple past tense.
3. Thomas Edison was a very clever man. ~~Invented~~ **He invented** the light bulb.	Use a subject with a simple past verb.
4. My baby sister ~~cryed~~ **cried** a lot last night.	Don't forget to change **y** to **i** and add –**ed**.
5. According to the radio report, two masked men ~~robed~~ **robbed** the bank about an hour ago.	If a verb ends in **consonant-vowel-consonant** (c-v-c), don't forget to double the consonant before adding –**ed**.

Grammar Lesson

Simple Past Tense of Irregular Verbs: Affirmative

do → **did**	make → **made**
eat → **ate**	see → **saw**
get → **got**	take → **took**

Rule 1. In the simple past tense, an irregular verb has one form, but it is difficult to predict the form. You have to memorize the correct form.

Rule 2. For irregular verbs, do not use –ed.

Rule 3. Use simple past tense for actions that happened in the past and are completely finished. Common time expressions for simple past tense include *yesterday, last _____ (last week)*, and *_____ ago (two weeks ago)*.

Connecting Grammar and Vocabulary

Many students make the mistake of studying long lists of irregular verbs, usually from big dictionaries on the Internet. Do not waste your time learning infrequent irregular verbs like *forsake* → *forsook* or *slay* → *slew*. Learn this list of 33 common irregular past tense verbs. (A longer list of 60 irregular verbs, which includes these 33, can be found in Appendix C.)

33 Frequently Used Irregular Past Tense Verbs					
Present	Past	Present	Past	Present	Past
1. begin	**began**	12. go	**went**	23. send	**sent**
2. bring	**brought**	13. have	**had**	24. sleep	**slept**
3. buy	**bought**	14. hear	**heard**	25. speak	**spoke**
4. choose	**chose**	15. leave	**left**	26. spend	**spent**
5. come	**came**	16. lose	**lost**	27. stand	**stood**
6. do	**did**	17. make	**made**	28. take	**took**
7. drink	**drank**	18. put	**put**	29. tell	**told**
8. eat	**ate**	19. read	**read**	30. think	**thought**
9. forget	**forgot**	20. say	**said**	31. understand	**understood**
10. get	**got**	21. see	**saw**	32. wake	**woke**
11. give	**gave**	22. sell	**sold**	33. write	**wrote**

Do Online Exercise 1.3. My score: _____ /10. _____ % correct.

BE CAREFUL!

Common Learner Errors	Explanation
1. My sister ~~goed~~ **went** to England last year.	Remember to use an irregular verb. Don't add –ed to an irregular verb.
2. Carlos ~~was took~~ **took** a trip to Miami last month.	Do not use **was** or **were** with simple past tense.
3. I got a bad grade on my math test. ~~Made~~ I **made** too many simple mistakes.	Use a subject with simple past irregular verbs.

Grammar Lesson

Simple Past Tense: Negative

Making a negative statement with regular and irregular verbs is easy. Study these two steps:

Step 1	Check for a **VERB** (not **be**).	The girl **wanted** the keys, so she **took** them.
Step 2	Put **did not** (OR **didn't**) before the base (simple) verb. (In regular verbs, the –ed moves from the verb to the word **did**.)	The girl **didn't want** the keys, so she **didn't take** them.

 ONE-MINUTE LESSON
When you talk about *tests*, be careful with **verbs** and **prepositions**: *We prepare for a test. We make 97 on a test* or *We get 97 on a test*. We can ask, *How did you do on your grammar test?* or *What did you make on your test?* or *What did you get on your test?*

Other examples:

Affirmative	Negative
I called John.	I **did not** call Sue.
We got off work at 6 PM.	We **didn't** get off work at 5 PM.
Pierre put on his watch.	Pierre **did not** put on his ring.
The class lasted for four months.	The class **didn't** last for a year.

<u>Rule 1.</u> To make a negative statement with a verb, add **did not** before the base (simple) form of the verb.

<u>Rule 2.</u> In informal English, it is possible to use a contraction for **did not: didn't.**

 BE CAREFUL!

Common Learner Errors	Explanation
1. Your cousin ~~no went~~ didn't go to the bank.	Remember to use **did not (didn't)** with the base form of the verb.
2. Nell and Vic ~~weren't like~~ didn't like the food at the party very much.	Do not use **was not (wasn't)** or **were not (weren't)** with the **VERB.** Use **did not (didn't)** only.
3. The meeting didn't ~~started~~ start on time.	If you have the helping verb **did,** don't use –ed with the verb. You need only one –ed or past time marker.

Grammar Lesson

Simple Past Tense: Making a Question

Making a question with regular and irregular past tense verbs (not *be*) is easy. Study these four steps:

Step 1	Check for a VERB (not be).	You **wanted** a cheese sandwich. You **ate** a sandwich for lunch.
Step 2	Put **did** at the beginning of the sentence.	**did** you wanted a cheese sandwich. **did** you ate a sandwich for lunch.
Step 3	Make sure the verb is in the base (simple) form.	did you **want** a cheese sandwich. did you **eat** a sandwich for lunch.
Step 4	Use a capital letter for the first word, and then change the period (.) to a question mark (?).	**Did** you want a cheese sandwich? **Did** you eat a sandwich for lunch?

Other examples:

Statement	Question
I **arrived** after you.	**Did** I **arrive** after you?
You **ran** four miles every day last week.	**Did** you **run** four miles every day last week?
He **worked** in Mexico one year.	**Did** he **work** in Mexico one year?
She **knew** all of the answers.	**Did** she **know** all of the answers?
It **snowed** last month.	**Did** it **snow** last month?
You and I **had** the same idea.	**Did** you and I **have** the same idea?

<u>Rule 1.</u> To make a question with a past tense verb (not be), add **did** before the subject.

<u>Rule 2.</u> Be sure to use only the base (simple) form of the verb.

BE CAREFUL!

Common Learner Errors	Explanation
1. ~~Were you watch~~ Did you watch the news last night?	Do not use **be (was, were)** with verbs in simple past tense.
2a. Did your car ~~needed~~ need a new radio? 2b. Did your car ~~had~~ have a problem?	Do not use **–ed** or the irregular past form of the verb in yes-no questions. Use only the base (simple) form of the verb. **Did** is past, and you only need a past tense form in one place in the verb.

EXERCISE 6. Simple Past Tense of Regular Verbs: Affirmative

Write the past tense forms of the verbs. Follow the example. Include the subject in your answer. Follow the example.

1. I want   I wanted   11. she listens   _____

2. they attend _____   12. I wait   _____

3. you repeat _____   13. he learns   _____

4. we talk   _____   14. they explain   _____

5. we need   _____   15. she uses   _____

6. it repeats _____   16. you like   _____

7. I count   _____   17. she adds   _____

8. they type   _____   18. I shop   _____

9. I watch   _____   19. we study   _____

10. you shout _____   20. he answers   _____

EXERCISE 7. Simple Past Tense of Irregular Verbs: Affirmative

Write the past tense forms of the verbs. Include the subject in your answer. Follow the example.

1. I drink   I drank   11. I send   _____

2. you give   _____   12. it eats   _____

3. they tell   _____   13. they have   _____

4. she reads   _____   14. he makes   _____

5. it begins   _____   15. you speak   _____

6. she gets   _____   16. he forgets   _____

7. we see   _____   17. I put   _____

8. I buy   _____   18. we come   _____

9. it takes   _____   19. you write   _____

10. it goes   _____   20. she chooses   _____

Do Online Exercise 1.4. My score: _____ /10. _____ % correct.

EXERCISE 8. Editing: Is It Correct?

If the sentence is correct, write a check mark (✔) on the line. If it is not correct, write X on the line and circle the mistake. Then change the sentence to make it correct. Write the change above the sentence. (*Hint:* There are eight sentences. Two are correct, but six have mistakes.)

Early Postage Stamps

_____ 1. The United Kingdom introduce the first stamp on May 1, 1840.

_____ 2. With this first stamp, the sender has to pay for the stamp.

_____ 3. Before this, the person who received the letter paid. In other words, the sender did not pay.

_____ 4. The first stamp no have the name of the United Kingdom on it because there was not any reason to have the country's name on it.

_____ 5. Even today, stamps from the U.K. did not have the name of the country on them.

_____ 6. In fact, the U.K. is the only country today that do not put its name on its stamps.

_____ 7. The U.S. begin using stamps in 1847.

_____ 8. In 1883, a stamp for a letter in the U.S. cost two cents, and this price did not change until 1933.

EXERCISE 9. Editing Errors with Simple Past Tense in a Paragraph

Read this short passage. There are eight mistakes. Circle the mistakes, and write the correction above the mistake.

My First Flight

Do you remember your first flight? My first flight were great. In January 2011, I fly with my family from Miami to New York. We get up very early that day. In fact, we wake up at 4 AM because our flight departed at 8 AM. Of course, I am a little nervous and a little afraid, but this did not bothered me. The flight attendant gived us some food, and we eat all of it. I enjoyed my first flight a lot, and I was so glad that my family traveled with me that day.

Grammar Lesson

Present Progressive Tense: Affirmative

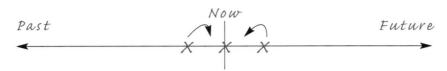

Example	subject	*be*	VERB + –ing
I am filling out an application.	I	am	filling
You're using the computer at this moment.	You	're	using
He is living in a house in Los Angeles.	He	is	living
She's renting an apartment in Burbank.	She	's	renting
It is raining right now.	It	is	raining
We are studying present progressive now.	We	are	studying
They're cutting onions for dinner.	They	're	cutting

<u>Rule 1</u>. In present progressive tense, a verb has three possible forms: am VERB + –ing, is VERB + –ing, are VERB + –ing.

<u>Rule 2</u>. We use am VERB + –ing with *I*; is VERB + –ing with *he, she, it*; are VERB + –ing with *you, we, they*.

<u>Rule 3</u>. It is necessary to include a subject (noun or pronoun).

<u>Rule 4</u>. Use simple present tense for actions that are happening now. Common time expressions for present progressive tense include phrases like *now, right now, today, tonight,* and *this _____* (*this year*).

<u>Rule 5</u>. We can use the present progressive tense with action verbs like *eat, do, read,* and *cry*. We do not use this tense with verbs that do not show an action. Four kinds of verbs that do not usually occur in present progressive tense are: senses (*hear, see, smell, feel, sound*), emotions (*like, love, need, prefer, want*), mental states (*believe, forget, remember, seem, think*), and possession (*belong, have, own, possess*).

> <u>Exception</u>: You can say *I'm having a good time* or *We're having a test* because *have* is an action in these two examples. You cannot say *I'm having a book* or *She's having a green pen* because *have* is not a real action in these examples.

<u>Rule 6</u>. For verbs that end in –e, drop the final –e before adding –ing: take → taking.

<u>Rule 7</u>. If a one-syllable verb ends in **consonant + vowel + consonant** (c-v-c), double the final consonant before adding *–ing*: **cut** → cu**tt**ing (but **read** → reading).

Rule 8. If a two-syllable verb ends in **consonant + vowel + consonant** (c-v-c), we double the final consonant before adding –ing if the pronunciation stress is on the second syllable:

open → ope<u>nn</u>ing	*begin → begi<u>nn</u>ing*
(o) pen [1st] 2nd	be (gin) 1st [2nd]
because we stress the 1st syllable	because we stress the 2nd syllable

 BE CAREFUL!

Common Learner Errors	**Explanation**
1. Kristin ~~makes~~ is making pancakes for breakfast now.	Remember to use present progressive when the action is happening now.
2. The earth ~~is taking~~ takes one year to go around the sun.	Don't use present progressive for actions that happen every day or all the time.
3. My baby sister ~~crying~~ is crying now. I don't know why.	Use a form of be with present progressive tense.
4. My baby sister is ~~cry~~ crying now. I don't know why.	You must use –ing with present progressive tense.
5. ~~eatting~~ eating ~~helpping~~ helping ~~takking~~ taking ~~openning~~ opening ~~cuting~~ cutting ~~comming~~ coming	Be careful with the spelling of the –ing verb.
6. I ~~am owning~~ own an old gold truck.	Use present progressive only when the verb shows action.

 ONE-MINUTE LESSON
The verb **take** has many meanings. Perhaps you know **take** *a test,* **take** *a bus,* **take** *a shower,* or **take** *it easy.* Another common way to use the word **take** is with time: *Cooking breakfast usually* **takes** *me 15 minutes* or *It* **took** *me 2 days to finish the work.*

Present Progressive Tense: Negative

Making a negative statement with present progressive is easy. You just follow the same rules for making the verb **be** negative. You add **not** after the form of **be**. You can also use contractions for informal language.

Affirmative	Negative
I am sitting in your chair.	I **am not** sitting in your chair. I'**m not** sitting in your chair.
You are helping Mike.	You **are not** helping Mike. You **aren't** helping Mike. You'**re not** helping Mike.
Maria is working at the bank this month.	Maria **is not** working at the bank this month. Maria **isn't** working at the bank this month. Maria'**s not** working at the bank this month.

<u>Rule 1</u>. We use the word **not** to make a negative sentence with the verb **be** in present progressive: **am not, is not, are not**.

<u>Rule 2</u>. There is no contraction for **am not**. It is possible to use contractions for **is not** and **are not**: **isn't, aren't**.

<u>Rule 3</u>. It is also possible to make a contraction with the subject and **be** before the word **not**: **I'm not, you're not (you aren't), she's not (she isn't)**, etc. There is no difference in meaning between these two forms of contractions.

 ## BE CAREFUL!

Common Learner Errors	Explanation
1. Mark ~~doesn't using~~ isn't using his cell phone right now.	Use **am not, isn't**, or **aren't**. Do not use **don't** or **doesn't**.
2. Tim ~~no is~~ is not taking the bus today.	Use **not** or **n't**. Don't use the word **no**.

 Do Online Exercise 1.5. My score: ____ /10. ____ % correct.

Present Progressive Tense: Making a Question

KEY
2

Making a question with present progressive is easy. You just follow the same rules for making a question with the verb **be**. You move the form of *be* before the subject.

Statement	Question
She's driving to the bank.	**Is she** driving to the bank? Where **is she** driving?
You and Jenna are eating fried fish.	**Are you and Jenna** eating fried fish? What **are you and Jenna** eating?

BE CAREFUL!

Common Learner Errors	Explanation
1. Why ~~are leaving Marco and Lena~~ are Marco and Lena leaving?	The subject goes just after **am**, **is**, or **are**. Do not move the subject to the end of the question.
2. ~~Do you using~~ Are you using this chair?	Use **am**, **is**, or **are**. Don't use **do** or **does**.

EXERCISE 10. Present Progressive: Affirmative

Fill in the blanks with the correct forms of the verbs. Follow the examples.

run	open	begin
I _am running_	I _____	I _____
you _are running_	you _____	you _____
he _____	he _____	he _____
she _____	she _____	she _____
it _____	it _____	it _____
we _____	we _____	we _____
they _____	they _____	they _____
Jo _____	Jo _____	Jo _____
Jo and I _____	Jo and I _____	Jo and I _____

EXERCISE 11. Comparing Simple Present and Present Progressive

Write the forms of **work** in present and progressive tenses. Notice the time words in each sentence.

Simple Present Tense	Present Progressive Tense
1. I ____work____ every day.	8. I _am working_ now.
2. You _____ at night.	9. You _____ right now.
3. He _____ all of the time.	10. He _____ today.
4. She _____ every day.	11. She _____ this week.
5. It _____ most of the time.	12. It _____ now.
6. We _____ every Monday.	13. We _____ hard this semester.
7. They _____ here every day.	14. They _____ here this morning.

EXERCISE 12. Simple Present and Present Progressive Forms

Write the correct forms of these verbs for simple present tense and present progressive tense. If a form is not common, write *not common* in the box. Follow the examples.

	Simple Present Tense		Present Progressive Tense	
	Affirmative	Negative	Affirmative	Negative
1. I/work	I work	I don't work	I am working	I'm not working
2. he/like	he likes	he doesn't like	not common	not common
3. they/want				
4. Ana/call				
5. we/watch				
6. you/get				
7. she/do				
8. it/begin				
9. they/sing				
10. he/prefer				

EXERCISE 13. Questions in Simple Present and Present Progressive

Make a question from each statement. Circle the time words. Decide if the verb in the statement is simple present tense or present progressive tense. This will help you write the question. Follow the examples.

1. A. Jill is swimming in the pool (now.)   *Is Jill swimming in the pool now?*

   B. Jill swims five laps (every day.)   *Does Jill swim five laps every day?*

2. A. Mr. Yoshida teaches history.   _____

   B. Mr. Yoshida is teaching Sue now.   _____

3. A. They're having a good time there.   _____

   B. They have a good time in
   Mr. Yoshida's class.   _____

4. A. It's snowing heavily now.   _____

   B. It snows a lot in January.   _____

5. A. Josh takes a shower at night.   _____

   B. Josh is taking a shower now.   _____

6. A. Mrs. Po is preparing lunch.   _____

   B. Mrs. Po prepares lunch every day.   _____

7. A. Henry and Mary study together.   _____

   B. Henry and Mary are studying.   _____

8. A: It's raining now.   _____

   B: It rains every other day in the
   summer.   _____

ONE-MINUTE LESSON
The words **every other** with a time word such as **day** or **week** mean "one time yes, one time no." If you get a paycheck every other week, that means you will receive 26 paychecks in a year. Common expressions are **every other day, every other week,** and **every other year.** Some students don't hear the expression correctly and are confused by it.

🔑 Grammar Lesson

Be Going To

Examples	subject	*be going to*	VERB
I'm **going to** take a trip to Miami in two more days.	I	'm going to	take
You're **going to** have a great time tonight.	You	're going to	have
At this rate, he **is going to** graduate soon.	he	is going to	graduate
She's **going to** call you at noon.	She	's going to	call
Do you think it's **going to** rain?	it	's going to	rain
We **are going to** eat dinner at Jack's later.	We	are going to	eat
They're **going to** get together at 6 tonight.	They	're going to	get

Rule 1. One usage of **be going to** + **VERB** is to talk about future plans.

Rule 2. We can also use **be going to** + **VERB** to talk about predictions based on current evidence. (A: "Oh, the sky is really dark." B: "Yes, it's going to rain soon.")

Rule 3. We use **will** + **VERB** to talk about future time, but the usage is more limited than **be** + **going to**. For example, you cannot use **will** for future actions that you have already planned. We usually ask, *What are you going to do tomorrow?* not *What will you do tomorrow?* In contrast, if the phone rings right now, you could say, *I'll answer it* (not *I'm going to answer it*) because you have no prior plan to answer the phone.

Rule 4. We use **am** with *I*; **is** with *he, she, it*; **are** for *you, we, they*.

Rule 5. It is necessary to include a subject (noun or pronoun) with this expression.

Rule 6. Common time expressions for **be going to** include *tomorrow, next _____ (next week)*, and *in _____ (in 5 minutes)*.

Rule 7. The negative of **be going to** is the same as the negative of **be**. Use *not* or a contraction *n't: We aren't going to drive there* OR *We're not going to drive there.*

Rule 8. Questions for **be going to** are the same as the question form of **be**. Move *be* before the subject: *Are most people going to vote tomorrow?* OR *Where is the meeting going to be?*

Rule 9. In spoken language, **going to** before the **VERB** often sounds like *gonna*. This is OK in informal spoken language, but we never write *gonna* in academic writing.

Connecting Grammar and Vocabulary

It is possible to use any verb after *be going to*, but you cannot learn thousands of verb combinations. You need the most common verbs for this grammar point. Memorize these two lists.

The 15 Most Commonly Used Verbs (in order of frequency) after *be going to*	
Spoken English	**Academic English**
1. be 6. take 11. come 2. have 7. happen 12. give 3. do 8. make 13. talk 4. get 9. see 14. try 5. go 10. say 15. tell	1. be 6. make 11. give 2. have 7. take 12. change 3. do 8. go 13. say 4. get 9. see 14. use 5. happen 10. die 15. come

Source: Based on information in the Corpus of Contemporary American English: www.americancorpus.org/

BE CAREFUL!

Common Learner Errors	Explanation
1. Guillermo ~~going~~ **is going** to study with Ana and Carla tonight.	Use a form of **be** with **going to** + VERB.
2. Laura ~~makes~~ **is making** chicken salad for lunch.	Remember to use present progressive when the action is happening now.
3. If we don't hurry up, we're ~~going be~~ **going to** be late.	Don't forget the word **to**.
4. Your application for a new passport is going to ~~takes~~ **take** four to six weeks.	The verb after **be going to** is the base simple form. Don't use **–s, –ed,** or **–ing** with the verb after **to**.
5. Written language example: Many people think those new laws are ~~gonna~~ **going** to be positive for the environment.	We often pronounce **going to** as *gonna*, but don't write *gonna*. It is not a written word.
6. Spoken language example: "I really think it's ~~gonna to~~ *gonna* OR **going to** rain soon."	If you want to say *gonna*, don't say *gonna to*. The pronunciation *gonna* means "going to," so the error *gonna to* really means "going to to." You can't use **to** twice.
7. Spoken language example: We're ~~gonna~~ **going to** New York tomorrow.	We never say *gonna* with a place. The pronunciation *gonna* in informal spoken English tells us that a verb follows.

EXERCISE 14. Mini-Conversations

Circle the correct words in these eight mini-conversations.

1. A: When are you going (get, getting, to get) a present for Joseph?

   B: Tomorrow I'm going (go, going, to go) shopping at the mall.

2. A: Can your sister speak German?

   B: No, but she (takes, is going to take) a German course before her trip.

3. A: Are you busy now? I need to see you.

   B: Yes, I am, but I'm (having, have, going to have) some free time after 5. Can you come back then?

4. A: What's wrong with your car? It sounds horrible.

   B: I don't know. (It makes, It's making, It's going to make) a strange noise, so I'm going to take it to the garage tomorrow morning.

5. A: Wow, today's weather was great, wasn't it?

   B: Yes, but I think (it rains, it's going to rain) tomorrow.

6. A: Why (do you cry, are you crying)? Is everything ok?

   B: Yes, everything is fine. I'm just cutting up onions now because (I use, I'm going to use, I will use) them to make soup for dinner.

7. A: How long (are you going to study, do you study) tonight?

   B: For about two or three hours. If I study more than that, (I go, I'm going, I'm gonna) to get really tired and then I'm not going to (am, is, be) able to concentrate.

8. A: Where are your sisters going to go for vacation?

   B: Sarah (am, is, are) not going to go anywhere, but Christine (visit, goes to visit, visits, is going to visit) our grandfather in Maine.

EXERCISE 15. Editing: Is It Correct?

If the sentence is correct, write a check mark (✓) on the line. If it is not correct, write X on the line and circle the mistake. Then change the sentence to make it correct. Write the change above the sentence. (*Hint:* There are eight sentences. Two are correct, but six have mistakes.)

Tomorrow's Weather Map

_____ 1. The weather in New York City today was very wet, but tomorrow it's going to sunny.

_____ 2. The high temperature in Los Angeles going to be 85 tomorrow.

_____ 3. The high temperature in Dallas going to be the same as the temperature in Los Angeles.

_____ 4. It's going to be extremely windy tomorrow in northern Arizona.

_____ 5. If you live in Detroit, you're probably not going like the weather report for tomorrow because it's going to be rainy and quite cool.

_____ 6. Residents of Denver are gonna be very happy with the beautiful weather they're going to have tomorrow.

_____ 7. There is going to be very heavy showers and some severe thunderstorms tomorrow afternoon in New Orleans and Houston.

_____ 8. Atlanta is going to have one more day of sunshine tomorrow before bad weather arrives the next day.

Do Online Exercise 1.6. My score: _____ /10. _____ % correct.

Present Perfect Tense: An Introduction

Present perfect tense is one of the most difficult tenses in English. It has several different meanings, but in this verb review, we are going to look at only one meaning: an action that began in the past and still continues now. Unit 5 covers this tense in greater detail.

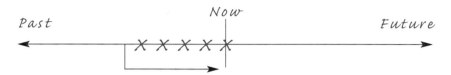

Example	subject	*have/has*	past participle
I have <u>lived</u> in this apartment for ten years.	I	have	lived
You have <u>worked</u> at the bank since 2007.	You	have	worked
He has <u>been</u> here since 8 AM today.	He	has	been
She's <u>taught</u> at Lincoln High since 1995.	She	's	taught
It has <u>taken</u> me six years to learn English.	It	has	taken
We've <u>known</u> Susan for about four years.	We	've	known
They've <u>played</u> the piano since they were ten.	They	've	played

<u>Rule 1</u>. Present perfect tense consists of **have** or **has** + **past participle** of a verb. (Contractions with 've and 's are possible.)

<u>Rule 2</u>. The past participle of a regular verb is the same as its past tense: **VERB + –ed**. The past participle of an irregular verb has many forms, but a common ending is **VERB + –en**. You can find more examples of past participle forms in **Appendix C**.

Regular Verbs			Irregular Verbs		
present	past	past participle	present	past	past participle
live	lived	lived	am, is, are	was, were	been
work	worked	worked	do	did	done
play	played	played	take	took	taken
want	wanted	wanted	go	went	gone

Rule 3. Use present perfect tense for a past action that continues to be true now. (This tense has several different uses, but this one is a good start.) Common time expressions for simple past tense include *for _____ (for ten years), since _____ (since 2005), so far,* and *until now.*

Rule 4. The negative of present perfect is **have not** or **has not**. The contractions *haven't* and *hasn't* can also be used: *We have not been here very long* OR *We haven't been here very long.*

Rule 5. To make a question with present perfect tense, move **have** or **has** before the subject: *Have you worked here since 2005?* OR *How long has Maria lived in China?*

EXERCISE 16. Review Verb Tenses in Sentences

Circle the correct form of the verb in these sentences.

1. The boys (are going to work, have worked, worked, work) here again tomorrow. They (are, were, have been, are going to be) here since last Monday.

2. Jim (is going to play, is not playing, played, plays) the piano at our party last week.

3. Ryan and Lee (are going to study, don't study, studied, study) a lot of vocabulary before next week's big exam.

4. We (are going to be, are being, were, are) on the plane in one hour from now.

5. Susan (is going to attend, is attending, attends, attend) class every day, and she gets really good grades.

6. They (are going to need, are needing, needed, need) a camera right now.

7. John, Mike, and Susan (are going to listen, are listening, listened, listen) to a news report on the radio now.

8. I (am going to assist, am assisting, assisted, assist) the doctor yesterday.

9. You need your umbrella if you're going outside because it (is going to rain, is raining, rained, rains) really hard right now.

10. Kirk and I (are going to visit, have not visited, visited, visit) Mrs. Jones in two more weeks.

Do Online Exercise 1.7. My score: _____ /10. _____ % correct.

EXERCISE 17. Contrasting Verb Forms in Situations

Read each sentence. Think about the time of the action, and then write the correct form of the verb on the line.

1. *play*

   a. They _____ chess now.

   b. We _____ chess yesterday.

   c. He _____ chess tomorrow.

   d. She _____ chess every day.

   e. I _____ chess since I was ten years old.

2. *study*

   a. She _____ grammar now.

   b. They _____ vocabulary last night.

   c. He always _____ spelling.

   d. I _____ grammar tomorrow.

   e. We _____ English for more than 20 years!

3. *do*

   a. You _____ the homework last night.

   b. I _____ the exercises every day.

   c. Last night they had a party for all their neighbors. They

   _____ the same thing on the first weekend

   of June since 1995!

   d. We _____ Lesson 1 right now.

   e. She _____ her homework tomorrow morning
   before class begins.

4. *need*

   a. We _____ some help last week.

   b. We _____ a rental car next week for our trip to
   San Diego.

   c. I always _____ more money.

   d. I _____ money right now.

   e. Since I first met Christina, she _____ a better job

   with a higher salary, but she still doesn't have a good job.

5. *be*

    a. I _____ a salesperson. It's my job.

    b. I _____ in Venezuela last year.

    c. I _____ in France next month.

    d. I _____ in Canada now.

    e. I _____ in this room for more than an hour, and I want to leave.

EXERCISE 18. Correct Verb Tense and Verb Form

Read these paragraphs, and then complete each sentence with the correct verb tense.

Tornadoes in the United States

Although tornadoes (occur) ❶ _____ all over the world, the U.S. (have) ❷ _____ more tornadoes every year than any other country. In 2011, the U.S. (experience) ❸ _____ some of the worst tornadoes on record. Scientists (record) ❹ _____ more than one thousand tornadoes in the first five months of the year alone, and the media (report) ❺ _____ 2011 as the deadliest tornado season since 1953. In Missouri, one tornado alone (kill) ❻ _____ more than 100 people, and it (be) ❼ _____ now the eighth deadliest tornado in U.S. history.

Within the United States, the majority of tornadoes (hit) ❽ _____ an area nicknamed "Tornado Alley." Tornado Alley (be) ❾ _____ a large area between the Appalachian Mountains and Rocky Mountains, and it (include) ❿ _____ the states of Oklahoma, Kansas, and Missouri. In fact, tornados (be) ⓫ _____ so common in this area that 90 percent of the tornadoes in the United States (happen) ⓬ _____ here.

EXERCISE 19. Sentence Study for Critical Reading

Read the numbered sentences. Then read the three answer choices, and put a check mark (✔) in the yes or no boxes in front of each sentence to show if that answer is true based on the information in the original sentence. If there is not enough information to mark something as yes, then mark it as no. Remember that more than one true answer is possible.

1. Mr. Jenks has worked at Brighton Gas for more than 20 years.

   ☐ yes ☐ no   a. Mr. Jenks quit his job 20 years ago.

   ☐ yes ☐ no   b. Mr. Jenks is still working at Brighton Gas.

   ☐ yes ☐ no   c. More than 20 years ago, Mr. Jenks started working at Brighton Gas.

2. Houston, Texas, became a city on June 5, 1837. Houston's population grew rapidly in the 1970s, and today Houston is one of the largest cities in the United States.

   ☐ yes ☐ no   a. Houston became a city more than 100 years ago.

   ☐ yes ☐ no   b. The population of Houston grew a lot in the 1960s.

   ☐ yes ☐ no   c. Houston is the largest city in the United States today.

3. In June and July, it rains a lot in Florida.

   ☐ yes ☐ no   a. This sentence is talking about right now.

   ☐ yes ☐ no   b. This sentence is talking about the whole summer.

   ☐ yes ☐ no   c. This sentence is talking about a usual event.

4. After the police get all the facts, they're going to try to figure out exactly why this bus crash took place.

   ☐ yes ☐ no   a. A police car and a bus had an accident.

   ☐ yes ☐ no   b. The police want to know why there was an accident.

   ☐ yes ☐ no   c. Right now they don't know how the accident happened.

5. Your brother has a great job. He is an assistant manager at First National Bank. He works at the branch on Jefferson Street near the high school.

   ☐ yes ☐ no   a. He works at a bank on Jefferson Street.

   ☐ yes ☐ no   b. He doesn't have a checking account at the bank.

   ☐ yes ☐ no   c. His place of employment is located on Jefferson Street.

6. My sister's computer is having some problems.

   ☐ yes ☐ no   a. This action is true all of the time.

   ☐ yes ☐ no   b. This action is happening now.

   ☐ yes ☐ no   c. This action is finished.

7. The grammar test is going to have only two sections with 30 questions each.

   ☐ yes ☐ no a. The test will have 30 questions.

   ☐ yes ☐ no b. The test will have more than one section.

   ☐ yes ☐ no c. The test will not have more than 60 questions.

8. Paella is a Spanish dish. It consists of rice that is cooked with many kinds of seafood. One interesting thing about this dish is that the shrimp are still in their whole shells.

   ☐ yes ☐ no a. Paella has rice in it.

   ☐ yes ☐ no b. Paella includes seafood.

   ☐ yes ☐ no c. Paella is a Spanish dish.

EXERCISE 20. Speaking Practice: Interviewing Classmates

First write your answers to the questions. Then work with a partner. Take turns interviewing each other. Pay attention to verb tenses in your answers. Ask your partner these questions:

1. What did you do last weekend?

   _____

   _____

2. Think of someone who is not here in this class. What do you think that person is doing right now?

   _____

   _____

3. What are your plans for next weekend? What are you going to do?

   _____

   _____

4. What are two of your hobbies? How long have you done these activities?

   _____

   _____

EXERCISE 21. Review Test 1: Multiple Choice

Circle the letter of the correct answer. Some are conversations.

1. "Was Raihan in math class yesterday?"

   "I'm not sure, but I think she _____ there."

       a. is   b. was   c. are   d. were

2. "_____ at Linda's house fun?"

   "Yes, it was. We had a good time there."

       a. The party was   c. Was the party

       b. The people were   d. Were the people

3. "Excuse me. Is this bus going to the mall?"

   "Yes, _____, but Bus 62 and 88 can take you there faster."

       a. it is   b. they are   c. it does   d. they do

4. "How long _____ here at Tennessee Bank?"

   "I started here in 1991, and I hope to continue here for many more years."

       a. do you work   c. have you worked

       b. are you working   d. did you work

5. "Do you spend a lot of time watching TV?"

   "Yes, we do. In fact, my sister and I _____ a horror movie right now, so can I call you back after the movie?"

       a. are watching   c. watch

       b. don't watch   d. aren't watching

6. "_____ work every day?"

   "No, I work from Tuesday to Saturday. I don't work on Sunday and Monday."

       a. Are you going to   c. Are you

       b. Do you   d. Did you

7. "Janice lives in an apartment."

   "Actually, that _____ true. Janice lived in an apartment before, but now she lives in a house."

       a. isn't   b. aren't   c. don't   d. doesn't

8. "_____ your score on the test the best in your class?"

   "No, Jane had 10 more points than I did."

       a. Had   b. Were   c. Did   d. Was

EXERCISE 22. Review Test 2: Production and Evaluation

Part 1.

Read this short passage. Fill in the blanks with the correct tense of the verb **be**.

I ❶ _____ a cat lover all my life. When I ❷ _____ a little boy, my

best pet ❸ _____ a cat. My cat's name ❹ _____ Sammy. Sammy

❺ _____ a beautiful cat. His feet ❻ _____ white, and his face and ears

❼ _____ black. His body ❽ _____ black and white. Sammy liked to

play outside. He ❾ _____ a really good pet. I have a picture of Sammy in

my photo album. This picture was taken in 2001. I want another

pet, so next week I'm going to go to the Animal Rescue

Shelter every day to see what kinds of animals

they have. Who knows? I wonder if my new pet

❿ _____ another black and white cat.

Sammy

Part 2.

Read each sentence carefully. Look at the underlined part in each sentence. If the underlined part is correct, circle the word *correct*. If it is wrong, circle the word *wrong*. Then write the correction above.

correct   wrong   1. Mark likes TV. He's <u>watch</u> a TV show right now.

correct   wrong   2. <u>Does Linda going</u> to the bank now?

correct   wrong   3. Mr. Wendell <u>teaches</u> French in Room 301 right now.

correct   wrong   4. The boys <u>are no doing</u> their homework now.

correct   wrong   5. People in Canada <u>drive</u> on the right-hand side of the road.

EXERCISE 23. Reading Practice: An Advice Column

Read the information in this letter a student wrote to Mr. Advice. In her letter, the student asks for help with a problem. After you read the letter, read Mr. Advice's answer. After reading both letters, answer the five comprehension questions on page 39. The grammar from this unit is underlined for you.

Dear Mr. Advice,

I need your help! I am a college student with a very difficult roommate. Let me tell you my problem. Two weeks ago, my roommate <u>began</u> guitar lessons. Unfortunately, she practices every night, and her practice place is our room!

Last Monday night <u>was</u> really bad. She <u>played</u> the guitar for four hours in a row. <u>Did she think</u> about me? No, she <u>didn't</u>. <u>Did she play</u> quietly? No, she <u>didn't</u>. She <u>didn't think</u> about me at all! I <u>went</u> to the store and <u>bought</u> some ear plugs, but they didn't help. Finally, I <u>spoke</u> to her about my problem. <u>Did she care</u>? No, <u>she didn't care</u> about my problem. She <u>told</u> me to put a pillow over my head! What can I do now?

Sincerely,

Awake in Toronto

Dear Awake in Toronto,

I'm so sorry to hear about your situation. It seems to me that you <u>gave</u> your roommate many chances to change, but she <u>didn't change</u> anything. You <u>told</u> her that her music is a problem. You <u>asked</u> her to play more quietly, but she <u>didn't do</u> that.

I think you should tell her that she cannot live with you any longer. Then you need to find another roommate. You <u>tried</u> your best. It's time to change things.

Sincerely,

Mr. Advice

1. In one sentence, what is the letter writer's problem? _____

   _____

2. When did the roommate start guitar lessons? _____

   _____

3. How long did the roommate play the guitar last Monday night? _____

   _____

4. What did Awake in Toronto purchase? _____

   _____

5. What did the roommate recommend to help Awake in Toronto sleep? _____

   _____

EXERCISE 24. Vocabulary Practice: Word Knowledge

Circle the word or phrase that is most closely related to the word or phrase on the left. Use a dictionary to check the meaning of words you do not know.

Vocabulary	Answer Choices	
1. average	special	usual
2. fiction	not new	not true
3. nearly 100	98	one hundred
4. a grade	a report	a score
5. wheat	in bread	in fish
6. a competition	a game	a job
7. a ring	on your finger	on your wrist
8. entire	all	none
9. shout	a quiet voice	a loud voice
10. hobbies	in your free time	in your work time
11. approximately	between 2 PM and 3 PM	at 2:15 PM exactly
12. put on	begin to sleep	begin to wear
13. my cousin	my aunt's son	my son's aunt
14. clever	modern	smart
15. whole	all	some
16. I win	I have 9, he has 3	he has 9, I have 3
17. snow	summer	winter
18. at the mall	where you can live	where you can shop
19. an expert	a person	a place
20. it lasted 3 hours	it was 3 hours long	it finished at 3 PM
21. depart	allow	leave
22. at least 20	17 or 18	27 or 28
23. choose	select	try
24. ten laps	shopping	swimming
25. the majority	a few	most
26. bother	cause problems	change clothes
27. concentrate	sing slowly	think hard
28. an application	for a job	for a sport
29. get together	explains several things	meet with people
30. positive	bad	good
31. export	come in	go out
32. hurry up	faster	slower
33. includes	compares	contains

EXERCISE 25. Vocabulary Practice: Collocations

Fill in each blank with the answer on the right that most naturally completes the phrase on the left. If necessary, use a dictionary to check the meaning of words you do not know.

Vocabulary	Answer Choices	
1. own a _____	car	cloud
2. _____ five hours	sound	spend
3. compete _____ someone	to	with
4. a _____ problem	cheap	serious
5. _____ biography	someone's	something's
6. according _____ the report	in	to
7. _____ mistakes	too many	too much
8. a _____ bulb	light	line
9. I _____ a bad grade	did	got
10. rob a _____	bank	plane
11. got _____ work	off	on
12. we were _____ a party	at	in
13. we didn't like it _____	very much	very really
14. _____ a trip	go	take
15. 3 times _____ week	for	per
16. two masked _____	men	onions
17. _____ a mistake	do	make
18. an _____ ago	hour	house
19. _____ to the bank	go	enter
20. _____ same idea	a	the
21. Can you _____?	kind	type
22. to _____ an apartment	relax	rent
23. it started on _____	money	time
24. _____ the news	listen	watch
25. scrambled _____	eggs	meat
26. I _____ two cars	bank	own
27. _____ the bus	sound	take
28. _____ fact	by	in
29. _____ fish	fried	ironed
30. most _____ time	of	of the
31. _____ a good time	have	make
32. _____ a shower	jump	take
33. work _____	easy	hard

EXERCISE 26. Writing Practice

Part 1. Editing Student Writing

Read these sentences about one student's family. Circle the 15 errors. Then write the number of the sentence with the error next to the type of error. (Some sentences may have more than one error.)

_____ a. no subject   _____ d. word order

_____ b. preposition (*at, on, in*)   _____ e. confusing *be* and *have*

_____ c. verb tense   _____ f. *much, many*

Three Members of My Family
1. I am going to talk about three people important. Are very important in my life.
2. My grandfather was born on 1908. Unfortunately, he passed away ago ten years.
3. He has worked at a bakery for more than 40 years.
4. My sister's name is Susan, and she has 32 years old.
5. My sister and her husband have much children, and they all live at Texas.
6. Right now my sister studies for a Master's degree in teaching reading. Is very smart.
7. My third special person is my daughter. Her name is Julietta.
8. Julietta finishes high school last year. Next month is going to enter college.
9. I have lucky to be a member of this family wonderful.
10. We have much reasons to be happy.

Part 2. Original Student Writing

Write several sentences about people in your family. Use each of these tenses at least once in your work: simple present, present progressive, simple past, *be going to,* and present perfect.

 Unit 2

Articles

Discover the Grammar

Read the recipe for chocolate chip cookies, and then answer the five questions.

1	I love to eat chocolate chip cookies. Making chocolate chip cookies is not
2	difficult. To make chocolate chip cookies, you need:
3	an electric mixer
4	a large mixing bowl
5	measuring cups and spoons
6	2 cups of flour
7	an egg
8	1¼ cups of brown sugar
9	a tablespoon of vanilla
10	a stick of butter
11	a cup of sugar
12	2 cups of chocolate chips
13	½ teaspoon of salt
14	OPTIONAL: Substitute a cup of peanut butter for the stick of butter.

1. Underline the five examples of the word *a*. What does the word *a* mean?

   _____

2. Circle the two examples of the word *an*. What does *an* mean?

   _____

3. What is the difference between *a* and *an*? When do we use *a* and when do we use *an*?

   _____

4. Put a box around the eight plural words. Do you find the word *a* or *an* before these plural words? _____ Why or why not? _____

   _____

5. Look at these common fruits. Write *a*, *an*, or Ø (the null symbol for no article). Be careful with plural nouns.

____ apples	____ cherries	____ peach
____ apricot	____ lemon	____ plums
____ avocado	____ mango	____ tangerine
____ banana	____ orange	____ watermelon

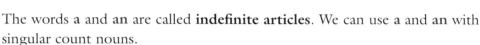 Grammar Lesson

Indefinite Articles *a* and *an*

The words **a** and **an** are called **indefinite articles**. We can use **a** and **an** with singular count nouns.

> **A** penguin is **a** small black and white bird.

> **An** umbrella is useful in rainy weather.

Count Nouns		Non-Count Nouns
singular	**plural**	
a penguin a cute penguin an ugly penguin	penguins cute penguins ugly penguins	information simple information useful information
an elephant a hungry elephant a sick elephant	elephants hungry elephants sick elephants	rice Thai rice Indonesian rice

<u>Rule 1</u>. Use **a** or **an** in a noun phrase that has a singular count noun (**a book, an egg**).

<u>Rule 2</u>. Use **a** before a singular count noun or an adjective (before a singular count noun) that begins with a consonant sound: /b/, "ch," /d/, /f/, /g/, /h/, /j/, /k/, /l/, /m/, /n/, /p/, /r/, /s/, "sh," /t/, /v/, /w/, /y/, /z/. (**a book, a child, a door, a feather,** etc.).

<u>Rule 3</u>. Use **an** before a singular count noun or an adjective (before a singular count noun) that begins with a vowel sound like *a, e, i, o, u*: **an apple, an egg, an island.**

<u>Rule 4</u>. Be careful with words that begin with the letter *h*. Sometimes the letter *h* has a consonant sound, as in *house, hamburger,* or *heavy*. Other times the letter *h* is silent, as in *hour* or *honest:* **a house, an hour**

<u>Rule 5</u>. Be careful with words that begin with the letter *u*. Sometimes the letter *u* has a consonant sound like /y/, as in *university, unit,* or *united*. Other times the letter *u* has a vowel sound, as in *umbrella, uncle,* or *ugly:* **a university, an umbrella.**

<u>Rule 6</u>. Plural nouns cannot have **a** or **an** because **a** and **an** mean "one."

<u>Rule 7</u>. Non-count nouns cannot have **a** or **an** because **a** and **an** mean "one," and non-count nouns cannot be counted.

BE CAREFUL!

Common Learner Errors	Explanation
1. I eat ~~banana~~ a banana and ~~apple~~ an apple for breakfast every morning.	A singular count noun always has **a** or **an** (or another determiner) before it. You must use some word before a singular count noun.
2. What is this letter? Is it ~~a~~ an E or is it ~~a~~ an F?	The word **an** goes before words that begin with a vowel sound.
3. (a) There are 60 minutes in ~~a~~ an hour. (b) I have ~~a~~ an uncle who lives in Hawaii.	Don't use **a** before words that begin with silent **h** or with the short sound of **u** as in *uncle* or *ugly*. Use **an** before vowel sounds. Pay attention to the sound, not just the letter.
4. Our teacher gives us ~~a very hard tests~~ very hard tests.	Don't use **a** or **an** with plural nouns.
5. I want to buy ~~a new~~ a new shirt.	Use **a** or **an** only if there is a noun.
6. I would like to get ~~an information~~ information (or **some information**) about renting a car.	Don't use **a** or **an** with non-count nouns. (It is possible to use **some** with non-count nouns.)

 ONE-MINUTE LESSON
Non-count nouns do not have a plural form. You cannot add **-s** to a non-count noun. Common mistakes: *homeworks, informations, furnitures.*

EXERCISE 1. Using *a* or *an* with Nouns

Complete each phrase by adding **a** or **an** before the noun or noun phrase. Some phrases have an adjective before the noun, but the same rules for **a/an** apply.

Things in a Classroom

1. _a_ test

2. ____ pencil

3. ____ eraser

4. ____ student

5. ____ computer

6. ____ old computer

7. ____ laptop

8. ____ teacher

9. ____ clock

10. ____ map

11. ____ pen

12. ____ door

13. ____ window

14. ____ hour

15. ____ answer

16. ____ exam

17. ____ university

18. ____ dictionary

19. ____ quiz

20. ____ world map

21. ____ U.S. map

22. ____ A on my test

23. ____ B on my test

24. ____ C on my test

25. ____ D on my test

26. ____ F on my test

27. ____ whiteboard

28. ____ error

29. ____ desk

30. ____ marker

EXERCISE 2. Using *a* or *an* with Noun Phrases

Complete each phrase by adding **a** or **an** before the noun phrase. These phrases have an adjective before the noun, but the same rules for **a/an** apply.

1. _an_ active person

2. _____ hard question

3. _____ university class

4. _____ aggressive animal

5. _____ very aggressive animal

6. _____ young boy

7. _____ delicious dinner

8. _____ very difficult test

9. _____ ugly painting

10. _____ history test

11. _____ orange car

12. _____ English test

13. _____ honest person

14. _____ huge house

15. _____ responsible parent

16. _____ awful day

17. _____ horrible grade on my test

18. _____ good grade on my test

19. _____ bad grade on my test

20. _____ excellent grade on my test

EXERCISE 3. Using *a* or *an* with Noun Phrases

Complete each phrase by adding **a** or **an** before the noun phrase. These phrases have an adjective before the noun, but the same rules for **a/an** apply.

Visiting an Amusement Park

1. _____ young boy
2. _____ delicious hot dog
3. _____ long line
4. _____ very long wait
5. _____ ugly costume
6. _____ horrible ride
7. _____ fast roller coaster
8. _____ expensive ticket
9. _____ haunted house
10. _____ huge park
11. _____ good show
12. _____ slow ferris wheel
13. _____ animal show
14. _____ cold soft drink

Do Online Exercise 2.1. My score: _____ /10. _____ % correct.

EXERCISE 4. Questions about Animals

Complete each phrase by adding **a** or **an** before the noun or noun phrase. Then work with one or two partners to answer the questions. Finally, check your answers on the Internet.

Questions That You Might Hear at a Zoo

1. "How many stripes does _____ adult zebra have?"

   Answer: _____

2. "Is _____ lion more dangerous than _____ tiger?"

   Answer: _____

3. "What do you call _____ baby cow?"

   Answer: _____

4. "How tall is _____ elephant?"

   Answer: _____

5. "Is it true that _____ kangaroo carries its baby in _____ pouch?"

   Answer: _____

6. "Is _____ cobra _____ poisonous snake?"

   Answer: _____

7. "Does _____ anteater really eat ants?"

   Answer: _____

8. "How many teeth does _____ alligator have?"

   Answer: _____

9. "What sound does _____ owl make?"

   Answer: _____

10. "How many bones are in _____ giraffe's neck?"

    Answer: _____

EXERCISE 5. Mini-Conversations

Circle the correct words in these eight mini-conversations.

1. A: I want to see (a, an) animal show.

   B: I think there is (a, an) bird show starting at 11:30 AM.

2. A: This is (a, an) long line!

   B: I know. I think the wait is (a, an) hour long!

3. A: That looks like (a, an) really scary roller coaster.

   B: Yes, it does! It has (a, an) upside-down section!

4. A: Is there (a, an) children's area of the park?

   B: Yes, there is. It has (a, an) arcade and (a, an) playground.

5. A: Look, there is (a, an) ice cream stand.

   B: I think it is closed. I don't see (a, an) attendant.

6. A: I wonder if the zoo section has (a, an) elephant!

   B: Let's find (a, an) park brochure. It will tell us.

7. A: Is there (a, an) fee for parking?

   B: Only if you want to park in (a, an) parking garage.

8. A: I see (a, an) open booth. Let's sit there.

   B: Okay. Wow, this must be (a, an) popular restaurant. It is so crowded.

Do Online Exercise 2.2. My score: _____ /10. _____ % correct.

EXERCISE 6. Speaking Practice: Using *a* or *an* with Singular Count Nouns

Work in pairs. Think of one thing that you see in your class right now. If you see an eraser, tell your partner, "I see an eraser." Your partner must repeat what you said and add what he or she sees. If your partner sees a big desk, he or she then says, "You see an eraser, but I see a big desk." You must then repeat what he or she just said and then add something. If you see a blue grammar book, then say, "You see a big desk, but I see a blue grammar book."

Instead of using the word *but*, use the word *and*. Continue this activity for two minutes. Try to name as many different things as possible, but be careful to use the word *a* or *an* each time.

EXERCISE 7. Using Articles with Count and Non-Count Nouns

Complete each phrase by adding **a, an**, or *no article* **(Ø)** on the line. Some phrases have an adjective before the noun or noun phrase, but the same rules for **a/an** apply.

❶ _____ Disaster Supply Kit

It is ❷ ____ good idea to keep ❸ _____ disaster supply kit in your house. This kit will help you a lot if there is ❹ _____ storm or ❺ _____ different problem. For example, in ❻ _____ hurricane, in ❼ _____ blizzard, or in ❽ _____ earthquake, you might be without ❾ _____ electricity and ❿ _____ water for ⓫ _____ days. ⓬ _____ good disaster supply kit will help you in case there is ⓭ _____ emergency. ⓮ _____ basic supply kit needs to have ⓯ _____ water and ⓰ _____ food. You also need ⓱ _____ weather radio and ⓲ _____ batteries. ⓳ _____ flashlight is also ⓴ _____ important item. ㉑ _____ whistle is ㉒ _____ good item to have to signal for ㉓ _____ help. Every disaster supply kit needs ㉔ _____ first aid kit with ㉕ _____ rubbing alcohol, ㉖ _____ bandages, ㉗ _____ medicine, and ㉘ _____ scissors. If you live in ㉙ _____ cold weather area, each person in your household needs ㉚ _____ sleeping bag, ㉛ _____ blanket, ㉜ _____ gloves, and ㉝ _____ thick socks.

Grammar Lesson

KEY
7

Definite Article *the*

The word **the** is called the **definite article**. We can use **the** with singular count nouns, plural count nouns, and non-count nouns. **The** can go with all types of nouns.

> **The** capital of South Korea is Seoul.

> **The** food that Ana cooked last night was delicious.

Count Nouns		Non-Count Nouns
singular	**plural**	
the answer the correct answer the lunch the Mexican lunch	the answers the correct answers the lunches the Mexican lunches	the information the correct information the food the international food

In this unit, you will study five different ways to use the word **the**.

 ## Meaning 1: Using *the* to Talk about a Specific Noun

Type of Noun	General	Specific
singular count noun	Playing a sport is good for you.	The sport that I like is soccer.
plural count noun	Playing sports is good for you.	The sports that he likes are soccer and tennis.
non-count noun	Football is good for you.	The football that we play in the U.S. is different from the football that they play in Mexico.

<u>Rule 1</u>. Use **the** with a noun that refers to a specific thing. Do not use **the** for a general meaning.

<u>Rule 2</u>. You can use **the** with all kinds of nouns (singular count, plural count, and non-count).

<u>Rule 3</u>. Do not use **the** to talk about a whole category.

BE CAREFUL!

Common Learner Errors	Explanation
1. I like to eat ~~the strawberries~~ **strawberries** as a snack.	For count nouns, do not use **the** to refer to the whole category. Just use a plural count noun with no article.
2. I am allergic to ~~the cheese~~ **cheese**.	For non-count nouns, do not use **the** to refer to the whole category. Just use the non-count noun with no article.
3. My favorite school subject is ~~the history~~ **history**, but I really like ~~history~~ **the history** of modern China.	Use **the** for specific nouns when there is a phrase after them. We often use **the** in the expression **the noun of noun** (*the history of China*).
4. ~~The Shakespeare~~ **Shakespeare** was a very famous author.	Do not use **the** with people's names.
5. ~~War of 1812~~ **The War of 1812** began in ~~the 1812~~ **1812** and ended in ~~the 1814~~ **1814**.	Use **the** with events or periods of time from history. Do not use **the** with one specific year.
6. Ladies and gentlemen, ~~next~~ **the next** flight to Los Angeles will leave from ~~the Gate 17~~ **Gate 17** at ~~the 3 o'clock~~ **3:00**.	Use **the** with words that show order (*first, second, next, last,* etc.). Do not use **the** with numbers, including time (*one, one o'clock,* etc.).
7. My favorite classes in school are ~~the English~~ **English**, ~~the tennis~~ **tennis**, and ~~the chemistry~~ **chemistry**.	Do not use **the** with: languages, sports, games, or school subjects.

ONE-MINUTE LESSON

Which is correct: *ladys* or *ladies*? *babys* or *babies*? *day* or *daies*? If you add –s to a word that ends in a consonant + –y, the –y changes to –i and you add –es: *babies, ladies, cities.* If the word ends in a vowel + –y, just add –s: *days, boys, buys.*

EXERCISE 8. Using Articles in Common Riddles

Work in pairs. Complete the riddles and jokes with **a, an, the,** or **Ø** for no article.

1. Q: What _____ building has _____ most stories?

   A: _____ library.

2. Q: What is _____ longest word in _____ English dictionary?

   A: _____ *smiles* because there is _____ mile between _____ two *s*'s!

3. Q: What is _____ eight-letter word that has only _____ one letter in it?

   A: Envelope!

4. Q: If you drop _____ yellow hat in _____ Red Sea, what does it become?

   A: Wet!

5. Q: What occurs once in _____ minute, twice in _____ moment, and never in _____ thousand years?

   A: _____ letter *m*!

6. Q: Four men sat in _____ room and played for hours. They played for _____ money, not for _____ fun. At _____ end of _____ evening, they all made _____ same amount of _____ money—but no one lost. How is this possible?

   A: _____ men were _____ musicians!

Bonus: Find two new jokes or riddles, and memorize them. Practice saying them out loud. Work on your expression and your timing. Then tell them to the class and your friends!

EXERCISE 9. Articles in Context

Read the conversation. Then then complete the sentences with **a, an, the,** or **Ø.**

Calling for Directions

Yuki: Hi, Keiko! Are you here in the park?

Keiko: Yes and no. Right now I am lost! I am looking for ❶ _____ main park entrance. Where are you?

Yuki: Nina, Marco, and I are at ❷ _____ big red ticket booth at ❸ _____ entrance. We are looking for you.

Keiko: I don't see it. What's near it?

Yuki: It's right in front of ❹ _____ Lost and Found office. It is on ❺ _____ Fun Street. There is ❻ _____ giant statue of a clown in front of ❼ _____ entrance. Do you see it?

Keiko: I don't see ❽ _____ clown statue, but I see ❾ _____ unicorn statue. Is that near you?

Yuki: I don't know. I have ❿ _____ park map. Let me check to see where you are. Okay, you are walking on ⓫ _____ Unicorn Way. Follow it until you get to ⓬ _____ Fun Street. There is ⓭ _____ merchandise cart at ⓮ _____ corner of Unicorn Way and Fun Street. Turn right and you will see us at the entrance!

Keiko: Oh, great! Thank you for ⓯ _____ directions!

ONE-MINUTE LESSON
We use **on** with streets: **on** *Fun Street.* We also use **on** with words that mean street: *avenue, road, highway,* and *way.* Example: *I live* **on** *Peach Avenue.*

Meaning 2: Talking about a Noun Again (Second Reference)

Type of Noun	1st Reference + 2nd Reference
singular count noun	1st 2nd I bought **an** apple yesterday. I ate **the** apple for breakfast.
plural count noun	1st 2nd We have many tests in this class, but **the** tests are not hard.
non-count noun	1st 2nd To make bread, you need flour and yeast. **The** bread will taste better if you add a lot of butter.
synonyms for a noun	1st 2nd Yesterday I was in a car crash. **The** accident was not my fault.

Rule 1. Use **the** with a noun when you are talking about it for the second (or third or fourth) time.

Rule 2. In writing, it is common to use synonyms because you do not want to repeat the same word every time. If you use a synonym, you must still use **the** with the synonym because it is the second reference.

BE CAREFUL!

Common Learner Errors	Explanation
1. We took a trip to Quebec last year. To prepare for ~~a trip~~ **the trip**, we learned a few expressions in French.	Be sure to use **the** with second and all additional references.
2. I watched ~~the good movie~~ a good movie on TV last night. The movie had a great ending.	Do not use **the** for the first reference of something.
3. What is the answer to our city's problem? One ~~answer~~ solution is to work with our neighbors more. In fact, I think this is the best ~~answer~~ plan for our community.	Use synonyms instead of repeating the same noun.

EXERCISE 10. Articles in Context

Complete the sentences with **a, an, the,** or **Ø.**

Roommates Hunting for a New Apartment

Ann: This is ❶ _____ nice apartment. I think we should take it. What do you think?

Zina: Hmmm . . . maybe. It has ❷ _____ large kitchen and ❸ _____ small balcony.

Ann: Yes, ❹ _____ kitchen is very large. It has ❺ _____ nice refrigerator and
          ❻ _____ microwave oven.

Zina: I really like ❼ _____ kitchen, too. ❽ _____ refrigerator is big. It has ❾ _____
          freezer, but I do not like that the apartment does not have ❿ _____ washer and
          ⓫ _____ dryer.

Ann: Yes, it does. ⓬ _____ washer is in ⓭ _____ closet in ⓮ _____ hallway.
          ⓯ _____ dryer is next to the washer.

Zina: Oh! Usually ⓰ _____washer and ⓱ _____ dryer are close to ⓲ _____ kitchen
          in apartments.

Ann: And ⓳ _____ balcony is nice. It's small, but I like ⓴ _____ balcony. It has ㉑
          _____ nice view of ㉒ _____ city.

Zina: I agree that ㉓ _____ view is great.

Ann: So what is your decision?

Zina: Let's take it! I really think this is ㉔ _____ best place for us!

EXERCISE 11. Articles in a Conversation

Complete the sentences with **a, an, the,** or **Ø.**

Zina: Hi, Ann! What did you do ❶ _____ last night?

Ann: I ate at that new restaurant on ❷ _____ Main Street ❸ _____ last night.

Zina: Really? How was it?

Ann: I liked it.

Zina: What did you eat?

Ann: I had ❹ _____ big salad and ❺ _____ double cheeseburger.

Zina: Well, how was everything?

Ann: ❻ _____ salad was very good. They give you a lot of tomatoes, and ❼ _____ tomatoes were very fresh.

Zina: That sounds good. I usually like to begin my dinner with ❽ _____ small salad.

Ann: ❾ _____ cheeseburger was great! You can't believe how much cheese they put on ❿ _____ cheeseburger. And ⓫ _____ cheese was cheddar, which is my favorite.

Zinna: Stop! My mouth is watering!

Meaning 3: Talking about a Noun that Both the Speaker and Listener Know

Examples	Notes
Ben: Hey, where's **the** newspaper?	They both know about the newspaper already.
Ana: It's on **the** table.	They both know which table Ana means.
Ben: Where are you going?	
Ana: To **the** bank. Do you want to come with me?	If Ana says *a bank*, then Ben does not know the bank's location. Saying **the** *bank* means Ana thinks Ben knows the bank already.

<u>Rule 1</u>. Use **the** when you are talking about a noun that your listener knows about.

<u>Rule 2</u>. Use **a** or **an** when you are not talking about a specific example of that noun.

　　　　I'm going to **the** *bank* = the speaker and listener know the same bank.

　　　　I'm going to a bank = the speaker is not referring to a specific bank.

BE CAREFUL!

Common Learner Error	Explanation
Please put ~~eggs~~ the eggs in ~~refrigerator~~ the refrigerator.	Be sure to use **the** when your listener is thinking of the same noun you are. We do not mean all eggs or any refrigerator. The speaker and listener can probably see (or imagine) the eggs and the refrigerator.

EXERCISE 12. Articles in a Longer Conversation

Read the conversation. Complete the sentences with **a, an, the,** or **Ø.**

Putting Away the Groceries

Rick: Wow, I can't believe how crowded that store was!

Ken: Gosh, I agree. Hey, can you help me put away these groceries?

Rick: Sure. Just tell me where things go.

Ken: OK, take everything out of the bags.

Rick: Here's ❶ _____ box of cereal.

Ken: Put ❷ _____ cereal in the top cabinet.

Rick: Here's a bag of sugar.

Ken: Put ❸ _____ sugar next to ❹ _____ cereal.

Rick: Here's a bag of chicken wings.

Ken: Put ❺ _____ chicken wings in the refrigerator.

Rick: And what about these four cans of tuna?

Ken: Put them in the top cabinet, too, next to ❻ _____ cereal and ❼ _____ sugar.

Rick: OK, I'm finished.

Ken: Thanks for your help. Are you hungry?

Rick: Actually, yes, I am.

Ken: How about ❽ _____ sandwich?

Rick: OK, I need some bread.

Ken: ❾ _____ bread is in that brown box next to the refrigerator.

Rick: OK, thanks. Here it is.

Meaning 4: Talking about a Noun with Only One Example

Examples	Notes
Jen: Hey, what's wrong with your car? *Tim*: There's a problem with **the** battery. *Jen*: So what are you going to do? *Tim*: I'm going to ask **the** mechanic for his advice.	A car has only one battery. When Tim says *the mechanic*, he means the same mechanic he talked to before. There is only one mechanic who is working on his car. If Tim says *a mechanic*, then he has not talked to a mechanic yet.

Rule 1. Use **the** when there is only one example of that noun.

Rule 2. Use **the** with ordinal numbers (*the 1st, the 2nd, the 3rd*) but not with regular numbers (*1, 2, 3*).

Rule 3. Use **the** with the parts of something.

BE CAREFUL!

Common Learner Errors	Explanation
1. What is ~~capital~~ **the capital** of Colombia?	Use **the** when there is only one example of that noun. (Countries have only one capital city.)
2. I went to Mary's new house last night. Her kitchen is beautiful. ~~Refrigerator~~ **The refrigerator** is white, ~~stove~~ **the stove** is black, and ~~a clock~~ **the clock** above ~~a door~~ **the door** is black and white.	Use **the** with the parts of something.
3. You and I have ~~same~~ **the same** last name.	Always use **the** with **same**: *the same name, the same reason*, etc.
4. The meeting took place on ~~21st~~ **the 21st**.	Use **the** with dates. Do not use **the** if the month is included first: *the 21st of May* but *May 21st*.

EXERCISE 13. Articles in Context

Read the paragraph about a famous dog race. Complete the sentences with **a, an, the,** or **Ø.**

A Famous Race

The Iditarod is **1** _____ famous dog sled race in **2** _____ Alaska that starts on **3** _____ first **4** _____ Saturday in **5** _____ March every **6** _____ year. It takes about 12 days to finish **7** _____ race. This dog race is **8** _____ 1,100 miles long and follows **9** _____ trail with **10** _____ same name. **11** _____ name "Iditarod" comes from **12** _____ Alaskan-Indian word for "far distance." During **13** _____ race, dogs pull **14** _____ sled that carries **15** _____ human driver called **16** _____ "musher." **17** _____ musher and **18** _____ dog team that finish **19** _____ race first win **20** _____ money. **21** _____ Iditarod is **22** _____ dangerous race because **23** _____ weather in Alaska is very cold and **24** _____ mushers and their dogs must cross **25** _____ frozen rivers and climb **26** _____ steep mountains.

Do Online Exercise 2.3. My score: ____ /10. ____ % correct.

EXERCISE 14. Using Articles in Conversations

Complete the six conversations with **a, an, the,** or **Ø.** Follow the examples.

Conversation A

Jim: How many Canadians won ❶ __*a*__ gold medal in the last Olympic Games?

Sue: I'm not sure. I know Jill Caruthers won ❷ __*the*__ 100-meter freestyle race.

Conversation B

Bill: Who was ❸ _____ first person to walk on ❹ _____ moon?

Ani: I think it was ❺ _____ Neil Armstrong.

Conversation C

Jill: It's hot in this room. Is something wrong with ❻ _____ air conditioner?

Ken: Yes, ❼ _____ thermostat is broken.

Jill: What's ❽ _____ thermostat?

Ken: It's ❾ _____ switch that controls ❿ _____ temperature in this room.

Jill: Can you fix it?

Ken: Well, we called ⓫ _____ repair shop, and they sent someone here. He said that he has to get ⓬ _____ new switch, and then he'll come back to fix it.

Conversation D

Ed: What time does ⓭ _____ first show start?

Luke: At ⓮ ____ 4:15. Do you want to go?

Ed: That's too early for me. When is ⓯ _____ next movie?

Luke: At ⓰ ____ 7:30. How's that?

Ed: That's perfect for me.

Conversation E

Pam: Guess what happened in my English class today.

Maria: I don't know. What?

Pam: In **17** _____ middle of class, **18** _____ teacher suddenly shouted as loudly as she could.

Maria: Why did she do that?

Pam: We were reading **19** _____ play by Shakespeare, and she wanted us to experience the words of the play.

Maria: So what happened?

Pam: Well, **20** _____ students immediately came to life. Everyone was suddenly paying attention to **21** _____ teacher and **22** _____ words of **23** _____ play.

Maria: So, it sounds pretty successful then.

Conversation F

Elly: Who was **24** _____ first person to sail around **25** _____ world?

Ann: I think it was **26** _____ Magellan from **27** _____ Portugal.

Elly: Yes. I believe that is **28** _____ correct answer.

ONE-MINUTE LESSON
When a word ends in **–ful**, it is probably an adjective. **Common** *–ful* **adjectives** that you should know are *beautiful, successful, colorful, wonderful, careful, awful,* and *helpful.*

Meaning 5: Talking about the Names of Places

Examples	Notes
I travel a lot. I have been in **Asia** and **Europe**. I have been in **the Philippines** and **Switzerland**. I have seen **the Pacific Ocean** and **Lake Geneva**. I have seen **the Gobi Desert** in **Mongolia** and **the Alps** in **France** and **Italy**. I have traveled on **the Danube River** in **Budapest**.	Some places need **the**, and some do not.

<u>Rule 1</u>. Use **the** with names of countries that sound plural because they end in –s or include the words *united, republic, kingdom,* or *union.* The majority of country names have no article at all.

<u>Rule 2</u>. Use **the** with buildings such as hotels and museums, but many building names have no article at all.

<u>Rule 3</u>. Use **the** with most bodies of water (except lakes).

<u>Rule 4</u>. Use **the** with chains of mountains, but an individual mountain name has no article at all.

<u>Rule 5</u>. Use **the** with deserts.

<u>Rule 6</u>. Use **the** with regions of a country: *the South, the coast,* etc.

<u>Rule 7</u>. The names of seasons do not require **the**: *I like summer* OR *I like the summer.*

BE CAREFUL!

Common Learner Errors	Explanation
1. Alaska is the largest state in ~~U.S.~~ the U.S.	Be sure to use **the** with country names that sound plural.
2. When my parents travel, they prefer to stay at ~~Hilton~~ the Hilton.	Be sure to use **the** with names of hotels.

EXERCISE 15. Articles with Place Nouns

Write **a, an, the,** or **Ø** before each place.

1. _____ Hawaii

2. _____ Hawaiian Islands

3. _____ Green Street

4. _____ Louvre

5. _____ Japan

6. _____ Japan and China

7. _____ Venezuela

8. _____ Africa

9. _____ Pacific Ocean

10. _____ United Nations

11. _____ Mississippi (= the river)

12. _____ Mississippi (= the state)

13. _____ United Kingdom

14. _____ Lake Michigan

15. _____ Himalaya Mountains

16. _____ Caribbean Sea

17. _____ Intercontinental Hotel

18. _____ Orinoco River

19. _____ Dead Sea

20. _____ Dominican Republic

21. _____ Greece

22. _____ North America

23. _____ Andaman Sea

24. _____ Argentina

25. _____ Quebec

26. _____ Asia

27. _____ United Arab Emirates

28. _____ Atlas Mountains

29. _____ Mojave Desert

30. _____ Gulf of Mexico

EXERCISE 16. Articles with Place Nouns

Write **a, an, the,** or Ø before each place.

1. _____ British Columbia
2. _____ Kingdom of Saudi Arabia
3. _____ Metropolitan Museum of Art
4. _____ Saudi Arabia
5. _____ Tate Gallery
6. _____ Republic of Colombia
7. _____ Colombia
8. _____ St. Lawrence River
9. _____ Persian Gulf
10. _____ Atlantic Ocean
11. _____ New Zealand
12. _____ Lake Titicaca
13. _____ Alps
14. _____ Amazon River
15. _____ Sarah's Diner
16. _____ Lake Geneva
17. _____ Mexico
18. _____ Mexico City
19. _____ Honolulu
20. _____ Sahara
21. _____ Missouri River
22. _____ Finland and Sweden
23. _____ Miami River
24. _____ Rome
25. _____ Rome and Athens
26. _____ Soviet Union
27. _____ Mediterranean Sea
28. _____ Nile
29. _____ Washington, DC
30. _____ Boston

 Do Online Exercise 2.4. My score: _____ /10. _____ % correct.

EXERCISE 17. Speaking Practice: Information Chart

Student A

Step 1. Work with a partner. Student A works here. Student B works on page 70.

Step 2. This chart lists well-known sites all over the world. It gives their locations and some facts about them. Your chart is missing some of the information, but your partner has this information. Take turns asking questions to complete this chart.

Step 3. When both of you have finished, compare books. Do not let your partner see your book until you have finished this activity.

Examples: *Where is the Louvre?*

How much does the Statue of Liberty weigh?

What is the name of the longest river in Africa?

Famous Sites	Location	Facts
the Empire State Building	New York City	• _____ tall • 102 floors
the Louvre	_____	• more than a million pieces of art
Ottawa	Canada	• _____
the Andes Mountains	South America	• the tallest mountains are _____ feet high
the Mississippi River	_____	• 2,340 miles long
Mexico City	Mexico	• 15,000,000 people
the _____	Egypt	• _____ miles long • the longest river in Africa
the Eiffel Tower	Paris	• built in _____ • 904 feet high
the Statue of Liberty	on Ellis Island _____	• _____ feet high • _____ pounds • built in 1884

EXERCISE 17. Speaking Practice: Information Chart

Student B

Step 1. Work with a partner. Student B works here. Student A works on page 69.

Step 2. This chart lists well-known sites all over the world. It gives their locations and some facts about them. Your chart is missing some of the information, but your partner has this information. Take turns asking questions to complete this chart.

Step 3. When both of you have finished, compare charts. Do not let your partner see your book until you have finished this activity.

Examples: *How long is the Mississippi River?*

When was the Statue of Liberty built?

What is the second reason that the Nile River is well known?

Famous Sites	Location	Facts
the Empire State Building	New York City	• 1,250 feet tall • _____ floors
the Louvre	Paris	• _____ pieces of art
_____	Canada	• the capital of Canada
the Andes Mountains	_____	• the tallest mountains are 20,000 feet high
the Mississippi River	the central U.S.	• _____ miles long
Mexico City	Mexico	• _____ people
the Nile River	_____	• 4,145 miles long • _____
the Eiffel Tower	Paris	• built in 1889 • _____ feet high
the Statue of Liberty	on Ellis Island _____ _____	• 301 feet high • 450,000 pounds • built in _____

EXERCISE 18. Mini-Conversations

Circle the correct words in these eight mini-conversations.

1. A: Do you have (a, an, Ø) idea for Marcia's birthday party?

   B: We should have (a, an, the, Ø) picnic in (a, the) big park by my house.

2. A: How much does (a, the, Ø) single-day ticket cost?

   B: $80.00, but there is (a, an, Ø) student discount.

3. A: I'm going to visit (Ø, the) Lake Como this summer.

   B: You're so lucky! I hear it's beautiful in (Ø, the, an) Italy then.

4. A: Who was (a, the, Ø) first woman to fly a plane across (Ø, the, an) Atlantic?

   B: (An, The) answer to your question is easy: (Ø, the) Amelia Earhart from (Ø, the) United States.

5. A: Can you recommend (a, an) hotel in (a, the) central area of (Ø, the) Smoky Mountains?

   B: Well, (Ø, the) hotel my wife and I like is Mountainview Lodge on (a, Ø, the) Pine Street in (a, Ø, the) small town in (a, Ø, the) eastern Tennessee.

6. A: Why were you so late for (a, Ø, the) meeting?

   B: There was (a, an) accident near my house. (A, The, Ø) traffic was terrible.

7. A: Did you take (a, Ø, the) final exam yesterday?

   B: Yes, and now I'm just waiting for (a, the, Ø) results.

8. A: Would you like to order (a, an, Ø) sandwich?

   B: Yes, I think I will have (a, the, Ø) cheeseburger.

Do Online Exercise 2.5. My score: ____ /10. ____ % correct.

Grammar Lesson

No Article (Ø)

A third possibility for using an article is **no article.** We use no article when we want to talk about the whole category of the noun, not just one example.

Tigers are dangerous.

My favorite color is **blue**.

Plural Count Nouns	Non-Count Nouns
tigers	information
verbs	blue

<u>Rule 1</u>. When you want to talk about a category or group in general, use **no article.**

<u>Rule 2</u>. Use **no article** before abstract nouns such as feelings or ideas.

BE CAREFUL!

Common Learner Errors	Explanation
1. Most people are afraid of ~~the snakes~~ snakes.	Do not use **the** with plural count nouns when you mean the category in general.
2. Joe's favorite foods are ~~the cheese~~ cheese and ~~the fresh bread~~ fresh bread.	Do not use **the** with non-count nouns when you mean the category in general.

EXERCISE 19. Speaking Practice: Interviewing Your Classmates about Their Eating Choices

Interview a classmate about how often he or she eats certain types of food or drinks certain beverages. Notice that there is no **the** before the food words because they are either plural count nouns or non-count nouns.

Step 1. Select a partner and write that person's name on the line.

Step 2. Predict what your partner's answers will be. Put a check mark (✔) in the box of the answer you predict.

Step 3. Interview your partner. Put a circle in the box for your partner's answers.

Step 4. Your partner will interview you now.

Step 5. Compare answers. Who was able to predict better?

My partner's name: _____

Question	Every Day	Almost Every Day	Sometimes	Almost Never	Never
How often do you eat sandwiches?					
How often do you eat pizza?					
How often do you eat scrambled eggs?					
How often do you eat in front of the TV?					
How often do you drink coffee?					
How often do you drink tea?					
How often do you eat rice?					
How often do you eat candy?					
How often do you eat pasta?					
How often do you drink milk?					

EXERCISE 20. Editing: Is It Correct?

If the sentence is correct, write a check mark (✓) on the line. If it is not correct, write X on the line and circle the mistake. Then change the sentence to make it correct. Write the change above the sentence. *(Hint:* There are twelve sentences. Four are correct, but eight have mistakes.)

Proverbs

_____ 1. You can't judge book by its cover.

_____ 2. Silence is golden.

_____ 3. When in the Rome, do as the Romans do.

_____ 4. Beauty is only skin deep.

_____ 5. When he came late again, that was straw that broke the camel's back.

_____ 6. Rome was not built in day.

_____ 7. The honesty is the best policy.

_____ 8. The love of money is root of all evil.

_____ 9. The blood is thicker than the water.

_____ 10. Best things in life are free.

_____ 11. Every cloud has a silver lining.

_____ 12. A leopard cannot change its spots.

EXERCISE 21. Sentence Study for Critical Reading

Read the numbered sentences. Then read the three answer choices, and put a check mark (✓) in the yes or no boxes in front of each sentence to show if that answer is true based on the information in the original sentence. If there is not enough information to mark something as yes, then mark it as no. Remember that more than one true answer is possible.

1. My cousin lives in Dubai now, but he was born in Istanbul, Turkey.
   - ☐ yes ☐ no   a. I have only one cousin.
   - ☐ yes ☐ no   b. My cousin does not live where he was born.
   - ☐ yes ☐ no   c. My cousin's birthplace is in Turkey.

2. Karla will be right back. She needs to use the phone in the kitchen.
   - ☐ yes ☐ no   a. Karla believes there are three phones in the kitchen.
   - ☐ yes ☐ no   b. Karla doesn't know if there is a phone in the house.
   - ☐ yes ☐ no   c. The phone in the kitchen is not working well.

3. Pierre is on the winning baseball team.
   - ☐ yes ☐ no   a. Pierre is a member of a baseball team.
   - ☐ yes ☐ no   b. Pierre's team is the winner.
   - ☐ yes ☐ no   c. Pierre's team won.

4. Hey, Donna! Come on. Come sit down now. It's 8:00, so it's time for the movie to start.
   - ☐ yes ☐ no   a. They are going to choose a movie to watch right now.
   - ☐ yes ☐ no   b. They are going to watch a movie.
   - ☐ yes ☐ no   c. This movie begins at 8 o'clock.

5. In the bowl on the table, there are six pieces of fruit: an apple, two pears, an orange, and two bananas.
   - ☐ yes ☐ no   a. The orange is between the pears and the bananas.
   - ☐ yes ☐ no   b. There are more bananas than apples.
   - ☐ yes ☐ no   c. There are more pears than bananas.

6. *Bob:* Mae, did you use the computer? I ask because it's still on.

   Mae: Yes, I did. I'm sorry that I forgot to turn it off.

   Bob: You hardly ever use the computer.

   Mae: Well, tonight I needed to finish a report for school.
   - ☐ yes ☐ no   a. Mae and Bob are talking about one computer, not two.
   - ☐ yes ☐ no   b. Both Mae and Bob finished their reports for school.
   - ☐ yes ☐ no   c. Mae and Bob got their computers at the same time.

7. They are moving to Florida, which is in the southern part of the United States.

   ☐ yes ☐ no a. Florida is in the southern part of the United States.

   ☐ yes ☐ no b. They are not living in Florida now.

   ☐ yes ☐ no c. They prefer to continue living in their current place.

8. The menu had prices ranging from $39.95 to $59.95.

   ☐ yes ☐ no a. The food at the restaurant costs $39.95 or $59.95.

   ☐ yes ☐ no b. There are many menus to choose from at the restaurant.

   ☐ yes ☐ no c. There is no steak dinner for $29.95 at the restaurant.

EXERCISE 22. Speaking Practice: Proverbs from Another Language to English

Step 1. Write a well-known proverb from another language.

_____

Step 2. Translate the proverb word by word into English. Do not worry if your translation is not good English.

_____

Step 3. Now write your translation in good English. Can you find an English proverb that has the same message even if it uses different words?

_____

_____

_____

_____

Step 4. Work with a partner or in a small group. Discuss your proverbs and their meanings in English.

EXERCISE 23. Review Test 1: Multiple Choice

Circle the letter of the correct answer. Some are conversations.

1. ____ English is a difficult language for some people to learn in school.

    a. a   b. an   c. the   d. Ø

2. I want to take ____ steamboat down the Mississippi River from Wisconsin to Louisiana.

    a. a   b. an   c. the   d. Ø

3. The students liked the movie starring ____ handsome actor Leonardo DiCaprio.

    a. a   b. an   c. the   d. Ø

4. "Is this ____ useful textbook?"

"Yes, it is. I'm sure you'll want to keep it for future reference."

    a. a   b. an   c. the   d. Ø

5. I plan to go on vacation to Arizona next year to see ____ Grand Canyon.

    a. a   b. an   c. the   d. Ø

6. She and her friend have ____ same taste in music.

    a. a   b. an   c. the   d. Ø

7. "How long did you have to wait in line at the driver's license office?"

"More than ____ hour! It was awful!"

    a. a   b. an   c. the   d. Ø

8. "Did you see the review of that video game?"

"I did! It was rated ____ best game of the year!"

    a. a   b. an   c. the   d. Ø

EXERCISE 24. Review Test 2: Production and Evaluation

Part 1.

Read this short passage. Put the words in parentheses in the correct order, and then fill in the blanks.

Formula One racing is ❶ _____ (popular a type of)

car racing. The name *formula* refers to ❷ _____ (a of set)

rules about how ❸ _____ (racers the drive) and control

their cars. Formula One cars are some of ❹ _____

(fastest racecars the) in the world. The cars race at speeds up to 220 miles

per hour. ❺ _____ (interesting fact an) about Formula

One racing is that the cars race on public streets, not tracks. A Formula

One race has five races. Only

❻ _____ (the the

with drivers) fastest times can race in the

fifth race. The most famous Formula One

race happens in Monte Carlo, Monaco,

and is called the Grand Prix.

Part 2.

Read the short passage. There are six mistakes. Circle the mistakes, and write the correction above the mistake.

Venice, Italy, is popular city for tourists to visit because of its beautiful

buildings and quiet canals. However, the sea level is rising, and Venice is slowly

sinking into Adriatic Sea. There has been a average of 100 floods per year.

Scientists say the water is rising because of global warming. Italy has a unusual

plan to save the city. The city hopes to build large gates that will fill with the air

when the water level rises and then push the water back. A plan is expensive, but

Italy hopes it will save Venice.

EXERCISE 25. Reading Practice: A Restaurant Review

Read this restaurant review. Notice the use of articles. Answer the seven questions on page 80. The grammar from this unit is underlined for you.

Lovers of Asian cuisine, there is a new restaurant in town for you: Splendor of the Orient, conveniently located downtown two blocks from the park and right on the west shore of the lake. The view from the dining room, of course, is beautiful. I recommend going for an early dinner so you can see the sunset. The location is spectacular.

My wife and I went on a crowded Friday evening, but the service was excellent. The host seated us at a table by the window. We could hear some noise from the kitchen, but it wasn't bad. A waiter arrived quickly, handed us the menu, and told us about the specials of the day. We both wanted an appetizer, so I chose a vegetable soup, and my wife chose a fresh salad. For our main dishes, I had the pineapple green curry from the menu, and my wife had fresh fish, one of the specials. I just had water to drink—I don't like any other taste to get in the way of my experience—and my wife had an iced tea. For dessert, we shared an ice cream dish with coconut ice cream and fresh mangos.

Our food was excellent. The curry was spicy, but not too spicy, so I could taste all of the subtle flavors. It was filled with vegetables, and the sweetness of the pineapple was a nice contrast to the hot curry. The fish my wife ordered was very good too, and it was well-prepared. The portions were a good size, and the service from the waiter was very good.

My only complaint was about the music. I like the atmosphere of an exotic Asian village in the countryside when I dine, not a noisy city disco, and certainly not an American disco. The music didn't go with the food at all, and at times it was difficult to hear my wife talk. I hope in the future that Splendor of the Orient will choose an authentic Asian music CD and play it at a reasonable volume.

Use the information from the reading, and then put a check mark (✔) in the rating box for each category. Then answer the seven questions.

	Poor	Fair	Good	Excellent
the food				
the service				
the portions				
the atmosphere				
the location				

1. Why does the writer recommend going to the restaurant for an early dinner?

   _____

2. How did the writer feel about the music?

   _____

3. Which dinner did the wife order?

   _____

4. Where is the restaurant located?

   _____

5. Why did the writer order water to drink?

   _____

6. What was a nice contrast to the hot curry in the writer's meal?

   _____

7. Overall, is this review positive or negative? Give three examples to support your answer.

   _____

   _____

   _____

   _____

   _____

   _____

EXERCISE 26. Vocabulary Practice: Word Knowledge

Circle the word or phrase that is most closely related to the word or phrase on the left. Use a dictionary to check the meaning of words you do not know.

Vocabulary	Answer Choices	
1. awful	bad	good
2. a blanket	for cooking	for sleeping
3. huge	very big	very small
4. aid	help	relax
5. actually	at this time; now	in fact; really
6. a snack	you believe it	you eat it
7. an envelope	at the bakery	at the post office
8. scary	I'm afraid	I'm tired
9. your lap	your body	your car
10. an author	a person	a place
11. yeast	in bread	in pasta
12. a disaster	a bad time	a good time
13. a pouch	a plane	a pocket
14. merchandise	in a class	in a store
15. a brochure	you read it	you wear it
16. a stripe	a lake	a line
17. ugly	not beautiful	not horrible
18. an owl	a bird	a fish
19. a section	a game	a part
20. crowded	many people	many reasons
21. flour	green	white
22. suddenly	quickly	slowly
23. an earthquake	the ground moves	the weather improves
24. a gate	a door	a plan
25. a fee	a calendar	a cost
26. a solution	an answer to a problem	a cause of a problem
27. take place	forget	happen
28. to sink	opposite of rise	opposite of turn
29. an attendant	a person	a place
30. a switch	in/out	on/off
31. dangerous	not free	not safe
32. a flood	a lot of furniture	a lot of water
33. an expression	a few coins	a few words

EXERCISE 27. Vocabulary Practice: Collocations

Fill in each blank with the answer on the right that most naturally completes the phrase on the left. If necessary, use a dictionary to check the meaning of words you do not know.

Vocabulary	Answer Choices	
1. I'm allergic _____ peanuts	to	with
2. _____ 11:30 AM	at	in
3. the building has three _____	stories	subjects
4. _____ socks	item	thick
5. she dropped her _____	evening	phone
6. an aggressive _____	animal	number
7. _____ for someone	like	look
8. two _____ batteries	flashlight	supply
9. a _____ crash	car	house
10. a grade _____ a test	in	on
11. _____ lost	I'm	I like
12. _____ you shortly	see	win
13. a haunted _____	cloud	house
14. an honest _____	man	toy
15. an amount of _____	money	people
16. a poisonous _____	alligator	snake
17. Lost and _____	Found	Gone
18. a _____ line of people	heavy	long
19. a sleeping _____	bag	box
20. a _____ booth	statue	ticket
21. a new plan _____ our country	for	than
22. a _____ and a dryer	cleaner	washer
23. a view _____ the city	at	of
24. a _____ garage	parking	sleeping
25. _____ away the groceries	get	put
26. prepare _____ a trip	for	to
27. to signal _____ help	by	for
28. a popular _____	conversation	restaurant
29. a subtle _____	flavor	town
30. _____ a trip	run	take
31. the main _____	dish	future
32. my mouth is _____	airing	watering
33. _____ careful	be	have

EXERCISE 28. Writing Practice

Part 1. Editing Student Writing

Read these sentences about one student's opinion about a favorite thing. Circle the 15 errors. Then write the number of the sentence with the error next to the type of error. (Some sentences may have more than one error.)

_____ a. missing article   _____ d. word order

_____ b. incorrect article   _____ e. verb tense

_____ c. subject-verb agreement   _____ f. preposition (*at, on, in*)

My Favorite Book
1. I love to read the books.
2. My favorite book are *Harry Potter and the Philosopher's Stone.*
3. This book was first Harry Potter book.
4. I have had this book since I first arrived in United States.
5. I get this book in a bookstore in the main train station at Paris.
6. To me, the story is really interesting because we can learn about the life amazing of the main character.
7. I think the most people who are my age have a copy of this book famous.
8. Characters are very good, and I really am liking the story in the book.
9. I'm not going to tell you an ending of the book, but I will say that it is a book wonderful.
10. If you need a idea for a gift for a nephew or niece, I highly recommend this book entertaining.

Part 2. Original Student Writing

Write sentences or a paragraph about a favorite thing or person. Underline the articles in your writing.

Unit 3

Irregular Past Tense Verbs

Discover the Grammar

Read the conversation between a husband (Stephan) and wife (Helena), and then answer the seven questions.

Line		
1	*Helena:*	Hi, honey, I'm home.
2	*Stephan:*	Hi, how are you? Did you have a good day at work today?
3	*Helena:*	Yes, it was pretty good. I worked in my office until 3, and then I
4		helped Belinda with a new job from 3 to 5.
5	*Stephan:*	Wow, you were really busy then, right? Did you go to the bank
6		today? I need some cash for tomorrow.
7	*Helena:*	Sorry. I didn't go to the bank. The car is making a funny noise.
8	*Stephan:*	A funny noise? What do you mean? I drove it yesterday, and it
9		sounded fine then.
10	*Helena:*	Well, it doesn't sound fine now. It sounds terrible. I thought you said
11		you were going to take it to the auto repair shop. Did you forget?
12	*Stephan:*	I called the shop. They were really busy, so I didn't take the car there.
13	*Helena:*	Then what did you do?

84

14	Stephan:	I just took the car to my cousin Joe's house. He knows a lot about
15		cars. He changed the oil and said the car was fine, but it still cost me
16		more than $50 for the oil change.
17	Helena:	Well, we'll have to call the mechanic tomorrow.
18	Stephan:	Ok, I'll take the car there, but I don't have any more cash. Do you
19		have some?
20	Helena:	No, I don't have any cash. Can you write a check?
21	Stephan:	No, I can't. I think I forgot my checkbook at the office.
22	Helena:	I can't believe you left it there again! Did you leave your briefcase
23		at work?
24	Stephan:	No, I didn't leave my briefcase at work. I brought it home, but my
25		checkbook isn't in my briefcase. I meant to put it in there, but I
26		forgot, so I think it's still in my desk drawer. Yes, that's where I think
27		I put it.

1. Find the one-word past tense forms of these 12 verbs in the conversation, and write them here. Then write the line number in parentheses.

are _____ ( )   forget _____ ( )   put _____ ( )

bring _____ ( )   is _____ ( )   say _____ ( )

cost _____ ( )   leave _____ ( )   take _____ ( )

drive _____ ( )   mean _____ ( )   think _____ ( )

2. Find the four past tense questions that begin with *did*. Write the line number and then copy the questions here. Put the subject and verb in the correct columns.

Line	Did	Subject	Verb	The rest of the statement
2	Did	you	have	a good day at work today?

3. How are past tense questions formed? When the question begins with *did*, what form of the verb do you use after the subject?

_____

_____

_____

4. Find the three past tense negative statements with *didn't*. Write the line number and then copy the negative statements here. Put the subject and verb in the correct columns.

Line	Did	Subject	Verb	The rest of the statement

5. How are past tense negative statements formed? When the negative statement has *didn't*, what form of the verb do you use after it?

_____

6. Change the statement into a negative statement and then a yes-no question.

Affirmative	She drove to the bank.
Negative	
Question	

7. What questions do you have about using the simple past tense in English?

_____

_____

_____

Grammar Lesson

Irregular Past Tense Verbs

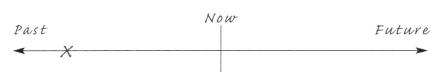

Past   *Now*   *Future*

Regular Past Tense	Irregular Past Tense
I work**ed** in my office from 8 to 3.	I just **took** the car to my cousin's house.
Then I help**ed** Belinda.	It **cost** me more than $75.
The car sound**ed** fine.	I **drove** the car to the office.
I call**ed** the shop.	I **forgot** my checkbook at the office
He chang**ed** the oil.	I **brought** the car home.

Simple Past Tense of Irregular Verbs: Affirmative

In simple past tense, more than 99 percent of all English verbs are regular: *attended, died, hoped, liked, worked*. Only about 175 English verbs are irregular in simple past tense. The number 175 may seem like a lot, but you should consider that there are thousands of verbs in the English language. In fact, 175 is a very small number.

These irregular past tense verbs are extremely common when talking about the past. In fact, some experts* say that about 57 percent of English speaking and writing about past events uses a very small number of these irregular verbs.

Irregular past tense verbs do not use *–ed*. Instead, they change in many different ways. Some people find it easier to learn these verbs in groups by the type of change. See Appendix C for irregular verbs in groupings.

*Source: Grabowski, E., and Mindt, D. A corpus-based learning list of irregular verbs in English *ICAME Journal, No. 19*, 5–22.

A Longer List of Irregular Past Tense Verbs					
Present	Past	Present	Past	Present	Past
1. become	**became**	27. go	**went**	53. sell	**sold**
2. begin	**began**	28. grow	**grew**	54. send	**sent**
3. bite	**bit**	29. hang	**hung**	55. set	**set**
4. blow	**blew**	30. have	**had**	56. shoot	**shot**
5. break	**broke**	31. hear	**heard**	57. shut	**shut**
6. bring	**brought**	32. hide	**hid**	58. sing	**sang**
7. build	**built**	33. hold	**held**	59. sits	**sat**
8. buy	**bought**	34. hurt	**hurt**	60. sleep	**slept**
9. catch	**caught**	35. keep	**kept**	61. speak	**spoke**
10. choose	**chose**	36. know	**knew**	62. spend	**spent**
11. come	**came**	37. lead	**led**	63. spread	**spread**
12. cost	**cost**	38. leave	**left**	64. stand	**stood**
13. cut	**cut**	39. lend	**lent**	65. steal	**stole**
14. do	**did**	40. let	**let**	66. stick	**stuck**
15. draw	**drew**	41. lie*	**lay**	67. swim	**swam**
16. drink	**drank**	42. lose	**lost**	68. take	**took**
17. drive	**drove**	43. make	**made**	69. teach	**taught**
18. eat	**ate**	44. mean	**meant**	70. tear	**tore**
19. fall	**fell**	45. meet	**met**	71. tell	**told**
20. feel	**felt**	46. put	**put**	72. think	**thought**
21. fight	**fought**	47. read	**read**	73. throw	**threw**
22. find	**found**	48. ride	**rode**	74. understand	**understood**
23. fly	**flew**	49. ring	**rang**	75. wake	**woke**
24. forget	**forgot**	50. run	**ran**	76. wear	**wore**
25. get	**got**	51. say	**said**	77. win	**won**
26. give	**gave**	52. see	**saw**	78. write	**wrote**

*lie = lie down (recline); not tell the truth = lie, lied

Rule 1. In the simple past tense, a regular verb ends in –ed (*add* → *added*) or –d (*use* → *used*).

Rule 2. An irregular verb does not use –ed, and the irregular form is difficult to predict. Some verbs change endings (*send* → *sent*), some verbs change the vowel (*get* → *got*), and some verbs do not change at all (*put* → *put*). In fact, there are many different ways to form an irregular past tense verb.

Rule 3. To learn irregular verbs, you have to memorize the correct forms and then practice them as much as possible. The good news is that the number of irregular verbs is small and they are very common, so you will see and hear the same irregular verbs a lot.

Rule 4. Use simple past tense for actions that happened in the past and are completely finished. Remember that common time expressions for simple past tense include *yesterday, last _____ (last week)*, and *_____ ago (two weeks ago)*.

Rule 5. To make a negative statement with a verb, add **did not** before the base (simple) form of the verb: *I* **went** *to the bank, but I* **did not go** *to the post office.*

Rule 6. In informal English, it is possible to use contractions for **did not: didn't.**

Rule 7. The question form is **did + SUBJECT + VERB: Did you go to the bank?**

Rule 8. To answer a yes-no question, use **did** for a short affirmative answer and **did not** or **didn't** for a short negative answer: *Yes, I* **did**. OR *No, I* **didn't**.

 BE CAREFUL!

Common Learner Errors	Explanation
1. My sister ~~goed~~ **went** to England last year.	Remember to use an irregular verb. Don't add **–ed** to an irregular verb.
2. Carlos ~~was took~~ **took** a trip to Miami last month.	Do not use **was** or **were** with simple past tense of irregular verbs.
3. I got a bad grade on my math test. ~~Made~~ **I made** too many simple mistakes.	Use a subject with a simple past irregular verb.
5. Your cousin ~~no went~~ **didn't go** to China.	For negatives, remember to use **didn't** (**did not**) with the base form of the verb.
6. Nell and Vick ~~weren't eat~~ **didn't eat** any food at the party.	For negatives, do not use **was not** (**wasn't**) or **were not** (**weren't**) with **VERB.** Use **did not** (**didn't**) only.
7. The meeting didn't ~~began~~ **begin** on time.	If you have the helping verb **did** in a question or a negative, don't use the past tense form of the verb. You need only one past time marker.
8. ~~Were~~ **Did** you get sick from last night's dinner?	Do not use **be** (**was, were**) with other verbs in simple past tense.
9. Did you watch TV last night? No, I ~~was~~ **did** not.	Do not use **was/were** as a short answer for **did** questions.
10. Did you like that movie? Yes, I ~~liked~~ **did**.	For yes-no questions in simple past tense, use only **did** or **didn't** in your answers. Do not use any other verb.

EXERCISE 1. Practicing Irregular Verb Forms

Write the past tense of the verbs.

1. win _____
2. see _____
3. forget _____
4. choose _____
5. mean _____
6. set _____
7. build _____
8. drink _____
9. buy _____
10. fly_____
11. hang _____
12. spread _____
13. go _____
14. have _____
15. make _____
16. bite _____
17. give _____
18. shut _____

EXERCISE 2. Irregular Past Tense Verbs in Context

Read this short story. Fill in the blanks with the correct past tense form of the verbs in the box. Several verbs are used more than once, and sometimes more than one verb is possible.

| **word list** | be | drink | forget | go | lose | read | take |
| | buy | feel | get | hear | put | ride | wake |

My Busy Day Yesterday

1. Yesterday I _____ up at 6:45 in the morning when I _____ the alarm clock ringing.

2. I _____ a hot shower, and I _____ ready for my busy day.

3. Then I _____ dressed in my new suit.

4. Because the weather _____ a little rainy in the morning, I also _____ on a raincoat.

Do Online Exercise 3.1. My score: _____ /10. _____ % correct.

5. A few weeks ago, I _____ my umbrella. Unfortunately, I _____ to buy a new one, so I _____ to work without it.

6. On my way to the metro station, I stopped at a convenience store and _____ an umbrella, a coffee, and a newspaper.

7. On the metro, I _____ the umbrella on the floor by my feet because it _____ wet.

8. I _____ my coffee and _____ the newspaper.

9. I _____ the metro to my usual stop.

10. I _____ off the subway and walked the short distance to my office, but without my umbrella again!

 EXERCISE 3. Speaking Practice: Testing Your Grammar Knowledge

Make a test for a classmate. What are ten of the most difficult irregular past tense verbs for you? Write the present tense of ten verbs on the lines on the left. Then give your book to a classmate. Your classmate will write the correct past tense on the lines on the right. Check your partner's answers.

	Present	*Past*
1.	_____	_____
2.	_____	_____
3.	_____	_____
4.	_____	_____
5.	_____	_____
6.	_____	_____
7.	_____	_____
8.	_____	_____
9.	_____	_____
10.	_____	_____

 Do Online Exercise 3.2. My score: ____/10. ____% correct.

Connecting Grammar and Vocabulary

Here are 50 of the most frequently used irregular verb forms in English. These fifty verbs are 87 percent of the irregular verbs in English.

If you want to improve your English, it is important for you to memorize an affirmative, a negative, a yes-no, and a *wh-* question for each of these common forms. Learn to read, write, say, and hear the four forms for each verb.

Affirmative	Negative	Yes-No Question?	Information Question?
1. He was	He wasn't	Was he . . . ?	When was he there?
2. You were	You weren't	Were you . . . ?	Why were you late?
3. They did	They didn't do	Did they do . . . ?	What did they do?
4. She had	She didn't have	Did she have . . . ?	Why did she have a key?
5. He said	He didn't say	Did he say . . . ?	What did he say?
6. You made	You didn't make	Did you make . . . ?	How many did you make?
7. I went	I didn't go	Did you go . . . ?	Where did you go?
8. They took	They didn't take	Did they take . . . ?	Which bus did they take?
9. They came	They didn't come	Did they come . . . ?	When did they come here?
10. You saw	You didn't see	Did you see . . . ?	Which movie did you see?
11. She knew	She didn't know	Did she know . . . ?	How did she know?
12. I got	I didn't get	Did you get . . . ?	When did you get here?
13. He gave	He didn't give	Did he give . . . ?	Why did he give it to you?
14. I found	I didn't find	Did you find . . . ?	Where did you find my keys?
15. I thought	I didn't think	Did you think . . . ?	What did you think?
16. He told	He didn't tell	Did he tell . . . ?	When did he tell you?
17. It became	It didn't become	Did it become . . . ?	When did it become impossible?
18. She left	She didn't leave	Did she leave . . . ?	Where did she leave her cell?
19. I felt	I didn't feel	Did you feel . . . ?	When did you feel sick?
20. We put	We didn't put	Did you put . . . ?	Where did you put the bag?
21. He brought	He didn't bring	Did he bring . . . ?	What did he bring?
22. It began	It didn't begin	Did it begin . . . ?	When did it begin to rain?
23. She kept	She didn't keep	Did she keep . . . ?	Where did she keep her cell?
24. I wrote	I didn't write	Did you write . . . ?	What did you write?
25. He let	He didn't let	Did he let . . . ?	When did he let you use his car?
26. I meant	I didn't mean	Did you mean . . . ?	What did you mean?
27. You set	You didn't set	Did you set . . . ?	When did you set the table?
28. They met	They didn't meet	Did they meet . . . ?	How did they meet?
29. We ran	We didn't run	Did you run . . . ?	Why did you run here?

30. I paid	I didn't pay	Did you pay . . . ?	How much did you pay?
31. She sat	She didn't sit	Did she sit . . . ?	Where did she sit?
32. I spoke	I didn't speak	Did you speak . . . ?	Who did you speak to?
33. I lay down	I didn't lie down	Did you lie down . . . ?	Why did you lie down?
34. He led	He didn't lead	Did he lead . . . ?	How long did he lead the group?
35. They read	They didn't read	Did they read . . . ?	Which book did they read?
36. It grew	It didn't grow	Did it grow . . . ?	How did that plant grow so fast?
37. You lost	You didn't lose	Did you lose . . . ?	When did you lose your keys?
38. He fell	He didn't fall	Did he fall . . . ?	How did he fall?
39. They sent	They didn't send	Did they send . . . ?	What did they send you?
40. I built	I didn't build	Did you build . . . ?	What did you build?
41. I understood	I didn't understand	Did you understand . . . ?	Which book did you understand better?
42. She drew	She didn't draw	Did she draw . . . ?	What did she draw?
43. It broke	It didn't break	Did it break . . . ?	When did it break?
44. I spent	I didn't spend	Did you spend . . . ?	How much did you spend?
45. He cut	He didn't cut	Did he cut . . . ?	How did he cut his finger?
46. It rose	It didn't rise	Did the sun rise . . . ?	When did the sun rise?
47. They drove	They didn't drive	Did they drive . . . ?	Where did they drive?
48. I bought	I didn't buy	Did you buy . . . ?	What did you buy?
49. He wore	He didn't wear	Did he wear . . . ?	Which tie did he wear?
50. We chose	We didn't choose	Did you choose . . . ?	What did you choose?

Source: Lancaster-Bergen Corpus, www.eslhq.com/forums/worksheets/esl-worksheets/most-common-irregular-verbs-english-1555/

EXERCISE 4. Editing: Is It Correct?

If the sentence is correct, write a check mark (✔) on the line. If it is not correct, write X on the line and circle the mistake. Then change the sentence to make it correct. Write the change above the sentence. (*Hint:* There are eight sentences. Two are correct, but six have mistakes.)

New York City Fashion Week

_____ 1. Last September, I go to Fashion Week in New York City.

_____ 2. Many people stood in line for hours for tickets to the main fashion show, but I already had my ticket.

_____ 3. For this fashion show that we saw, six famous designers make new clothes for the models to wear.

_____ 4. I saw a lot of beautiful dresses and take about 50 pictures.

_____ 5. After the great show, I meet my favorite designer.

_____ 6. She was so nice. She give me an invitation to a party after the show.

_____ 7. I went to the party, and it was amazing. There I was with so many famous people. I feel like a really important person!

_____ 8. I thought my trip to New York City Fashion Week was amazing!

Do Online Exercise 3.3. My score: _____ /10. _____ % correct.

EXERCISE 5. Can You Guess the Truth?

Use this list of 30 common irregular past tense verbs to write six negative sentences in the past about anything about yourself. Make three of the sentences true and three of the sentences false. Use a different verb in each sentence. Circle T if your sentence is true and F if it is false. Then read your sentence to see if your partner can guess if your sentence is true or false. Take turns guessing. Who can guess more correct answers?

ate	flew	left	sent	took
began	found	lent	shot	tore
bought	gave	lost	sold	went
did	got	made	spent	wrote
drank	had	rode	stole	woke
drive	hurt	saw	stuck	won

Example: (T) F   I began high school when I was 13 years old.

1. T F _____
2. T F _____
3. T F _____
4. T F _____
5. T F _____
6. T F _____

After you finish: Were there any surprises? Are there any interesting facts?

EXERCISE 6. Speaking Practice: The Shopping Bag Game

Look at the shopping bags. Work with a partner. Each partner chooses one of the sixteen shopping bags. Take turns asking yes-no questions to find out which bag is your partner's bag. If Student B's answer is yes, Student A continues asking questions. If the answer is no, then Student B asks questions. The first student to guess the price of his or her partner's shopping bag is the winner. Use "Did you buy _____?" and "Yes, I bought _____" or "No, I didn't buy _____" in your conversations.

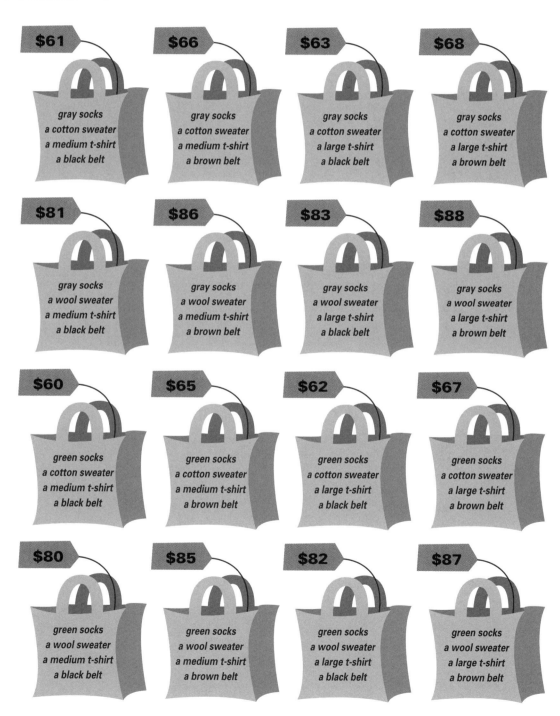

$61
gray socks
a cotton sweater
a medium t-shirt
a black belt

$66
gray socks
a cotton sweater
a medium t-shirt
a brown belt

$63
gray socks
a cotton sweater
a large t-shirt
a black belt

$68
gray socks
a cotton sweater
a large t-shirt
a brown belt

$81
gray socks
a wool sweater
a medium t-shirt
a black belt

$86
gray socks
a wool sweater
a medium t-shirt
a brown belt

$83
gray socks
a wool sweater
a large t-shirt
a black belt

$88
gray socks
a wool sweater
a large t-shirt
a brown belt

$60
green socks
a cotton sweater
a medium t-shirt
a black belt

$65
green socks
a cotton sweater
a medium t-shirt
a brown belt

$62
green socks
a cotton sweater
a large t-shirt
a black belt

$67
green socks
a cotton sweater
a large t-shirt
a brown belt

$80
green socks
a wool sweater
a medium t-shirt
a black belt

$85
green socks
a wool sweater
a medium t-shirt
a brown belt

$82
green socks
a wool sweater
a large t-shirt
a black belt

$87
green socks
a wool sweater
a large t-shirt
a brown belt

EXERCISE 7. Sentence Study for Critical Reading

Read the numbered sentences. Then read the three answer choices, and put a check mark (✓) in the yes or no boxes in front of each sentence to show if that answer is true based on the information in the original sentence. If there is not enough information to mark something as yes, then mark it as no. Remember that more than one true answer is possible.

1. Yesterday Choi went fishing with his grandfather at the lake. However, Choi forgot his fishing pole!

   ☐ yes ☐ no   a. Choi caught a fish.

   ☐ yes ☐ no   b. Choi saw his grandfather yesterday.

   ☐ yes ☐ no   c. Choi was at the lake, but his grandfather could not go there.

2. The contestant who stood the longest won the contest and the prize.

   ☐ yes ☐ no   a. The contest is still going on.

   ☐ yes ☐ no   b. One person received the prize.

   ☐ yes ☐ no   c. All the contestants sat down at the same time.

3. Caroline didn't understand how to do the homework. She asked Tom to meet her at a coffee shop to help her, but Tom had a cold and didn't show up.

   ☐ yes ☐ no   a. Tom helped Caroline with her homework.

   ☐ yes ☐ no   b. Caroline needed help with her homework.

   ☐ yes ☐ no   c. Caroline thought that Tom understood the homework.

4. A man in Germany built the first car in 1885. It became the most popular mode of transportation in the world. Today, there are about 600 million cars in the world, and this number is increasing at a very fast pace.

   ☐ yes ☐ no   a. Someone built the first car more than one hundred years ago.

   ☐ yes ☐ no   b. The man who built the first car made 600 million cars.

   ☐ yes ☐ no   c. In 1880, there were no automobiles on the roads.

5. Louise didn't do her homework yesterday, so her teacher didn't give her a good grade. In fact, she received a zero.

   ☐ yes ☐ no   a. Louise didn't go to school.

   ☐ yes ☐ no   b. The teacher gave Louise a bad grade.

   ☐ yes ☐ no   c. Louise did not turn in her homework yesterday.

6. My weekend was very busy. I saw a horror movie that was nearly three hours long, and then I went swimming at Jeanine's house. She has a great pool.

   ☐ yes ☐ no   a. I spent more time swimming than watching the movie.

   ☐ yes ☐ no   b. I went swimming after I saw the movie.

   ☐ yes ☐ no   c. The movie that I saw was horrible.

7. Maria made some beautiful dresses for her grandchildren. For the oldest grand-daughter, she chose to make a green one. For the youngest granddaughter, she chose to make a yellow one.

     yes   no   a. Maria made more than one dress.

     yes   no   b. The dress for the youngest granddaughter is yellow.

     yes   no   c. Maria's mother made the dresses for her granddaughters.

8. Marcos and Lucas drove to the mountains and went hiking for the weekend. They had to come home early because Marcos fell and broke his glasses. He's okay now, but his left ankle is sore.

     yes   no   a. Marcos and Lucas live in the mountains.

     yes   no   b. Lucas went hiking after Marcos did.

     yes   no   c. Marcos had a problem, but he stayed in the mountains all weekend.

REVIEW   **EXERCISE 8. Review Test 1: Multiple Choice**

Circle the letter of the correct answer. Some are conversations.

1. "What's wrong? What's the problem?"

   "Driving a stick shift ____ really difficult. The car stalled three times during my driving test."

        a. was   b. didn't   c. did   d. wasn't

2. How did Hazel choose that university? ____ other students who studied there?

        a. Was she know   c. Is she knowing

        b. Did she know   d. Did she knew

3. Last night I put up three new pictures on the living room wall. I ____ to borrow a hammer and some small nails from my neighbor to do this.

        a. was have   b. was had   c. had   d. haved

4. Paolo ____ his sister to swimming practice after school last week. He followed his mom's instructions and never let her out of his sight.

        a. took   b. takes   c. has taken   d. was took

5. When she was on vacation in Indonesia, Dodie ____ to practice yoga every day. However, the weather was so nice that she spent most of her time at the beach.

        a. tryed   b. was tryed   c. tried   d. was tried

6. Ted: "Tom, the vegetables from your garden are delicious!"

   Ann: "Yes, Tom, they were great. You always ____ great vegetables."

   Tom: "Thank you both. I spend a lot of time in my garden."

       a. grew   c. are going to grow

       b. are growing   d. grow

7. The police arrested the young man for stealing two radios from the store, but he says that he ____ anything. He denies everything.

       a. wasn't stole   c. doesn't stole

       b. not stole   d. didn't steal

8. "Did you take part in the race this past weekend?"

   "No, I ____. I was out of town, so I couldn't compete."

       a. don't   b. didn't   c. wasn't   d. watched

 EXERCISE 9. Review Test 2: Production and Evaluation

Part 1.

Read this short passage. Fill in the blanks with a form of the verb in parentheses.

Every Friday night I ❶ _____ (go) to my salsa class. The class

❷ _____ (meet) downtown in a dance studio. Some of my other friends

usually come, too. We usually ❸ _____ (practice) new routines

together. Last night we ❹ _____ (choose) new dancing costumes for

our upcoming performance. Raquel ❺ _____ (fight) to have green

shirts, but I ❻ _____ (not like) those shirts at all. I ❼ _____

(think) they were too expensive. In the end, most people ❽ _____ (agree)

with me.

 ONE-MINUTE LESSON

The expression **(not) at all** is a strong negative. *I don't speak Spanish* **at all** means that you do not know even one word of Spanish. *I didn't like the movie* **at all** means that you did not like any of the movie, not even one part of it. When you use **at all**, you should put *not* with the verb. It is possible to use the whole phrase in answer to a question. If someone asks you, *Do you speak Spanish?* you can answer, *Not at all.* (It is impossible to use only *at all* without the word *not* or another negative word somewhere.)

Part 2.

Read this short passage. There are six mistakes with verbs. Circle the mistakes, and write the correction above the mistake.

Do you remember your first visit to the ocean? Can you recall what you first felt when your eyes saw the endless water? In July 2010, I go with my family from Chicago to Miami. It was the first time that I saw the ocean. Wow! The ocean waves was so blue and warm. They looked beautiful, just like in a postcard. I jumped in the water and swimmed like a fish. Then I lied down on the white sand and heard the sound of the waves for the first time. It was an awesome feeling. Listening to the waves as they crashed one after the other was so relaxing. Later that afternoon, my family and I make a sandcastle and took lots of pictures. I felt so happy at the beach with my family. We had such a nice time! In fact, when the sun set, I really didn't wanted to go home to Chicago.

EXERCISE 10. Reading Practice: The Internet

Read the information in this letter a student wrote to Ms. Advice. In her letter, the student asks for help with a problem. After you read the letter, read Ms. Advice's answer. After reading both letters, answer the five comprehension questions on page 103. The grammar from this unit is underlined for you.

Dear Ms. Advice,

It is difficult for me to imagine what life <u>was</u> like before the Internet. I am a university student, and I use the Internet every day. These days, if I need to know a fact or a date for a research project, or if I want to communicate with friends and family, I just go online. Whether I need a telephone number or I want to know what time a movie starts, the answer is just a click away. It <u>wasn't</u> like that in the past. Things <u>were</u> very different indeed. In fact, my mother always talks about life before the Internet.

When my mom was in college, the Internet <u>didn't exist</u>, and students' lives <u>were</u> much different than they are today. Whenever students <u>had</u> to do research papers, they <u>went</u> to the library and <u>spoke</u> with the librarian. After they <u>searched</u> for several hours through the stacks and stacks of books and finally <u>found</u> the information that they <u>wanted</u>, they <u>had</u> to check the books out, which were generally very large and often quite heavy. This process <u>took up</u> most of one day if they <u>were</u> lucky. It <u>was</u> often necessary to go back to the library several times to get all the information they <u>needed</u>. Today, students just type their topic into a search engine like Google, and thousands of related web pages appear. Click, read, save, delete, click, and then at once a new web page appears. You don't even have to change out of your pajamas to get the information you need to help you with your paper.

Here is my question: When <u>was</u> the last time you <u>wrote</u> a letter? When <u>was</u> the last time you <u>bought</u> a stamp? How long has it been since you <u>sent</u> a letter in the mail? My mother wants me to write her letters instead of emails. For me, the whole process of going to the post office, buying envelopes, and buying stamps is very inconvenient. To me, an email is better than a letter. My mom receives an email from me every day and reads all of my important news. If I write her a letter, she will only hear my news once a week. I still can't understand why she wants letters instead of emails.

Sincerely,
Enjoying Emails

Dear Enjoying Emails,

Chances are, if you <u>were</u> born after 1990, you have almost never received a handwritten letter in the mail. The first and perhaps most important change since the invention of the Internet is personal communication. Nothing will ever replace the joy of receiving a postcard from a family member or friend overseas. People waited for personal letters with a lot of anticipation. It was a big event to get a letter. However, being able to chat with the same friend online and view pictures of the trip on his personal travel page is also good.

Your mom prefers letters because they make her feel special. In the past, when people wrote letters, they <u>had</u> to sit down in a quiet place. They <u>thought</u> about the best way to share their news and express their feelings. People <u>chose</u> their words very carefully. When people <u>got</u> a letter in the mailbox, it <u>was</u> a surprise. Usually there <u>were</u> only bills and ads, but a letter <u>was</u> a nice piece of happy news. It <u>made</u> them smile. Today, when people send an email, they can do it from anywhere. They can even write an email on their phones while they are buying coffee. Today, however, there are only bills and ads in the mailbox, and people can also check their email on their phone. There is usually no special treat waiting in the mailbox when they get home.

Even though you don't want to write a letter, I hope you can understand now the excitement that a letter can bring. My advice for you is to compromise. Yes, it is time-consuming to write a letter every day, so perhaps this is not practical. However, maybe you could write a letter once a week. This way, your mother can feel appreciated and special. Remember that your mother is always thinking about you, so it is good to show her that you are thinking about her. Also, if you make better use of email by attaching lots of recent photos, perhaps your mom will see some of the advantages that email offers.

Good luck,

Ms. Advice

1. What problem is this person having with her mother?

_____

_____

_____

2. Do you prefer letters or emails? Why?

_____

_____

_____

3. Why did people prefer letters in the past?

_____

_____

_____

4. What advice did Enjoying Emails get about writing letters?

_____

_____

_____

5. Can you think of three advantages that email can offer that traditional letters cannot?

_____

_____

_____

_____

_____

_____

ONE-MINUTE LESSON
When we want to talk about a future event that we want to happen or that we are happy about happening, we use the expression **look forward to** + the action. For example, if you have a vacation in Hawaii next week, you can say, *I'm* **looking forward** *to my vacation next week.* If you want to use a verb after this expression, you must add *–ing* to the verb. You can also say, *I'm* **looking forward** *to going to Hawaii next week.* At the end of a job interview, you can tell the person, *Thank you for meeting me today. I* **look forward** *to hearing from you next week about the job.*

EXERCISE 11. Vocabulary Practice: Word Knowledge

Circle the word or phrase that is most closely related to the word or phrase on the left. Use a dictionary to check the meaning of words you do not know.

Vocabulary	Answer Choices	
1. spread	water on the floor	water in a cup
2. a mechanic	a person	a thing
3. win	not find	not lose
4. amazing	negative	positive
5. fall	go down	go up
6. cash	food	money
7. however	and	but
8. a contest	a competition	a discussion
9. a drawer	in a car	in a desk
10. build	make	take
11. a mode	a section	a way
12. stick	drink little by little	put together with glue
13. a click	using a computer	using a dictionary
14. a stack	books next to books	books on top of books
15. improve	from bad to good	from good to bad
16. a garden	animals	plants
17. both	two	zero
18. steal	burn	rob
19. a costume	you eat it	you wear it
20. wool	fruit	hair
21. time-consuming	a little time	a lot of time
22. bite	with your fingers	with your teeth
23. let	bother	permit
24. wet	air	water
25. at once	very quickly	very slowly
26. shut	close quickly	open quickly
27. waves	at the beach	at the studio
28. a race	crying	running
29. a contestant	a person	a thing
30. a hammer	cans	nails
31. hiking	talking	walking
32. agree	look the same	think the same
33. a belt	pants	ears

EXERCISE 12. Vocabulary Practice: Collocations

Fill in each blank with the answer on the right that most naturally completes the phrase on the left. If necessary, use a dictionary to check the meaning of words you do not know.

Vocabulary	Answer Choices	
1. take a trip _____ a place	for	to
2. _____ hiking	ran	went
3. didn't _____	say	said
4. _____ a noise	do	make
5. _____ in line	drive	stand
6. sound _____	cousin	fine
7. _____ up at sunrise	slept	woke
8. rode a _____	bicycle	television
9. an auto repair _____	shop	store
10. what did you _____	do	did
11. an alarm _____	clock	watch
12. make a gift _____ someone	for	to
13. on _____	time	times
14. let's _____ fishing	do	go
15. I didn't _____ to do that.	mean	sound
16. win a _____	prize	score
17. _____ good	beautiful	pretty
18. the _____ stalled	river	truck
19. a convenience _____	shop	store
20. I was on _____.	trip	vacation
21. don't _____	go	went
22. a wool _____	sweater	t-shirt
23. out of _____	city	town
24. an oil _____	change	repair
25. Do you know _____ cook?	how to	to
26. _____ a good day	do	have
27. tear _____	a box of cookies	a piece of paper
28. hang the pictures _____ the wall	in	on
29. do something _____ advance	at	in
30. extremely _____	sister	small
31. _____ dressed	get	make
32. _____ in your homework	put	turn
33. _____ a shower	make	take

EXERCISE 13. Writing Practice

Part 1. Editing Student Writing

Read these sentences about one student's opinion about a job interview. Circle the 15 errors. Then write the number of the sentence with the error next to the type of error. (Some sentences may have more than one error.)

_____ a. wrong irregular past tense form　　_____ d. word order

_____ b. wrong verb tense　　　　　　　　　_____ e. article

_____ c. mistake with negative　　　　　　　_____ f. no subject

Job Interviews Make Me Nervous
1. Last year decided to find a new job, so I went to several interviews before I finally found the perfect company for me. 
2. I started by looking on the Internet for job openings in my town, and I found an opening at bank.
3. I sended my resume for this job, and someone called me for a interview the next day!
4. I waited in the lobby and drank coffee before my interview.
5. I was so nervous that I spilled cup of hot coffee on the front of my new shirt white.
6. As soon as I spilled my coffee, the interviewer comed to meet me.
7. I no had any time to clean my shirt. Was so embarrassed.
8. We walked to his office and start the interview.
9. During the interview, something lucky happens.
10. I telled a funny story, and the man laughed so hard that he spilled his coffee on his shirt, too.
11. In the interview, we both had big coffee stains on our shirts, but we not care.
12. It was strange day for me. I was nervous and spilled coffee on my shirt, but in the end, I get the job.

Part 2. Original Student Writing

Write sentences about a past problem. Tell what the problem was, where it happened, when it happened, why it happened, or how you solved the problem. Underline all irregular verbs.

Unit 4

Present Perfect Tense

Discover the Grammar

Read the conversation between two friends, and then answer the four questions.

Line	
1	*Paolo*: So, Kate, you've just returned from England, right?
2	*Kate*: Yes, I went to London. Have you ever gone there?
3	*Paolo*: Oh, sure. I've been there at least five times. I've also visited Paris, Rome,
4	and Amsterdam.
5	*Kate*: Oh? I've never been anywhere else in Europe.
6	*Paolo*: How about South America? Have you ever taken a boat ride down the
7	Amazon River?
8	*Kate*: No, I haven't.
9	*Paolo*: Or Africa? Have you ever ridden an elephant? Have you ever seen lions
10	and zebras in the wild?
11	*Kate*: Well, no, I've never traveled as far as Africa. I went to Chicago once,
12	though, to see my cousins.

13	*Paolo*:	And Asia! Have you climbed Mt. Everest? I climbed it last year. Or what
14		about the Great Wall of China? I've walked on it three times.
15	*Kate*:	No, no, I haven't. It's a bit hard to travel with a full-time job and classes.
16		Do you have a job?
17	*Paolo*:	I don't have one right now—it makes it too hard to travel!

1. In Line 2, you see *went* and *have gone*. Both of these come from the verb *go*. Is there any difference in meaning here?

   _____

   _____

2. In Line 13, you see *have climbed* and *climbed*. Both of these come from the verb *climb*. Is there any difference in meaning here?

   _____

   _____

3. In Line 2 and Line 9, you see the question *Have you*, but in Line 16, you see the question *Do you have*. Why are these two questions with *have* so different?

   _____

   _____

   _____

4. The new verb tense in this conversation is called the **present perfect tense.** It consists of the verb *have* or *has* with the **past participle**. Some past participles end in *–ed*. These are called *regular*. Others have many different endings. These are *irregular*. Put the ten different past participles in the correct category. In parentheses, write the original base verb form. (<u>Hint</u>: Find the verb form after *have*.)

Regular Past Participles	Irregular Past Participles
a. _____returned_____ (return)	a. _____gone_____ (go)
b. _____ ( )	b. _____ ( )
c. _____ ( )	c. _____ ( )
d. _____ ( )	d. _____ ( )
e. _____ ( )	e. _____ ( )

Grammar Lesson

Present Perfect Tense

Examples	subject	*have/has*	past participle
I have <u>lived</u> here since 1999.	I	have	lived
Have you ever <u>flown</u> in a helicopter?	you	have	flown
He has <u>waited</u> for this chance for many years.	He	has	waited
She has never <u>had</u> any problems with her car.	She	has	had
It has <u>taken</u> me a long time to learn English.	It	has	taken
We have just <u>arrived</u> here.	We	have	arrived
They have <u>been</u> in China for more than 2 years.	They	have	been

<u>Rule 1</u>. In present perfect tense, a verb has two forms: **has + PAST PARTICIPLE** and **have + PAST PARTICIPLE**. We use **have + PAST PARTICIPLE** with *I, you, we, they*; **has + PAST PARTICIPLE** with *he, she, it*.

<u>Rule 2</u>. The past participle of a regular verb is the same as the simple past tense form. If the verb is one syllable and ends in **consonant + vowel + consonant** (c-v-c), we double the final consonant before adding **–ed.** We do the same for a two-syllable verb if it ends in **consonant + vowel + consonant** (c-v-c) and the pronunciation stress is on the second syllable:

open → ope<u>ne</u>d	*occur → occu<u>rr</u>ed*
(o) pen [1st] 2nd	oc (cur) 1st [2nd]
because we stress the 1st syllable	because we stress the 2nd syllable

<u>Rule 3</u>. The past participle of an irregular verb is impossible to predict. There are some irregular verbs with similar past participles, so you should try to learn these verbs in their groups. For example, some verbs do not change (*put, put, put*), some change –d to –t (*send, sent, sent*), and others change a vowel in the middle (*sing, sang, sung*). Studying these patterns can help you learn these verbs better. (See a listing in this unit and also Appendix C.)

<u>Rule 4</u>. Present perfect tense has several distinct usages. Three common usages include:
   a. an action that began in the past but continues now (*we* **have lived** *here for 10 years*)
   b. a past (often recent) action that is important to now (*she* **has** *just* **eaten** *lunch*)
   c. a past action that occurred at an indefinite time in the past (*I* **have worked** *in Dubai*)

Rule 5. Common time expressions for present perfect tense include *since _____, for _____, so far, until now, ever, always, never, just, recently, already, yet, before, the best, the worst*. Never use present perfect tense with a specific past time.

Rule 6. To make a negative statement with a verb, add **not** after **have** or **has**. (*We have not gone to the bank yet.*) In informal English, it is possible to use the contractions **haven't** and **hasn't**.

Rule 7. The question form is **have/has + SUBJECT + PAST PARTICIPLE** (*Have you gone to the bank?*). In other words, you invert the **SUBJECT** and **have/has**.

Rule 8. To answer a yes-no question, use **have** or **has** for a short affirmative answer and **have not (haven't)**, **has not (hasn't)** for a short negative answer: *Yes, we have.* OR *No, we haven't.*

 BE CAREFUL!

Common Learner Errors	Explanation
1. I ~~study~~ have studied English since I was 10 years old.	Don't use simple present tense for an action that began in the past and still continues.
2. In 2010, I ~~have lived~~ lived in Bogota, Colombia.	Don't use present perfect tense for a specific past time.
3. My sister and I ~~gone~~ have gone to India twice.	Remember to use **have** or **has** with the past participle.
4. We ~~didn't have eaten~~ haven't eaten at the new restaurant on Green Street yet.	Do not use **don't, doesn't,** or **didn't** to form the negative in present perfect tense.
5. ~~Did you have eaten~~ Have you eaten sushi?	Do not use **do, does,** or **did** in the question form in present perfect tense.

EXERCISE 1. Regular and Irregular Verb Forms

Write the correct forms for these four verbs for the present perfect tense.

Regular Verbs		Irregular Verbs	
work	live	be	have
I _____	I _____	I _____	I _____
you _____	you _____	you _____	you _____
he _____	he _____	he _____	he _____
she _____	she _____	she _____	she _____
it _____	it _____	it _____	it _____
we _____	we _____	we _____	we _____
they _____	they _____	they _____	they _____

Grammar Lesson

Past Participles

KEY
3

The **past participle** is the second part of the present perfect tense. In order to understand and use present perfect tense well, you need to know common past participle forms.

All verbs in English have three basic forms: present, past, and **past participle**. The past and past participle forms of **regular verbs** use –ed. These two forms are the same. The past and past participle forms of **irregular verbs** are different. Common endings for the past participle forms of irregular verbs include –en (*been*), –ne (*gone*), or –n (*seen*), but there are many possibilities. Some irregular forms are the same for both past and past participle (*send, sent, sent*).

Regular Verbs	Irregular Verbs
I have <u>worked</u> here since 1999.	I have <u>been</u> here since 1999.
You have <u>changed</u> the schedule again.	You have <u>gone</u> to Alaska before, right?
He has <u>waited</u> for this chance for many years.	He has <u>done</u> the same job since 2005.
She has <u>climbed</u> Mt. Fuji in Japan.	She has <u>had</u> cats all her life.
It has <u>rained</u> twice this week.	It has <u>taken</u> me a long time to learn English.
We have already <u>watched</u> that TV show.	The best movie we have ever <u>seen</u> is *Jaws*.
They have <u>lived</u> in many countries.	Laws about texting have <u>gotten</u> tougher.

60 Commonly Used Irregular Past and Past Participle Forms of Verbs

Present	Past	Past Participle
1. be	was/were	been
2. become	became	become
3. begin	began	begun
4. break	broke	broken
5. bring	brought	brought
6. build	built	built
7. buy	bought	bought
8. catch	caught	caught
9. choose	chose	chosen
10. come	came	come
11. cost	cost	cost
12. cut	cut	cut
13. drink	drank	drunk
14. drive	drove	driven
15. do	did	done
16. eat	ate	eaten
17. fall	fell	fallen
18. feel	felt	felt
19. find	found	found
20. fly	flew	flown
21. forget	forgot	forgotten
22. freeze	froze	frozen
23. get	got	gotten
24. give	gave	given
25. go	went	gone
26. have	had	had
27. hit	hit	hit
28. hold	held	held
29. keep	kept	kept
30. know	knew	known
31. leave	left	left
32. lend	lent	lent
33. let	let	let
34. lose	lost	lost
35. make	made	made
36. meet	met	met
37. put	put	put
38. read	read	read
39. ride	rode	ridden

40.	run	ran	run
41.	say	said	said
42.	see	saw	seen
43.	sell	sold	sold
44.	send	sent	sent
45.	show	showed	shown
46.	sing	sang	sung
47.	sit	sat	sat
48.	sleep	slept	slept
49.	speak	spoke	spoken
50.	spend	spent	spent
51.	steal	stole	stolen
52.	swim	swam	swum
53.	take	took	taken
54.	teach	taught	taught
55.	tell	told	told
56.	think	thought	thought
57.	understand	understood	understood
58.	wear	wore	worn
59.	win	won	won
60.	write	wrote	written

EXERCISE 2. Practicing Past Participles

Write the past participle forms of the verbs.

Present	Past	Past Participle
1. be	was/were	_____
2. make	made	_____
3. forget	forgot	_____
4. show	showed	_____
5. sit	sat	_____
6. hit	hit	_____
7. steal	stole	_____
8. take	took	_____
9. tell	told	_____
10. think	thought	_____
11. lose	lost	_____
12. see	saw	_____
13. freeze	froze	_____
14. sing	sang	_____
15. sleep	slept	_____
16. leave	left	_____
17. swim	swam	_____
18. teach	taught	_____
19. break	broke	_____
20. run	ran	_____

Do Online Exercise 4.1. My score: ____ /10. ____ % correct.

EXERCISE 3. Practicing Past Participles

Write the past and past participle forms of the verbs.

Present	Past	Past Participle
1. say	_____	_____
2. wear	_____	_____
3. write	_____	_____
4. begin	_____	_____
5. ride	_____	_____
6. speak	_____	_____
7. buy	_____	_____
8. catch	_____	_____
9. drink	_____	_____
10. eat	_____	_____
11. choose	_____	_____
12. win	_____	_____
13. become	_____	_____
14. bring	_____	_____
15. come	_____	_____
16. spend	_____	_____
17. put	_____	_____
18. meet	_____	_____
19. drive	_____	_____
20. fall	_____	_____

EXERCISE 4. Finding Patterns in Past Participles

Some people find it easier to learn the past participles in small groups according to pronunciation or spelling patterns. Write the past participles that belong in these groups. Follow the examples. (Some verbs may be used twice.)

1.

long *i*	long *o*	*–en*
drive	drove	driven

2.

present	*–aught*	*–aught*
catch	caught	caught

3. All three forms are the same.

cost	cost	cost

4.

long *e*	long *o*	*–en*
freeze	froze	frozen

5.

present	past	present + *–en*
eat	ate	eaten

6.

present	*–ought*	*–ought*
bring	brought	brought

7.
short *i*	short *a*	short *u*
begin	began	begun

8.
present	past	same as present
become	became	become

9.
present	past	present + −*n*
drive	drove	driven

10.
present (−*d*)	past (−*d* → −*t*)	same as past (−*d* → −*t*)
build	built	built

ONE-MINUTE LESSON

I drove, I didn't drive, Did you drive . . . ? Treat the most common irregular verbs as new vocabulary and memorize them! Be sure you memorize all three forms: affirmative, negative, and question. Try to imagine which subject (*I? you? they?*) you will probably need the most for your communication in English.

Do Online Exercise 4.2. My score: _____ /10. _____% correct.

EXERCISE 5. Speaking Practice: Testing Your Present Perfect

Step 1. Inside each pair of parentheses given, write one verb from the list on pages 113–14.

Step 2. Write the correct present perfect form according to the subject (noun or pronoun).

Step 3. Work with a partner. Student A reads one verb and subject combination. Student B then has to give the correct form. Then Student B gives a verb from his or her paper.

Example: A: "go, you"

B: "You have gone."

A: "That's correct." (now Student B reads a verb and subject)

B: "eat, the cats"

A: "The cats have eaten."

Step 4. If you want to make this exercise more challenging, try to make a more complicated sentence. For example, you could say, "You have gone to the bank many times" or "The cats have already eaten."

1. (   ) Mr. Lee _____

2. (   ) she _____

3. (   ) the teacher _____

4. (   ) you _____

5. (   ) Julia _____

6. (   ) you _____

7. (   ) she _____

8. (   ) Sue and Jo _____

9. (   ) you _____

10. (   ) they _____

Present Perfect

Grammar Usage 1: A Past Action or Situation that Continues Now

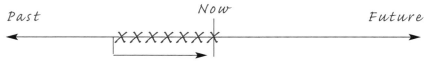

Examples	Key Words
José: How long **have** you **worked** at Carpet World?	how long
Cara: I've **been** there for 18 years. In fact, I've **worked** there longer than any of my supervisors!	for ___
José: What do you do there?	
Cara: I used to work in manufacturing, but since 2010, I've **been** with the sales force in the front office.	since ___
José: Have you ever met the president of the corporation?	
Cara: Actually, no, I've never **met** him. He never comes to the office.	never

We can use present perfect to talk about a past action or situation that continues now. (It can be affirmative or negative; the important thing is that it still continues.) In this example, Cara tells José that she has been at this same company for 18 years. This means that the action began 18 years ago and still continues today.

The words **since** and **for** are common with this usage of present perfect tense. The word **since** goes with the name of the beginning of the time period and **for** goes with the name of a duration of time: I've **lived** here since 1995. I've **worked** here for six years.

See pages 110–11 for the eight rules for present perfect tense.

EXERCISE 6. *since* vs *for* with Time Words

Write **since** or **for.**

1. _____ yesterday
2. _____ six weeks
3. _____ six o'clock
4. _____ March
5. _____ two months
6. _____ noon

7. _____ a few days
8. _____ my birthday
9. _____ one minute
10. _____ a decade
11. _____ 1993
12. _____ late last night

EXERCISE 7. Sentences with *since* and *for*

Read the two sentences. Then write a new sentence using **since** or **for.** Follow the examples.

1. I live on Madison Avenue. I moved there five months ago.

   I have lived on Madison Avenue for five months.

2. I live on Madison Avenue. I moved there in 2000.

   I have lived on Madison Avenue since 2000.

3. The shop around the corner has apples on sale. The sale started on Monday.

   _____

4. We know the shop's manager. We met her ten years ago.

   _____

5. The manager owns a BMW. She bought it in 1997.

   _____

6. I began to work at the office behind the shop two years ago. I still work here.

   _____

7. My cousin has a huge house. He purchased it when he moved here.

   _____

8. My boss plays tennis. He learned how to play in 1992.

   _____

9. My upstairs neighbor teaches French. Her first year was 1991.

   _____

10. His wife is a university professor. She began that job in the fall of 1997.

    _____

 ONE-MINUTE LESSON
We met her ten years ago. Most time words come before the noun: **at** 5 *PM,* **on** *Monday,* **in** *July.* Remember that the word **ago** is different in that it goes after the noun: *ten years* **ago,** *two hours* **ago,** *just a minute* **ago.**

EXERCISE 8. Using Time Words to Compare Verb Tenses

Read each situation, and circle the correct verb tense.

Situation A Today is Thursday. Joe arrived here three days ago.

1. Joe (arrives, arrived, has arrived) on Monday.

2. Joe (is, was, has been) here for three days.

3. Joe (is, was, has been) here since Monday.

4. Joe (isn't, wasn't, hasn't been) here for a week.

5. Joe (isn't, wasn't, hasn't been) here on Sunday.

6. Joe (isn't, wasn't, hasn't been) on a flight to Paris now.

Situation B Claudia is home with her husband. They got married five years ago. They are eating dinner together, but last night she was at a new restaurant with three of her friends.

1. Claudia (is eating, eats, ate, was eating, has eaten) at a restaurant last night.

2. Claudia (is eating, eats, ate, was eating, has eaten) at a new restaurant last night.

3. Claudia (is eating, eats, ate, was eating, has eaten) at a new restaurant this year.

4. Claudia (is eating, eats, ate, was eating, has eaten) with three friends last night.

5. Claudia (is eating, eats, ate, was eating, has eaten) dinner with her husband tonight.

6. For five years, Claudia (is eating, eats, ate, was eating, has eaten) dinner with her husband almost every night.

Situation C It is raining today. It also rained yesterday and the day before yesterday. No one knows when the rain will stop.

1. It (is raining, rains, rained, was raining, has rained) for the past three days.

2. It (is raining, rains, rained, was raining, has rained) two days ago.

3. It (is raining, rains, rained, was raining, has rained) for almost 72 hours.

4. It (is raining, rains, rained, was raining, has rained) at this very moment.

5. It (is raining, rains, rained, was raining, has rained) when I woke up at 7:00 this morning.

6. It (is raining, rains, rained, was raining, has rained) since I woke up at 7:00 this morning.

 Do Online Exercise 4.3. My score: _____/10. _____% correct.

Present Perfect

KEY 3

Grammar Usage 2: Recent Past Action or Situation that Is Important to the Current Situation

Examples	Key Words
Amber: It's hot in here. Why don't you turn on the air conditioner?	
James: Actually, I've just **turned*** it on. We have to wait a few minutes to feel it. Can I help you with the reports?	just
Amber: Thanks, but I've already **finished*** them. Here they are.	already

*In these examples, simple past tense can be used here without changing the meaning.

We can use present perfect to talk about a past action that happened a short time ago and that is still important to the current situation. In this example, Amber is complaining about the temperature in the room right now. James explains to Amber that he has turned on the air conditioner. When James uses the phrase **has turned on**, it means that the action is finished but that it is still important to the current situation.

In other words, there is a connection between his action and the current situation in the room. This kind of sentence often uses the word **just** to show that the action has just happened.

See pages 110–11 for the eight rules for present perfect tense.

ONE-MINUTE LESSON

I've just turned it on. The word **just** has several different meanings, but the two most common ones are "only" and "recently." When **just** means "only," it is used in front of a noun or pronoun: **just** *five*, **just** *me*, **just** *coffee*. When **just** means "recently," it is frequently used in the middle of present perfect tense: *I've* **just** *eaten*, she *has* **just** *arrived*, it *has* **just** *rained*. (Remember that it also possible to use simple past tense, especially in informal conversation.)

EXERCISE 9. Using *just* in Conversations

Practice using **just**, present perfect, and contractions in these conversations. Use words from the word list.

word list	ask	come	cook	finish	realize	take

Conversation A

Sam: I ❶ _____ some spaghetti a little while ago. Would you like some?

Dean: No, thanks. I ❷ _____ eating lunch.

Sam: OK, but if you change your mind, be sure to let me know.

Conversation B

Pete: Hey, the next time that you go to the post office, would you pick up some stamps for me?

Gwen: Why, of course, but it's too bad you didn't ask me sooner. I
❸ _____ back from the post office.

Conversation C

Keith: Hey, Jim. Can you give me a ride to the bus stop now?

Jim: I'm sorry, but my boss ❹ _____ me to help her. Why don't you ask Sandy for a ride? I think she's about to go home.

Conversation D

Karen: Excuse me, sir. Has Flight 663 left yet?

Ed: Yes, it ❺ _____ off about ten minutes ago. Why do you ask?

Karen: Well, I ❻ _____ that I left my carry-on bag on the plane.

Ed: No problem. Here it is. Someone found it and turned it in to us.

Present Perfect

Grammar Usage 3: Past Experience, Indefinite Past Time

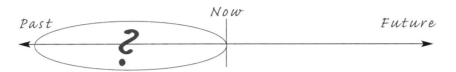

Examples	Key Words
Katie: Susan has just gotten back from China. She told me she had a great time.	
Sean: That's wonderful news. She must be tired. That was really a long trip.	
Katie: I wonder how many hours it is from here to China. **Have** you ever **gone** there?	ever
Sean: No, I've never **gone** there, but my uncle **has traveled** there many times. In fact, he went there last month. He has to go there on business.	never many times
Katie: **Have** you **talked** to your uncle recently?	recently
Sean: No, he **hasn't returned** from China yet. He gets back next week.	yet

We can use present perfect tense to talk about a past experience. In this situation, one person wants to know if a second person has ever done a particular action (**go to China**). In this example, Katie is telling Sean that Susan has just returned from China. Katie wants to know if Sean has traveled to China at any time before now. She uses the common question, **Have you ever . . . ?**

Notice that **went** is in simple past tense because it refers to a specific past event. In other words, **went** refers to definite past time, but **have gone** refers to indefinite past time.

See pages 110–11 for the eight rules for present perfect tense.

EXERCISE 10. Using Present Perfect and Contractions in Conversations

Use present perfect tense in these conversations. Add **ever** in questions. Add **never** in the answers if it is appropriate. Use words from the word list.

word list	be	eat	have	hear	study	think	travel

Conversation A

Khalid: ❶ _____ tempura?

Laura: No, I haven't. What is it?

Khalid: It's a Japanese dish. It's fried vegetables and seafood.

Laura: Really? I ❷ _____ of it.

Khalid: You ought to try it. It's great.

Conversation B

Vic: ❸ _____ a foreign language?

Carl: Yes, I studied French when I was in college.

Vic: ❹ _____ a chance to use it? I mean,
❺ _____ to France?

Carl: Unfortunately, no. I ❻ _____ abroad.

Conversation C

Diego: I'm sorry I'm late, but I had car trouble again this morning.

Jean: Why do you keep that old car? ❼ _____ about getting a new car?

Diego: Sure, I've thought about it, but I ❽ _____ enough money to buy one. Every car I've ever bought was a used car.

Do Online Exercise 4.4. My score: _____ /10. _____ % correct.

EXERCISE 11. Speaking Practice: *Have You Ever . . . ?*

You are at a meeting or party, and there are 16 people in the room. You will be one of these 16 people. You have done four special things that no one else in the room has done.

Step 1. Work with a partner. Choose a person that you will be from page 128, but do NOT let your partner know your choice.

Step 2. Take turns asking yes-no questions to try to guess your partner's four special things. If the answer to a question is yes, the person answering has to make up an extra sentence to add to the conversation. This extra information should probably be in the past tense. In English conversation, it is common to move from present perfect (general information) to past tense (specific information).

Step 3. If the answer is yes, then the questioner can continue asking. If the answer is no, the turn passes to the other student. Remember to use *Have you ever . . . ?* in your conversations. Practice English grammar!

Step 4. The first partner to finish is the winner!

> <u>Example</u>:   *A:* Have you ever gone to France?
>
>   *B:* No, I have never gone to France. (So it's Student B's turn to ask a question.)
>
>   *B:* Have you ever ridden an elephant?
>
>   *A:* Yes, I've ridden an elephant. I went to Thailand in 1985, and I rode an elephant there. (So Student B continues asking.)
>
>   *B:* Have you ever gone to Egypt?
>
>   *A:* No, I haven't gone to Egypt. (So it's Student A's turn again to ask a question.)

Nydia	Luz	Mary	Alberto

went to France
flew on a 747
drove a BMW
rode on a horse
	went to France
	flew on a 747
	drove a Toyota
	   truck
	rode on a horse
		went to France
		flew on the
		   Concorde
		drove a BMW
		rode on a horse
			went to France
			flew on the
			   Concorde
			drove a Toyota
			   truck
			rode on a horse

Cindy	**James**	**Simon**	**Kevin**

went to France
flew on a 747
drove a BMW
rode on an elephant
	went to France
	flew on a 747
	drove a Toyota
	   truck
	rode on an elephant
		went to France
		flew on the
		   Concorde
		drove a BMW
		rode on an elephant
			went to France
			flew on the
			   Concorde
			drove a Toyota
			   truck
			rode on an elephant

Chris	**Markus**	**Silvio**	**Temara**

went to Egypt
flew on a 747
drove a BMW
rode on a horse
	went to Egypt
	flew on a 747
	drove a Toyota
	   truck
	rode on a horse
		went to Egypt
		flew on the
		   Concorde
		drove a BMW
		rode on a horse
			went to Egypt
			flew on the
			   Concorde
			drove a Toyota
			   truck
			rode on a horse

Melissa	**Ana**	**Julian**	**Lukas**

went to Egypt
flew on a 747
drove a BMW
rode on an elephant
	went to Egypt
	flew on a 747
	drove a Toyota
	   truck
	rode on an elephant
		went to Egypt
		flew on the
		   Concorde
		drove a BMW
		rode on an elephant
			went to Egypt
			flew on the
			   Concorde
			drove a Toyota
			   truck
			rode on an elephant

EXERCISE 12. Making Sentences with *yet*

Read the situation, and then write a negative sentence with **yet.** Follow the example.

Situation 1. Ben always eats dinner at 7:00 PM. It's 6:45 PM now.

Ben hasn't eaten dinner yet.

Situation 2. The weather report predicted rain for today. The sky is dark, but the ground is completely dry.

_____

Situation 3. The monitor says the plane will arrive in ten minutes. The plane is still in the air.

_____

Situation 4. Joe set his alarm clock for 6 AM. It's now 5:50 AM.

_____

Situation 5. I wanted to speak with Dr. Adams yesterday, but I didn't have time. I need to speak to her.

_____

Situation 6. The big game is tomorrow. I forgot to buy my ticket yesterday. I still need a ticket!

_____

Do Online Exercise 4.5. My score: _____ /10. _____ % correct.

EXERCISE 13. Asking Questions with *ever*

Write five questions practicing **ever** + present perfect. Use the words in parentheses. Write your six questions. Write your own answers on the first answer line (S1). Then interview a classmate. Take turns asking each other questions. Write your partner's answers on the second answer line (S2). Follow the example.

1. (really bad) movie / see

   [?] _Have you ever seen a really bad movie?_____

   S1: _Yes, I have. It was "Jaws." I hated it._____

   S2: _____

2. (incredibly long) trip / take

   [?] _____

   S1: _____

   S2: _____

3. (really good) food / eat

   [?] _____

   S1: _____

   S2: _____

4. (amazingly beautiful) place / visit

   [?] _____

   S1: _____

   S2: _____

5. (extremely interesting) book / read

   [?] _____

   S1: _____

   S2: _____

6. (incredibly easy) job / have

   [?] _____

   S1: _____

   S2: _____

EXERCISE 14. Present Perfect with *time*

Circle the correct verb form.

1. *Andy:*   Here's today's newspaper.

   Sue: Andy, this is not today's paper. This is the second time that you (gave, have given) me yesterday's paper.

2. *Koji:*   Can you remember the first time that you (met, have met) Tim?

   Beth: Yes, I can. It (was, has been) 1993. We (were, have been) both in high school.

3. *Gina:*   I don't know if I'll ever be able to remember all these people's names! It's the third day that I (saw, have seen) Frank and Tony, but I still have trouble remembering their names.

   Lim: Don't worry about it. I'm not very good with names either.

4. *Coach:*   Wes, is there a problem? That is the fourth time that you (dropped, have dropped) a ball in this game. Are you trying to set a new record?

   Wes: Sorry, coach. I guess my mind is somewhere else today.

5. *Mother:*   Is that the third paper that you (had, have had) to do this month?

   Bernadette: Yes, but it's the first paper that the teacher (asked, has asked) us to complete on the computer.

   Mother: So what are you worried about now?

   Bernadette: I'm not good at using the computer.

   Mother: You have to practice! This seems like the hundredth time that I (told, have told) you that you need to practice!

EXERCISE 15. Simple Past or Present Perfect?

Put a check mark (✔) by the expressions to show if they are only for past tense, only for present perfect tense, or possible with both. Follow the examples.

	Past Only	Present Perfect Only	Both OK	
1.	✔			in 1995
2.		✔		so far
3.			✔	today
4.				until now
5.				just
6.				for the last two years
7.				for two years
8.				last month
9.				ever
10.				since Monday
11.				a week ago
12.				never
13.				at noon
14.				before last Monday's class

EXERCISE 16. Simple Past and Present Perfect in Context

Read the statement, and then write the verb in parentheses in the correct tense. Use simple past or present perfect. Follow the examples.

(go) 1. I _____have gone_____ to Mexico many times, and I hope to go again some day.

2. I _____went_____ to Mexico in 2006 and 2007.

(eat) 3. _____ you ever _____ octopus?

4. When you lived in Japan, _____ you ever _____ octopus?

(see) 5. Did you like that movie the first time that you _____ it?

6. This is the first time that I _____ a movie with that actor in it.

(have) 7. The people who live next to us _____ a lot of parties this year.

8. In fact, they _____ a party last night.

(fly) 9. The last time that you went to New York, _____ you _____ on Northeast Airlines?

10. How many times _____ you _____ on Northeast Airlines?

Connecting Grammar and Vocabulary

It is possible to use thousands of verbs in present perfect tense. It is useful for you to learn some of the verbs commonly used in present perfect tense.

Memorize these forms so that you write them or say them easily in English.

22 Frequent Present Perfect Examples	
12 Examples from Spoken English	**10 Examples from Academic English**
1. have **been**	1. have **been**
2. have **gone**	2. have **shown**
3. have **done**	3. have **had**
4. have **had**	4. have **made**
5. have **come**	5. have **seen**
6. have **said**	6. have **become**
7. have **thought**	7. have **done**
8. have **called**	8. have **come**
9. have **made**	9. have **taken**
10. have **seen**	10. have **given**
11. have **taken**	
12. have **put**	

Source: Biber, D., et al. (1999). *Longman Grammar of Spoken and Written English*. London: Longman.

EXERCISE 17. Editing: Is It Correct?

If the sentence is correct, put a check mark (✔) on the line. If it is not correct, write X on the line and circle the mistake. Then change the sentence to make it correct. Write the change above the sentence. (*Hint:* There are eight sentences. Two are correct, but six have mistakes.)

Janet's Pets

_____ 1. I have been an English teacher for 20 years. I have taught in three schools. Two were in the U.S., and the current one is in Mexico.

_____ 2. I have been in Mexico for eight years. I worked in a small school.

_____ 3. My wife's name is Janet. She came from the United States with me to live in Mexico.

_____ 4. She has worked as a teacher for the past 15 years. Before that, she working as a veterinarian's assistant.

_____ 5. She loves animals. She says she loved animals all of her life.

_____ 6. Her favorite animal is called a macaw. She has raising macaws for the past 10 years.

_____ 7. Her macaws are with us for a long time. In fact, one is over 50 years old!

_____ 8. She does not like frogs, though. She does not like frogs since one jumped on her head when she was little.

EXERCISE 18. Mini-Conversations

Circle the correct words in these eight mini-conversations.

1. A: Hey, Mom! Can I go to a party tonight at Serena's house?

   B: Well, (have you, has you) finished your chores?

2. A: Have you ever (flew, flown) on a jet with two aisles?

   B: Yes, I have. I flew on a jumbo jet when I went to Japan last year.

3. A: Do you have any dirty clothes that need to be washed?

   B: No, but thanks for asking. I (have, has) already washed mine.

4. A: Have you (fed, feeding, feed) the dog this afternoon?

   B: I tried, but he wasn't hungry.

5. A: We have to clean the house today.

   B: Yes, the living room needs to be vacuumed. By the way, (has, have) you seen the vacuum cleaner anywhere?

6. A: How is it that you know so many Spanish words?

   B: When I (am, was, have been) eleven years old, my family lived in Peru. I learned Spanish in school there.

7. A: I love this town. I was born here, and I guess I will die here.

   B: Do you mean that you (live, are living, lived, have lived) here your whole life? I find it hard to believe that you never moved to another town.

8. A: What are you doing?

   B: I'm getting ready to go see a movie with Jack. Do you want to go to the movie with us? We're going to see that new movie *Happy People* tonight.

   A: No, thanks. I've got a lot of work to do, and I've already (see, saw, seen) that movie.

Do Online Exercise 4.6. My score: _____ /10. _____ % correct.

EXERCISE 19. Sentence Study for Critical Reading

Read the numbered sentences. Then read the three answer choices, and put a check mark (✓) in the yes or no boxes in front of each sentence to show if that answer is true based on the information in the original sentence. If there is not enough information to mark something as yes, then mark it as no. Remember that more than one true answer is possible.

1. Samara and Sandra have sung together in a band since 1996.

   ☐ yes ☐ no   a. Samara and Sandra are singers.

   ☐ yes ☐ no   b. They now sing in different bands.

   ☐ yes ☐ no   c. The band started in 1996.

2. Samara's brother has taken drum lessons since he was 10 years old. He's played in the band since 2008.

   ☐ yes ☐ no   a. Samara's brother plays the drums.

   ☐ yes ☐ no   b. He took lessons when he was 6 years old.

   ☐ yes ☐ no   c. He joined the band in 2008.

3. Sandra's younger sister has played the guitar since she took lessons in college. She's played in the band since 2009.

   ☐ yes ☐ no   a. Sandra's younger sister plays the guitar.

   ☐ yes ☐ no   b. She didn't learn to play guitar by herself.

   ☐ yes ☐ no   c. She joined the band in 2009.

4. Tony went to college to be a sound engineer, and he has managed the band's sound system since 2006. This has been his only job in the band.

   ☐ yes ☐ no   a. Tony studied sound engineering at college.

   ☐ yes ☐ no   b. Tony does the band's lighting system.

   ☐ yes ☐ no   c. Tony joined the band in 2006.

5. Mr. Downs has owned a shirt printing shop since 1985. He made the band's first shirt in 1986 and has made them ever since.

   ☐ yes ☐ no   a. Mr. Downs owns part of the band.

   ☐ yes ☐ no   b. Mr. Downs bought his shop in 1985.

   ☐ yes ☐ no   c. Mr. Downs bought his shop in 1986.

6. Linda is a makeup artist and has done the band's makeup since they played their first show.

   ☐ yes ☐ no   a. Linda is a makeup artist.

   ☐ yes ☐ no   b. Linda's boss thinks her work is not so good.

   ☐ yes ☐ no   c. Linda started doing makeup four years before the band got together.

7. Sandra's dad has loved rock music since the 1960s, and he's gone to almost all of his daughter's concerts.

   [ ] **yes** [ ] **no**   a. Sandra's dad loves rock music.

   [ ] **yes** [ ] **no**   b. He just started listening to rock music recently.

   [ ] **yes** [ ] **no**   c. He hardly ever misses one of his daughter's concerts.

8. Samara's mom likes only classical music, and she started playing the violin when she was five years old. She definitely prefers to go to classical music concerts.

   [ ] **yes** [ ] **no**   a. Samara's mom doesn't like rock music.

   [ ] **yes** [ ] **no**   b. She started playing the violin when she was five years old.

   [ ] **yes** [ ] **no**   c. When she goes to a music concert, she would rather go to a classical concert than a rock concert.

EXERCISE 20. Speaking Practice: Talking about Grammar

Step 1. Work with a partner. One of you is Student A and is responsible for the A sentences, and the other is Student B and is responsible for the B sentences. Sentences 4–8 are on page 138.

Step 2. Read the pair of sentences. Both A and B have an underlined part. Which one is correct, and which one is wrong?

Step 3. Circle the letter of the wrong sentence. Then write your reason on the line.

Step 4. Compare your answers. Discuss any differences. Can you both explain why you say a sentence is wrong?

1. (A) I <u>have gone</u> to France twice. I am in France now.

   (B) I <u>have gone</u> to France twice. I was there last month.

   Reason: _____

2. (A) I <u>have done</u> my homework already. I finished it three hours ago.

   (B) I <u>have done</u> my homework already. I am working on it now.

   Reason: _____

3. (A) I <u>have called</u> my brother recently. In fact, I am on the phone with him now.

   (B) I <u>have called</u> my brother recently. In fact, I just hung up with him about 15 minutes ago.

   Reason: _____

4. (A) I <u>have said</u> before that it was a bad idea! I warned them earlier today.

   (B) I <u>have said</u> before that it was a bad idea! I am warning them right now.

   Reason: _____

5. (A) I <u>haven't seen</u> that movie. I plan to see it soon.

   (B) I <u>haven't seen</u> that movie. I watched it last week.

   Reason: _____

6. (A) I <u>haven't gone</u> to the supermarket this week. I probably spent a lot of money on groceries!

   (B) I <u>haven't gone</u> to the supermarket this week. I am probably going to spend a lot of money on groceries!

   Reason: _____

7. (A) I <u>have made</u> a delicious cake. Would you like a slice?

   (B) I <u>have made</u> a delicious cake. Can you help me mix the cake batter?

   Reason: _____

8. (A) I <u>have taken</u> a train ride up the East Coast. I wonder if I will like traveling on a train.

   (B) I <u>have taken</u> a train ride up the East Coast. It was so beautiful. I can't wait to go again.

   Reason: _____

EXERCISE 21. Review Test 1: Multiple Choice

Circle the letter of the correct answer. Some are conversations.

1. "So how long ____ there? I can't believe you're still there!"

   "Well, I started there in 1980. You do the math."

     a. do you work   c. have you worked

     b. did you work   d. are you working

2. "Have you ever ____ anything?"

   "No, never."

     a. won   b. build   c. stole   d. make

3. "How many movies do you think you ____ in your life?"

     a. see   c. have seen

     b. saw   d. are seen

4. I don't have a car now. In fact, I ____ a car since 1996.

     a. haven't had   c. don't have

     b. didn't have   d. didn't had

5. "My stomach hurts."

   "I ____ some medicine yesterday. Would you like some?"

     a. have bought   b. was buying   c. was buying   d. bought

6. We've discussed our ideas for the meeting ____ the past month, so it's time to make a decision.

     a. for   b. by   c. since   d. with

7. "Do you know Rob Douglas?"

   "Why of course I do. I ____ him for a long time."

     a. have met   b. have known   c. met   d. known

8. "Hi, I'm here to pick up the checks for my department staff."

   "I'm sorry, but you're a little bit early. They're not ready ____."

     a. some   b. yet   c. already   d. all

EXERCISE 22. Review Test 2: Production and Evaluation

Part 1.

Read this short passage. Circle the correct answer in the parentheses.

Our Anniversary

Each year for our anniversary, my husband and I ❶(are taking, take, will take) a trip. We ❷(have gone, will go, go) to Aruba, Florida, the Blue Ridge Mountains, and Nantucket. We ❸(has, have) eaten lobster, we have ❹(took, taken, take) a boat to see whales, and we have ❺(go, going, gone) hiking in the Grand Canyon. My husband ❻(haven't been, hasn't been, wasn't) on a cruise, so this year we are going to take a cruise to the Bahamas. I ❼(am taking, have taken, took) many small cruises, but never a big one!

Part 2.

Read this short passage. There are six mistakes. Circle the mistakes, and write the correction above the mistake.

The day after tomorrow, four of my friends are going to coming to my new apartment for dinner. This dinner is a housewarming party for me because I have moved into this place just two weeks ago. It has been a lot of work to set up this apartment, but now that the place is ready, I have invite some of my best friends over for dinner. I didn't decide on the menu yet, but it is going to be something pretty simple. I'm really looking forward to getting together with my friends again. I also want to show them my new place, and I want to catching up on their news. I was so busy with my new place that I have not kept up with any of my friends' news. We're going to have a good time together for sure.

EXERCISE 23. Reading Practice: Fill in the Chart

Read these two emails between two sisters. Then complete the questions in the chart on page 143. The grammar from this unit is underlined for you.

To: Tina Miller <tinam@jmail.com>
From: Ana Miller <amiller@presperf.com>
Subject: New York

Hi, Tina!
I'm having a great time in New York City! In fact, I think it's one of the most interesting cities I've ever visited. I saw the Statue of Liberty yesterday, and I went to Chinatown today. I haven't seen a Broadway show yet, but I have tickets for tomorrow night. Have you ever been to the Metropolitan Museum of Art? Well, I'm going on Thursday. I can't wait! I'm sorry I haven't called you.

I'll see you on Friday. Don't worry if you are running a few minutes late. I'll just wait outside the baggage claim area for you.

Love, Ana

To: Ana Miller <amiller@presperf.com>
From: Tina Miller <tinam@jmail.com>
Subject: Can't meet you at the airport

Dear Ana,

I haven't had any emails from you. I hope you are OK. I've sent you two messages so far. Did you get them? I hope nothing bad has happened. Anyway, I just wanted to tell you that I won't be able to pick you up at the airport on Friday. My boss has scheduled an important meeting, and I can't miss it. Take a taxi, and I'll see you at home on Friday.

Tina

Based on the two emails, identify who each statement is describing.

	Ana	Tina	Neither Ana nor Tina
1. Hasn't been able to get Internet access.			
2. Asked if anything bad has happened.			
3. Has not received an email from her sister.			
4. Went to a Broadway show yesterday.			
5. Thinks that New York City is boring.			
6. Wants her sister to pick her up at the airport on Friday.			
7. Sent her sister two email messages.			
8. Can't miss an important meeting.			
9. Is in New York now.			
10. Will be in New York Friday.			

EXERCISE 24. Vocabulary Practice: Word Knowledge

Circle the word or phrase that is most closely related to the word or phrase on the left. Use a dictionary to check the meaning of words you do not know.

Vocabulary	Answer Choices	
1. behind	in back of	in front of
2. frozen	egg	ice
3. current	future	present
4. distinct	general	specific
5. a supervisor	a person	a thing
6. this kind	this size	this type
7. though	and	but
8. pick up	go to a place and take	go to a place and stay
9. climb	go down	go up
10. realize	introduce	understand
11. manufacture	make	sing
12. about to eat	ten minutes ago	in ten minutes
13. hold	on your feet	in your hands
14. a stew	a person	a thing
15. so far	past to present	present to future
16. a neighbor	a person	a thing
17. lend	clean	money
18. a veterinarian	a person	a place
19. jumbo	huge	tiny
20. purchase	buy	cut
21. a monitor	information	zoo
22. the fall	a location	a season
23. feed	give food	give time
24. a manager	a menu	a person
25. a frog	an animal	a person
26. a concert	food	music
27. staff	money	people
28. vacuum	a fish	a room
29. predict	about the future	about the past
30. a stove	in the bathroom	in the kitchen
31. a whale	huge	tiny
32. warn	bad news	good news
33. would rather	finish	prefer

EXERCISE 25. Vocabulary Practice: Collocations

Fill in each blank with the answer on the right that most naturally completes the phrase on the left. If necessary, use a dictionary to check the meaning of words you do not know.

Vocabulary	Answer Choices	
1. more _____ two years	than	that
2. _____ far	so	such
3. I'm _____ a little late	running	saying
4. _____ about	what	when
5. for both _____	year	years
6. _____ sale	in	on
7. in _____ wild	a	the
8. I met him _____	for ten years	ten years ago
9. a _____ student	university	university's
10. a bit _____	difficult	question
11. for the _____ three days	before	past
12. be sure to _____ me know	let	make
13. flown in a _____	helicopter	trouble
14. change _____ mind	the	your
15. turn _____	it on	on it
16. ask him _____ a ride	by	for
17. at _____	least	less
18. they're _____ to eat	about	next
19. I _____ him since 2000	know	have known
20. go to Boston on _____	business	a car
21. extremely _____	money	rich
22. a full-time _____	job	trip
23. have trouble _____ something	to remember	remembering
24. be worried _____ something	about	for
25. _____ the drums	mean	play
26. you _____ to try it some time	ought	should
27. _____ done it yet	have	haven't
28. climb _____	a car	a tree
29. since _____	2010	one year
30. I've just _____	eating	eaten
31. the _____ office	mail	post
32. a few _____	time	times
33. _____ me a ride	give	take

EXERCISE 26. Writing Practice

Part 1. Editing Student Writing

Read these sentences about one student's visit to a former professor. Circle the 14 errors. Then write the number of the sentence with the error next to the type of error. (Some sentences may have more than one error.)

_____ a. singular-plural   _____ d. word order

_____ b. no subject   _____ e. article

_____ c. verb tense   _____ f. pronoun

A Visit to My Old Professor
1. A few month ago, I went to visit Mr. Harding, my old English teacher from the high school.
2. When was in high school, he has been my favorite teacher because he understood all my problem with English.
3. When it was time for me to go to college, he has given me some advice important about choosing a good university.
4. I think about his class all the time, and I still remembered something she once told me: "Education is the key to success."
5. Since high school, my English improved tremendously.
6. Two years ago, I enrolled in courses to get master's degree, but I don't finish my degree yet.
7. When I saw her a few months ago, my teacher laughed and said, "You have certainly grown since the last time I have seen you!"
8. I am so happy that visited Mr. Harding.

Part 2. Original Student Writing

Imagine you are in a foreign country. You have been there two or three months. A good friend from your hometown has just found out that you are in this country. She didn't know that you were not in your home country any longer. Your friend wrote you this email. Write a reply to your friend's letter.

Dear (your name),

Hi, how are you doing? What are you doing in [the country that you want]? I was talking to our good friend Adele last night, and she mentioned very casually that you were in [the country]. I couldn't believe it! How come I didn't know?

So how long have you been there? Do you like it? What are you doing there? Why did you go there? Why didn't I know that you were going there? How long are you going to stay?

I never thought that you were the kind of person who would want to live in a foreign country. What is the country like? What are the people like? What is the strangest thing that you have seen there?

I'm full of questions, and I hope you are full of answers! Write me back as soon as you can. I want to know how you've been.

Your friend,

Patricia

Be sure to practice the present perfect tense. Try to use present perfect at least three times and simple past tense at least three times. For example, you might write, _How have you been?_ or _I didn't realize you weren't here. How long have you been there?_ Underline the grammar point that you have used so the teacher can see what you are trying to practice.

Unit 5

Adverbs of Frequency

Discover the Grammar

Read the conversation between a university student and a reporter who is talking about her job, and then answer the five questions.

Line		
1	*Reporter:*	So, Lily, you're majoring in journalism, right?
2	*Student:*	Yes, that's correct. I'm graduating next June, and I'm looking for
3		jobs now.
4	*Reporter:*	Well, it's <u>never</u> too early to do that!
5	*Student:*	I know! So I'd like to ask you a few questions about what it's like to
6		work for a newspaper.
7	*Reporter:*	Sure, go ahead.
8	*Student:*	Well, my first question is a basic one. Do you pretty much do the
9		same thing every day?
10	*Reporter:*	No, not really. I <u>rarely</u> do the same thing from one day to the next.
11	*Student:*	Could you explain that a little bit more?
12	*Reporter:*	Well, I mean that I <u>always</u> have a story that I'm working on, but the
13		stories are always different, so I never see the same people. I visit
14		different people, go to different places, and do many different things.
15		My job has a lot of variety.

16	*Student*:	How often are you in your office?
17	*Reporter*:	Well . . . some of the time . . . I mean, my computer is there, and
18		that's where I write my stories, but sometimes I go interview people
19		in their homes or offices. Actually, I spend a lot of time in my car
20		going to and from interviews.
21	*Student*:	How do you stay in touch with the newspaper then?
22	*Reporter*:	Oh, I always take my cell phone with me.
23	*Student*:	Do you <u>usually</u> have a laptop with you, too?
24	*Reporter*:	No. I don't like to use a laptop when I'm interviewing. I <u>sometimes</u>
25		take notes on paper, but I usually use a little voice recorder. Then I
26		type my stories as soon as I get back to the office.
27	*Student*:	So you don't use email much?
28	*Reporter*:	Oh, yes, I do. I always check my email before I leave home in the
29		morning, again when I get to the office, before and after lunch, and
30		again before I go home in the evening.
31	*Student*:	Wow, that's a lot! Do you check your email on weekends, too?
32	*Reporter*:	Yes, I usually check my email on weekends. I will answer personal
33		emails, but I have a rule that I never answer business emails on the
34		weekend or a holiday.

1. Look at the five underlined words in the conversation. These words are called **adverbs of frequency** because they tell us how frequent an action is. Study the meaning of these frequency words, and then write these five words in the boxes. List them in order from the most frequent (all of the time) to the least frequent (not at any time).

Most Frequent				**Least Frequent**
← 100% of the time —————— 50% of the time —————— 0% of the time →				

2. Locate the three sentences that include the word *never*. Write the line number of those sentences. Then circle the order of the subject, verb, and *never*.

Line	Word Order
a. _____	S + V + *never* OR S + *never* + V
b. _____	S + V + *never* OR S + *never* + V
c. _____	S + V + *never* OR S + *never* + V

3. Locate the four sentences that include the word *always*. Write the line number of those sentences. Then circle the order of the subject, verb, and *always*.

Line	Word Order
a. _____	S + V + *always* OR S + *always* + V
b. _____	S + V + *always* OR S + *always* + V
c. _____	S + V + *always* OR S + *always* + V
d. _____	S + V + *always* OR S + *always* + V

4. Based on your answers for Questions 2 and 3, where do you think these adverbs of frequency usually appear in a sentence? Does the verb matter?

_____

_____

_____

5. One of these frequency words can come before the subject. Can you find an example of the frequency word that can come before the subject?

Line	Frequency Word	Subject	Verb

Grammar Lesson

Adverbs of Frequency

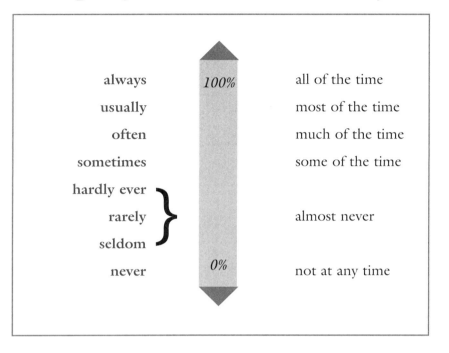

Placement of Adverbs of Frequency in a Sentence	
after *be*: *be* + frequency	**before other verbs: frequency + VERB**
I <u>am</u> **always** hungry when I first wake up. Mohamed <u>is</u> **usually** late to class. You <u>are</u> **often** the first to arrive at work. I <u>am</u> **sometimes** shy around new people Carlos <u>is</u> **rarely** absent from school. Zeke and Ana <u>are</u> **seldom** on time. We <u>are</u> **never** at school after 5 PM.	I **always** <u>use</u> a pencil in math class. He **usually** <u>goes</u> to school by bike. My teacher **often** <u>arrives</u> early. We **sometimes** <u>play</u> tennis at night. Carlos **rarely** <u>misses</u> school. They **seldom** <u>fail</u> a test. I **never** <u>eat</u> a big breakfast.

Questions with Adverbs of Frequency	
A: Do you **ever** take a bus to work? B: Yes, but not usually. I prefer to drive my own car when I can.	Meaning: Do you take a bus to work *at any time*? The answer is probably yes or no with an adverb of frequency.
A: **How often** do you take a bus to work? B: Maybe once or twice a week.	Meaning: How many times during a certain period of time do you take a bus? The answer is probably a number with a period of time.

Rule 1. Adverbs of frequency are words that tell how often something happens: **always, usually, often, sometimes, rarely, seldom, never.**

Rule 2. In a sentence, an adverb of frequency usually comes after **be** but before other verbs. When a verb has two parts (**has eaten**), the adverb of frequency occurs between the two parts (**has never eaten**).

Rule 3. The word **sometimes** can occur in all three places: in front of a sentence, in the middle of a sentence, or at the end of a sentence.

> **Sometimes we practice together.**
>
> **We sometimes practice together.**
>
> **We practice together sometimes.**

Rule 4. To ask about the frequency of an action, use **ever** or **How often:** *Do you ever play golf? How often do you play golf?*

Rule 5. Negative adverbs of frequency such as **rarely, seldom,** and **never** should be used with an affirmative verb. Double negatives are not possible.

 BE CAREFUL!

Common Learner Errors	Explanation
1. We ~~usually are~~ **are usually** the first people to arrive at work each morning.	Adverbs of frequency usually come after the verb **be.**
2. It ~~takes usually~~ **usually takes** me only ten minutes to make a tuna sandwich.	Adverbs of frequency usually come before verbs (other than **be**).
3. The price of gas ~~never has been~~ **has never been** as high as it is now.	When a verb has two parts (**is using, has used**), adverbs of frequency usually come between the two parts.
4. I ~~don't never~~ **never** text while driving.	Double negatives are not possible.

EXERCISE 1. The Meanings of Adverbs of Frequency

Fill in the blanks with the correct adverbs of frequency.

Adverb of Frequency	Meanings
1. _____	all of the time
2. _____	most of the time
3. _____	much of the time
4. _____	some of the time
5. _____	almost never
6. _____	almost never
7. _____	almost never
8. _____	not at anytime

EXERCISE 2. Understanding Adverbs of Frequency

Read each situation, and then answer the question.

1. Jorge usually does his homework. Raul always does his homework. Diego never does his homework. Who is the best student? _____

2. The weather in Florida is rarely cold. It is sometimes cold in Mississippi. It is usually cold in Alaska. If you don't like cold weather, which state might be a good place for you to live? _____

3. Nedra seldom walks to work. Carol often walks to work. Betty walks to work sometimes. Who might drive to work more than walk there? _____

4. I usually put sugar in my coffee. Rich sometimes puts sugar in his tea. Gabrielle always puts sugar on her cereal. Who uses sugar the most frequently? _____

5. My grandmother sometimes takes a walk after dinner. My brother always runs five miles every morning. I hardly ever exercise. Who gets the most exercise?

   _____

6. Ramon rarely watches American television. Ivan usually listens to public radio in English. Nadia seldom sees English movies. Nadine prefers to talk to her friends in her native language. Who probably hears the most English in a day? _____

7. Joe is seldom late to work. Adam is usually late to work. Steve is rarely late to work. Who will the boss most likely give a warning to first? _____

8. Maddie often spends three hours per day reading e-books on her e-reader. Her dad is a professor, and he usually reads a chapter in his textbook two nights per week. Her grandfather used to read the newspaper, but now he seldom does. Who probably reads the most? _____

EXERCISE 3. Writing Sentences with Adverbs of Frequency

Write a new sentence using an adverb of frequency word in place of the information in the parentheses. Circle the verbs. Follow the example.

Breakfast at My House

1. My family eats breakfast together. (This happens every morning.)

   My family always (eats) breakfast together.

2. My sister Mariana makes scrambled eggs for breakfast. (This happens most of the time.)

   _____

   _____

3. She adds potatoes and green peppers to her eggs. (This happens much of the time.)

   _____

4. There isn't any meat in her scrambled eggs. (She is a vegetarian.) (<u>Hint</u>: You can use the word *because* if you want.)

   _____

5. My brother Lucas eats a couple of pieces of toast with butter and jam. (He does this every day.)

   _____

6. He has a huge cup of black coffee with his toast. (He does this about half the time.)

   _____

7. He is a quiet guy, so he doesn't talk much at the breakfast table. (He is quiet most of the time, and he almost never talks.)

   _____

8. My family doesn't start the day without having breakfast together. (This does not happen at any time.)

   _____

   Do Online Exercise 5.1. My score: ____ /10. ____ % correct.

EXERCISE 4. Word Order with Adverbs of Frequency

Read these sentences, and then circle the most common word order.

My Classmate Yvonne

1. Yvonne amazes me. She (never is, is never) sad. She (always seems, seems always) so happy.

2. She (always eats, eats always) with a small group of friends.

3. They (always meet up, meet up always) to study together.

4. She (sometimes picks up, picks up sometimes) her friends and takes them to class.

5. She (always arrives, arrives always) on time when she makes plans with her friends.

6. Yvonne (always is, is always) available to give very good advice to people.

7. She (seldom says, says seldom) anything bad about anyone.

8. She (never gossips, gossips never).

9. Yvonne (never goes, goes never) to parties on a school night.

10. She and her friends (seldom are, are seldom) late to class.

11. Her answers in English class (usually are, are usually) right. She is great at English!

12. In addition to being great at English, Yvonne (always has, has always) her books with her in class. She is very prepared!

EXERCISE 5. Speaking Practice: How Often Do You . . . ?

Step 1. You will interview another student. Choose someone. Write that person's name here:

_____

Step 2. Read the ten statements labeled a – j. Without talking to your partner, guess how often your partner does these things. Write your guesses as adverbs of frequency in the column My Guess: *always, usually, often, sometimes, seldom/rarely, never.*

	My Guess	My Partner's Answer
a. How often do you check your email on Saturday?	_____	_____
b. How often are you late for class?	_____	_____
c. Do you ever use social media sites?	_____	_____
d. How often do you call your parents?	_____	_____
e. Do you ever listen to news on the radio in the morning?	_____	_____
f. How often do you exercise?	_____	_____
g. How often do you see your best friend?	_____	_____
h. Do you ever skip breakfast?	_____	_____
i. How often do you drink coffee?	_____	_____
j. How often do you stay up late?	_____	_____

Step 3. Now interview your partner. Write your partner's answers in the column on the right. Did you guess correctly? Give yourself one point for every correct guess. Which of you had the most points?

Correct guesses _____

ONE-MINUTE LESSON
Make sure you understand the grammar of making questions that begin with **How often**, like **How often do you call your parents?** This is a very useful tool in speaking fluency.

Do Online Exercise 5.2. My score: _____ /10. _____ % correct.

EXERCISE 6. Adverbs of Frequency in Context

Circle the correct word order in this paragraph. Sometimes more than one answer is correct.

Our Garden

At our house, we have a great urban garden. My husband ❶ (wakes usually up, usually wakes up, wakes up usually) at 7 AM every day. ❷ (Sometimes he, He sometimes) goes for a run, but ❸ (usually he, he usually) waters the garden. He ❹ (asks never, never asks) us to help him that early because we ❺ (usually are, are usually) getting ready for school. Our kids ❻ (seldom are, are seldom) late for school and ❼ (often are, are often) there pretty early.

❽ (Sometimes it, It sometimes) rains in the afternoon. In the summer, it ❾ (usually storms, storms usually) between 2 PM and 4 PM in the afternoon. It ❿ (rains rarely, rarely rains) in the wintertime, so my husband or our children will have to water the garden then. In the fall, we ⓫ (have usually, usually have) lots of big pumpkins that we ⓬ (always carve, carve always) to get the seeds for roasting. In the spring, we ⓭ (sometimes have, have sometimes) cucumbers that we pickle in jars. In early summer, we ⓮ (have often, often have) beautiful red strawberries that we pick and turn into jam. It ⓯ (sometimes is, is sometimes) a lot of hard work, but we don't have to make as many trips to the grocery store.

ONE-MINUTE LESSON
Many words can work as a noun and as a verb. Their meanings are connected. *You* **water** *the garden with* **water.** *You* **plant** *a* **plant.** *Leaves* **fall** *in the* **fall.** However, sometimes the meanings are not connected. For example, *you* **take** *a* **trip,** but *you* **trip** *on a* **rock.**

EXERCISE 7. Editing: Is It Correct?

If the sentence is correct, put a check mark (✔) on the line. If it is not correct, write X on the line, and circle the mistake. Then change the sentence to make it correct. Write the change above the sentence. (*Hint:* There are twelve sentences. Four are correct, but eight have mistakes.)

Going to the Pharmacy

_____ 1. When I go to the doctor, I don't rarely need a prescription.

_____ 2. Sometimes I need a prescription if I have a bad infection.

_____ 3. At my old pharmacy, there was a long line always.

_____ 4. When I went there, they sometimes make a mistake with my prescription, so I changed pharmacies.

_____ 5. The cashiers at my new pharmacy are always nice and helpful.

_____ 6. They rarely having a problem filling my prescription.

_____ 7. There usually no is a long wait at my pharmacy.

_____ 8. I often visit the store to pick up extra things while I am waiting for my prescription.

_____ 9. I sometime call in my order if I need a refill.

_____ 10. Someone from the pharmacy often call me to ask if I like the service.

_____ 11. I don't never have any questions about my refills.

_____ 12. My pharmacy sometimes offers free flu shots, but I hate to get shots.

ONE-MINUTE LESSON
The verb after **have a problem** (and similar expressions) is usually with –ing. (This is not a verb tense.) *I had a* **hard time waking up** *today. She* **had no trouble driving** *her new car. We* **had an awful time getting** *a driver's license.*

Do Online Exercise 5.3. My score: _____ /10. _____ % correct.

EXERCISE 8. How Often Do They . . . ?

Answer the questions about the information in the chart. Follow the examples.

Name	Go Running?	Watch TV?	Eat Vegetables?
Marcia	yes/every day	yes/almost every day	yes/all of the time
Boris	yes/rarely	yes/on Sundays	yes/one meal a day
Diego	no/never	yes/only at night	no/never

1. Does Marcia ever eat vegetables?   *Yes, she does.*
2. How often does Marcia eat vegetables?   *all of the time*
3. Does Boris ever go running?   _____
4. How often does Boris go running?   _____
5. Does Diego ever watch TV?   _____
6. How often does Diego watch TV?   _____
7. Does Marcia ever go running?   _____
8. How often does Marcia go running?   _____
9. Does Diego eat vegetables?   _____
10. How often does Diego eat vegetables?   _____

ONE-MINUTE LESSON

The verb **go** is used in front of several activities, but the action word ends in **–ing**. Common examples include: **go bowling, go fishing, go hunting, go jogging, go shopping, go sightseeing, go window shopping**. A very important one is **go swimming**. We don't say, "Let's swim." We say, "**Let's go swimming**." If someone asks you what you did yesterday, you should say, "**I went swimming**," never "I swam."

EXERCISE 9. Mini-Conversations

Circle the correct words in these eight mini-conversations.

1. A: Yuck! Does it (always rain, rain always) so much here?

   B: Yes, it (usually does, does usually).

2. A: Where I'm from, it (rarely storms, storms rarely).

   B: Oh, it (doesn't often, does often not) storm here, but it rains frequently.

3. A: That's good. I don't like storms because they (scare usually, usually scare) me!

   B: I'm (not never scared, never scared) of storms.

4. A: Well, what are you afraid of?

   B: I (sometimes am, am sometimes) scared of spiders, but only the big ones.

5. A: Me, too. I'm lucky that I (see seldom, seldom see) them around here.

   B: What other things are you afraid of?

6. A: I (am often not, am not often) frightened, so let me think. . . .

   B: How about clowns?

7. A: No, clowns (do not usually, not usually) scare me.

   B: What about big dogs?

8. A: Yes! Big dogs (always scare, scare always) me! I (always get, get always) afraid whenever one of them gets too near me.

   B: Well, the good news is that you (see seldom, seldom see) any dogs in this neighborhood. Most people have a cat or no pets at all.

Do Online Exercise 5.4. My score: _____ /10. _____ % correct.

EXERCISE 10. Sentence Study for Critical Reading

Read the numbered sentences. Then read the three answer choices and put a check mark (✔) in the yes or no boxes in front of each sentence to show if that answer is true based on the information in the original sentence. If there is not enough information to mark something as yes, then mark it as no. Remember that more than one true answer is possible.

1. My brother was very out of shape. He worked out only half a dozen times or so per year. He bought a new bike but never rode it.

   ☐ yes ☐ no   a. My brother often worked out at a gym.

   ☐ yes ☐ no   b. My brother almost never did any exercises.

   ☐ yes ☐ no   c. His only exercise was riding a bike.

2. Until fairly recently, my brother had red meat every night. He hardly ever ate a salad. He got fast food and French fries for lunch at least four days per week.

   ☐ yes ☐ no   a. My brother always ate red meat for dinner.

   ☐ yes ☐ no   b. He usually ate a salad with his meals.

   ☐ yes ☐ no   c. He ate fast food a lot.

3. Not surprisingly, my brother has gained a lot of weight in the past two years. His knee hurt sometimes, so he had to see a special doctor for the pain every other month.

   ☐ yes ☐ no   a. My brother lost 15 pounds in the past two years.

   ☐ yes ☐ no   b. His knee hurt every day.

   ☐ yes ☐ no   c. He saw the doctor every other month.

4. The doctor immediately understood my brother's knee problem. He said that many overweight people come to his office. He sees some of them every week for pain in their joints.

   ☐ yes ☐ no   a. The doctor had many overweight patients.

   ☐ yes ☐ no   b. The doctor rarely saw the overweight patients.

   ☐ yes ☐ no   c. The doctor often saw overweight patients for their chest pains.

5. My brother's doctor also sees many people who have heart and breathing problems because of their weight. My brother could not breathe well at night. He woke up every night because it was difficult for him to breathe.

   ☐ yes ☐ no   a. The doctor treats overweight people with heart and breathing problems.

   ☐ yes ☐ no   b. My brother had difficulty breathing at night.

   ☐ yes ☐ no   c. My brother woke up because he could not breathe.

6. The doctor told my brother to lose 40 pounds, so now my brother rides his bicycle every morning. In the evening, he and his wife walk three miles around the lake near their house.

[ ] yes [no]   a. My brother exercises more now than he used to do.

[ ] yes [no]   b. My brother often swims in the lake near his house.

[ ] yes [no]   c. My brother usually walks with his wife.

7. In addition to increasing his exercise, my brother also stopped eating red meat. He now eats a salad with lunch and dinner.

[ ] yes [no]   a. My brother never works out now.

[ ] yes [no]   b. My brother never eats red meat.

[ ] yes [no]   c. My brother always eats a salad each day.

8. After he lost the 40 pounds, he decided to start a fitness club at work. His club meets once per week. They also have walking buddies who exercise during their lunch hours every day.

[ ] yes [no]   a. My brother's fitness club is at his work.

[ ] yes [no]   b. My brother's fitness club meets every other week.

[ ] yes [no]   c. Members of the fitness club walk every work day.

EXERCISE 11. Speaking Practice: How Do You Learn New Vocabulary?

Read each of these ways of learning new vocabulary. How often do you use these ways to learn new words? Write the answer that is true for you. (Write *always, usually, often, sometimes, seldom, never.*) Then work with a partner. Take turns asking and answering these questions. Begin each question with *Do you ever . . . ?* If the answer is yes, then ask, *How often do you . . . ?*

1. I draw a picture of the meaning. _____

2. I write the meaning down in a special notebook. _____

3. I mark new words with different colors of ink. _____

4. When I study vocabulary, I repeat the word aloud. _____

5. I make an example sentence with the new word. _____

6. I try to use new words in conversation. _____

7. I look up the meaning of new words in a bilingual dictionary. _____

8. I circle or underline new words when I find them. _____

9. I write each word several times (perhaps five times). _____

10. I write a translation of the word next to the English word. _____

EXERCISE 12. Review Test 1: Multiple Choice

Circle the letter of the correct answer. Some are conversations.

1. Lupe asked, "How often do you eat cereal for breakfast?"

   Juan Carlos replied, "____."

    a. Ever   b. Never   c. At all of the time d. Yes, I do

2. Gustavo almost never comes to class on time. He ____ almost always late.

    a. is   b. are   c. comes   d. come

3. Ana asked, "Does Dimitry ever eat salad for lunch?"

   Olga answered, "Yes, ____."

    a. always   b. ever   c. seldom   d. at any time

4. Mr. Hobbs almost never has coffee in the morning. He ____ coffee then.

    a. seldom has   c. doesn't seldom have

    b. has seldom   d. seldom doesn't have

5. Kristina is absent every Monday. She ____ to class then because she is tired.

    a. ever comes   c. never comes

    b. comes ever   d. comes never

6. Mary asked, "____ study by yourself?"

   Damaris replied, "Yes, I don't like to study with anyone else."

    a. Ever do you   c. Do ever you

    b. Always do you   d. Do you always

7. Nadya asked, "____ do you read the newspaper?"

   Jose said, "Almost every day. I like to read it in the morning before I go to work."

    a. However   c. Almost always

    b. Ever   d. How often

8. Which sentence does **not** have correct grammar?

    a. Zina often plays tennis.

    b. Always Farah and I are late.

    c. The winter here can be very cold sometimes.

    d. Meat almost never costs less than vegetables.

REVIEW **EXERCISE 13. Review Test 2: Production and Evaluation**

Part 1.
Each sentence has two blanks. Fill in one of the blanks in each sentence with the correct adverb of frequency: *always, usually, often, sometimes, rarely, never, ever.* The other blank does not need an adverb of frequency. Which blank needs the adverb?

1. My days are pretty routine. I am on time for school every day. I _____ arrive _____ on time.

2. When you were in school, did you _____ go _____ by bus?

3. Our teacher wears a tie some of the time. He _____ wears _____ a tie.

4. Students _____ eat _____ lunch off campus. It is not allowed.

5. Tom never fails a test. His score _____ is _____ above 70.

6. Lunch in the college cafeteria is expensive, so I _____ eat _____ it there. The last time was about two months ago.

7. Wendy is a very smart student. She _____ makes _____ a mistake on a test. Her test average is almost 100.

8. I can't drive, so I _____ drive _____ a car from home to campus.

Part 2.
Read this short passage. There are six mistakes. Circle the mistakes, and write the correction above the mistake.

   Bill is late for work often on Monday. He is late for work because he always read the Monday morning paper before he go to the office. He enjoys reading the paper, so he takes his time. Unfortunately, he often takes too much time. Bill drinks always coffee in the morning, but he hardly ever takes it black. He drinks coffee without sugar rarely. Sometimes he is late because he goes to work by bus. He doesn't never drives to work.

EXERCISE 14. Reading Practice: Matching People with Their Actions

Read the postings to an Internet bulletin board with advice for online shoppers. Notice the underlined adverbs of frequency. Then fill in the chart on page 166. The grammar from this unit is underlined for you.

<u>Never</u> buy an item at the first site you visit! It's <u>always</u> a good idea to check several sites. In fact, the first site I go to <u>rarely</u> has the best price. I don't know why that is.
Sally Shopper

It's <u>usually</u> not a good idea to buy an item too quickly. Take a few days to think about it, and, as Sally Shopper says, to check other sites. You can <u>often</u> find a better price later.
Cautious Carl

I disagree with Carl. <u>Often</u> items sell out, or sales end. <u>Sometimes</u> you get lucky, sure, but if you don't buy an item when you see it, you might never find it again!
Bargain Hunter

I think it's important to read other customers' reviews of the product. You can usually learn a lot that way. Of course advertisers <u>always</u> say their products are great. I want to hear from a real person who has experience with using that product. I <u>seldom</u> buy a product online if there aren't any reviews.
Buyer B-ware

Even great products <u>sometimes</u> have problems, so make sure you only buy from a site that has a good return policy. It's important to be able to get your money back or to get your item replaced.
Cautious Carl

I <u>never</u> like to give out my credit card number online. Isn't that risky? <u>Sometimes</u> I read stories in the newspaper about identity theft. Am I just worrying too much?
Nellie

Nellie, I <u>rarely</u> worry about security with online payments. Just make sure that when you check out, you see the https:// at the beginning of the website address. That means that the site is secure. However, if you feel nervous, then just check the site's contact information. You can <u>often</u> find a phone number, and then you order over the phone. Or you can <u>usually</u> pay by check through the mail. Of course, that almost <u>always</u> takes longer.
Thrifty1

Put a check mark (✔) in the column to match the names of the people with the descriptions. Sometimes more than one answer is possible. Sometimes none is possible.

	Bargain Hunter	Buyer B-Ware	Cautious Carl	Nellie	Sally Shopper	Thrifty1
1. I rarely worry about paying online.						
2. I posted a message on this board.						
3. I believe in moving quickly if you see something you want to buy.						
4. I disagree with Cautious Carl.						
5. I talked about security.						
6. I recommend going to different sites to see if they have better prices.						
7. I always look for what other people say about a product before I buy.						
8. I bought a used car online.						

EXERCISE 15. Vocabulary Practice: Word Knowledge

Circle the word or phrase that is most closely related to the word or phrase on the left. Use a dictionary to check the meaning of words you do not know.

Vocabulary	Answer Choices	
1. an interview	2 people	2 places
2. get to school	arrive	leave
3. once	one time	two times
4. check your email	read your email	write your email
5. a couple	one	two
6. carve	with a knife	with a dictionary
7. a chapter	in a book	in a car
8. a reporter	a person	a place
9. a pharmacy	drugs	students
10. rarely	seldom	usually
11. fail	bad	good
12. a campus	a bank	a school
13. seeds	usually big	usually small
14. skip lunch	not eat lunch	not pay for lunch
15. enjoy	hate	like
16. a theft	review	rob
17. risky	dangerous	wonderful
18. an item	a person	a thing
19. variety	different	same
20. to roast	in the bathroom	in the kitchen
21. scared	afraid	population
22. breathe	air	water
23. prefer	like less	like more
24. turn into	become	persuade
25. stay up	don't talk	don't sleep
26. kids	children	dictionaries
27. a refill	more of something	less of something
28. a cucumber	you eat it	you read it
29. shy	rarely talks	usually talks
30. bored	bad	good
31. several	one	more than one
32. smart	famous	intelligent
33. a clown	a person	a place

EXERCISE 16. Vocabulary Practice: Collocations

Fill in each blank with the answer on the right that most naturally completes the phrase on the left. If necessary, use a dictionary to check the meaning of words you do not know.

Vocabulary	Answer Choices	
1. _____ ahead	go	take
2. pretty _____ the same	many	much
3. a few _____	question	questions
4. from one day _____ the next	for	to
5. How many _____	time	times
6. Do you _____ a lot of exercise?	get	make
7. _____ plans with someone	do	make
8. stay _____ touch	in	on
9. _____ a tie	fair	wear
10. I _____ a salad for lunch	have often	often have
11. in _____ to	addition	subtraction
12. _____ peppers	black	green
13. _____ the evening	at	in
14. _____ ever	hardly	seldom
15. to _____ a prescription	die	fill
16. play _____	golf	the golf
17. a _____ storm	bad	pretty
18. _____ lucky	get	run
19. have _____ flu	a	the
20. spend two hours _____	shop	shopping
21. be scared _____	at	of
22. _____ a picture	draw	wear
23. I disagree _____ you	to	with
24. _____ doing that	enjoy	want
25. get ready _____ school	for	to
26. _____ into the price of a new car	looking	watching
27. _____ the weekend	in	on
28. how _____	always	often
29. while _____	drive	driving
30. majoring in _____	business	hobbies
31. a grocery _____	shop	store
32. _____ a mistake	do	make
33. _____ up	prefer	wake

EXERCISE 17. Writing Practice

Part 1. Editing Student Writing

Read these sentences about one student's opinion about his nephews. Circle the 15 errors. Then write the number of the sentence with the error next to the type of error. (Some sentences may have more than one error.)

_____ a. no subject   _____ d. word order

_____ b. article   _____ e. negative

_____ c. no verb   _____ f. verb tense

My Nephews
1. My younger brother had two sons.
2. I visit almost always them during the month of July because that is when I can take a vacation from work. 
3. The older boy is five years old, and he full of energy!
4. That child is on the go always. Some people say is like lightning.
5. He never sleeps, and he kept all of us very busy.
6. The younger one is still baby, and he slept most of the time.
7. My brother and his family live in Albany. They chose to live in this city because like it very much.
8. They do no usually travel because their boys very young.
9. The boys usually hate to travel by car because they can't stand to sit in one place for a very long time.
10. Boys like to travel by train, and they took a train trip about ten times so far.
11. My brother points often out interesting things to the boys while they are on the train.
12. I always happy to see them when I can get away from work!

Part 2. Original Student Writing

Write sentences or a paragraph about a person or family. You can write about a real person, or you can make up a story. Practice using adverbs of frequency. Underline at least five examples of frequency words in your writing.

A. **Dallas Grandmother Robs DC Bank**

B. **Gas Price at 10-Year Peak**

C. **Cigarette Smokers to Pay More for Health Insurance**

Unit 6

Nouns Used as Adjectives

Discover the Grammar

Read the three newspaper headlines, and then answer the eight questions.

1. In your own words, what does Headline A mean?

   _____

   _____

   _____

2. Compare Headline A with "A Grandmother from Dallas Robs a Bank in DC." Both are possible, but why do you think the original is more common?

   _____

   _____

   _____

3. In your own words, what does Headline B mean?

   _____

   _____

   _____

4. If the writer is talking about 10 years, why is there no letter –*s* in the word *year* in this headline?

_____

_____

_____

5. In your own words, what does Headline C mean?

_____

_____

_____

6. Smokers smoke cigarettes. Notice that cigarettes ends in –*s*, but there is no –*s* in the headline. Can you explain this lack of –*s*?

_____

_____

_____

7. Identify each underlined word as a noun or an adjective.

    a. My <u>grandmother</u> lives in <u>Dallas</u>. _____ _____

    b. <u>Dallas Grandmother</u> Robs DC Bank _____ _____

    c. The <u>price</u> of <u>gas</u> has never been higher in the last ten <u>years</u>.

    _____ _____ _____

    d. <u>Gas Price</u> at 10-<u>Year</u> Peak. _____ _____ _____

    e. My uncle smokes <u>cigarettes</u>. _____

    f. <u>Cigarette</u> Smokers to Pay More for Health Insurance _____

8. In English, it is common for a noun to be in front of another noun. In this case, the first noun is working as an adjective. Translate these noun + noun expressions into your language. Do you need any extra words? How is the translation in your language different from English?

    a. cigarette smokers   _____

    b. health insurance   _____

    c. a Dallas grandmother   _____

    d. the gas price   _____

    e. a 10-year peak   _____

    f. a DC bank   _____

Grammar Lesson

Nouns Used as Adjectives

Noun	Noun Working as an Adjective
That factory produces cars.	It is a car factory.
The shop on Main Street sells doughnuts.	It is a doughnut shop.
He has a book that discusses history.	It is a history book.

<u>Rule 1</u>. When a noun is working as an adjective, there is no special ending. The noun and the adjective form can look the same.

<u>Rule 2</u>. When a plural noun is used before another noun, it is an adjective. We do not use the –s. A factory that makes cars is a car factory.

<u>Rule 3</u>. When the plural noun has a number with it, we drop the –s, keep the number, and add a hyphen: **a child who is three years old** → **a three-year-old child.**

<u>Rule 4.</u> When there are a true adjective (*comfortable*) and a noun used as an adjective (*a* cotton *t-shirt*), the true adjective goes first: *a* comfortable cotton *t-shirt*.

Possible Meanings of Nouns Used as Adjectives

Noun-Adjective	Meaning	Other Examples
a <u>gold</u> <u>ring</u> N^1 N^2	N^2 is made of N^1	a plastic fork, a diamond necklace
<u>basketball</u> <u>shoes</u> N^1 N^2	N^2 is for the purpose of N^1	a wedding ring, a pencil case
a <u>love</u> <u>story</u> N^1 N^2	N^2 is about N^1	a war movie, a history report
<u>cafeteria</u> <u>food</u> N^1 N^2	N^2 comes from N^1	home cooking, a New York accent
<u>winter</u> <u>colds</u> N^1 N^2	N^2 is at the time of N^1	a morning meeting, a Tuesday deadline
a <u>school</u> <u>event</u> N^1 N^2	N^2 happens at N^1	a beach party, a lake picnic
a <u>bread</u> <u>store</u> N^1 N^2	N^2 makes/sells N^1	a coffee shop, a fast-food restaurant

Connecting Grammar and Vocabulary

Most of the time, there is no descriptive word in front of a noun. We use just the noun with an article, a possessive adjective, or a number: *the man, my aunt, ten books.*

If people put a descriptive word in front of a noun, the most usual kind of word to go in front of that noun is an adjective: *a clean shirt, a large coffee, a delicious dinner.*

The second most common kind of word to go in front of a noun is another noun (acting as an adjective): *a cheese sandwich, a leather belt, a baby seat.*

When you see these noun + noun combinations, they sometimes look easy to understand because both nouns may be short, common words. However, the meanings of these noun + noun combinations can be difficult and confusing.

For example, a **coffee shop** is a shop that *sells* coffee, but a **war movie** is not a movie that *sells* wars. A **steak knife** is a special knife for *cutting* steak, but a **Texas accent** is not an accent for *cutting Texas*!

These noun + noun combinations are especially common in newspaper writing, as you have seen in the headlines on page 170. In fact, noun + noun phrases make up about 40 percent of examples where there is a descriptive word in front of a noun. These combinations also make up about 30 percent of similar examples in academic English. In science, we have *cell division*; in math, we have *square roots*; and in art, we study *oil paintings.* Therefore, to read the newspaper and your academic books, you need to be able to understand these noun + noun phrases.

Source: Biber et al., 1999, *Longman Corpus of Spoken and Written English*, p. 589.

 ## BE CAREFUL!

Common Learner Errors	Explanation
1. I ate a ~~sandwich of cheese~~ a cheese sandwich.	Put the two nouns together. Do not use a preposition such as **of** to connect them.
2. Is there a ~~shoes store~~ shoe store near here?	When a noun is used as an adjective, it cannot have a plural form because adjectives are never plural.
3. She has a ~~two years old~~ two-year-old child.	When a plural noun with a number is used as an adjective, do not use the –s and do not forget the hyphen.
4. She gave me a ~~cookie's recipe~~ cookie recipe.	Put the two nouns together. This is not a possessive example, so do not use an apostrophe.

EXERCISE 1. Understanding Noun + Noun Phrases

In your own words, explain the meaning of these phrases. Follow the example.

1. a watch store   *a store that sells watches*
2. a flight attendant _____
3. a kitchen appliance _____
4. a flower garden   _____
5. a garden flower   _____
6. a pocket watch   _____
7. a gold ring   _____
8. an engine problem   _____
9. a math teacher   _____
10. a wool jacket   _____

EXERCISE 2. Understanding Noun + Noun Phrases

In your own words, explain the meaning of these phrases.

Things You Might See in a Pet Store

1. a bird cage   _____
2. a cash register   _____
3. a goldfish bowl   _____
4. a litter box   _____
5. a hamster wheel   _____
6. aquarium lights   _____
7. a rabbit hut   _____
8. a cat collar   _____
9. a turtle tank   _____
10. a flea spray   _____
11. dog treats   _____
12. bird toys   _____

EXERCISE 3. Understanding Longer Noun + Noun Phrases

In your own words, explain the meaning of these phrases.

1. a Rolex watch store _____

2. a downtown watch store _____

3. vanilla cream _____

4. vanilla ice cream _____

5. Madagascar vanilla ice cream _____

6. a small dog treat _____

7. washing machine repair _____

8. a camera repair shop _____

9. a vintage camera repair shop _____

10. an egg sandwich _____

11. an auto insurance application form _____

12. a ten-day vacation package _____

13. a strawberry yogurt drink _____

14. a saltwater swimming pool cleaner _____

15. a practice exam _____

16. my university gym membership _____

17. a holiday pumpkin pie _____

18. a plastic computer screen _____

ONE-MINUTE LESSON

Longer strings of **noun + noun** are common in English. Understanding the complete phrase can seem difficult. However, you should remember that the most important word is the last word because that is what the item is: **An auto insurance application form** is **a form.**

Do Online Exercise 6.1. My score: _____ /10. _____ % correct.

EXERCISE 4. Scrambled Noun/Adjective + Noun Phrases

Write these words in the correct order to produce the correct noun phrase. Follow the example.

1. flower plastic ten pots   *ten plastic flower pots* _____

2. first-class ticket train a _____

3. recent your match tennis _____

4. Chinese older vase an _____

5. reading your glasses black _____

6. last committee the college meeting _____

7. Thai spicy a vegetable dish _____

8. black buffalo water four _____

9. McIntosh shiny apple a red _____

10. trend fall the hot latest _____

EXERCISE 5. Writing Noun/Adjective + Noun Phrases

Answer the questions using a noun/adjective + noun phrase. Include **a, an**, or **Ø**. Follow the example.

1. What do you call a garden for flowers? <u>a</u> <u>flower</u> <u>garden</u>

2. What do you call a flower from a garden? ___ _____ _____

3. What do you call a watch that you keep in a pocket? ___ _____ _____

4. What do you call a pocket that you keep your watch in? ___ _____ _____

5. What do you call a station where buses arrive? ___ _____ _____

6. What do you call a fork for eating salad? ___ _____ _____

7. What do you call a spoon for eating soup? ___ _____ _____

8. What do you call a lamp that is on a desk? ___ _____ _____

9. What do you call clothing for babies? _____ _____

10. What do you call a cover for a magazine? ___ _____ _____

11. What is a cup for coffee? ___ _____ _____

12. What do you call a table where you play cards? ___ _____ _____

13. What do you call a counter where passengers can check in? ___ _____ _____

14. What do you call an exam in a history course? ___ _____ _____

15. What do you call a tree that grows apples? ___ _____ _____

16. What do you call trees that grow apples? _____ _____

17. What is a headline in a newspaper? ___ _____ _____

18. What are headlines in a newspaper? _____ _____

19. What do you call a student at a university? ___ _____ _____

20. What do you call students at a university? _____ _____

21. What is a cake that is made of chocolate? ___ _____ _____

22. What is a cake that we usually eat with coffee? ___ _____ _____

EXERCISE 6. Noun Phrases in Context

Circle the correct word order.

Things You Might Hear in Class

1. In today's (class lecture, lecture class), we will hear about the (brain human, human brain).

2. On tomorrow's (history exam, exam history), you will find fifty (short-answer questions, questions short-answer) and two (questions essay, essay questions).

3. To understand history in 1935, it is important to look at a (map world, world map).

4. You can see how many students are registered by looking at the (list class, class list).

5. Many students wish they had the (answer key, key answer) to their current textbooks.

6. In physics, you will study the nature of (compounds chemical, chemical compounds).

7. Your professors expect to see (writing college-level, college-level writing) from you.

8. Please check the course catalog for the latest (modern art electives, art electives modern).

9. Please open your (biology molecular textbooks, molecular biology textbooks) to page 213.

10. Our last (day class, class day) is May 29th. We have our (exam final, final exam) the next day.

EXERCISE 7. Speaking Practice: Noun + Noun Phrases at a Garage Sale

Step 1. Work with a partner or in a small group.

Step 2. Read the list of items for sale. Make sure you understand what each item is.

Step 3. Then work together to choose which five things you will buy. You can choose only five.

Step 4. Each group will explain their five items. Be prepared to defend your choices. Why do you need to buy these items?

Garage Sale
Saturday afternoon

All things must go!

baseball gloves	computer manuals
tennis balls	coffee cups
flower pots	old fashion magazines
romance novels	a rice cooker
music CDs	muffin pans
computer things	a card table
garden plants	plastic picture frames
living room furniture	a vacuum cleaner
kitchen plates	an ironing board
wine glasses	10 salad plates
baby clothes	a garden hose

 Do Online Exercise 6.3. My score: _____ /10. _____ % correct.

EXERCISE 8. Editing: Is It Correct?

If the sentence is correct, write a check mark (✓) on the line. If it is not correct, write X on the line, and circle the mistake. Then change the sentence to make it correct. Write the change above the sentence. (*Hint:* There are twelve sentences. Four are correct, but eight have mistakes.)

A Movie Addict

_____ 1. One of my hobbies is watching movies.

_____ 2. In fact, you could say that I am addicted to watching movies.

_____ 3. I love to collect a few specific kinds of movies, especially horrors movies.

_____ 4. I can watch four or five hours of horror movies in a row, so I admit that I am a horror movies addict.

_____ 5. A home, we have a TV cable service that has a special channel that shows nothing but horror movies.

_____ 6. There are many great horror movies on this special channel, but that is not how I prefer to watch horror movie.

_____ 7. Because I am addicted to watching movies, my mom gave me a player DVD several years ago.

_____ 8. It was a birthday gift, and I use that gift almost every day.

_____ 9. I think that the quality sound on my machine is outstanding.

_____ 10. For horror movies, the sound is a factor very important in scaring the audience.

_____ 11. When you watched your last horror movie, were you frightened more by the visuals or the sounds?

_____ 12. If I had a week off from work, I think I would spend all seven days watching the horror movies on my DVD player.

Do Online Exercise 6.4. My score: ____ /10. ____ % correct.

EXERCISE 9. Mini-Conversations

Circle the correct words in these eight mini-conversations.

1. A: Hey, there's Lena! Look at her (pink beautiful, beautiful pink) sweater.

   B: Oh, I see it! It is bright!

2. A: Hey, Steve! Who is your (new English, English new) teacher?

   B: It's Mrs. Ladner.

3. A: Where can we eat lunch?

   B: How about that (little Greek, Greek little) restaurant on the corner of Hillcrest and Orange?

4. A: Terri, what does your sister do for a living?

   B: She's a (public school, school public) teacher.

5. A: Can you hand me that (mixing bowl, bowl mixing), please?

   B: Do you mean this (large green, green large) one?

6. A: How many (ticket bus, bus ticket, tickets bus, bus tickets) did you buy?

   B: Two.

7. A: Where do you want to meet again?

   B: How about the (red brick, brick red) building in front of the library?

8. A: Hey, are you on the (social new, new social, news socials, socials news) website?

   B: No, I'm not. I'm worried about the (privacy risks, risks privacy).

ONE-MINUTE LESSON
Remember that the noun with **How many** is always plural. **How many tickets?**
How many people? How many questions?

EXERCISE 10. Sentence Study for Critical Reading

Read the numbered sentences. Then read the three answer choices, and put a check mark (✔) in the yes or no boxes in front of each sentence to show if that answer is true based on the information in the original sentence. If there is not enough information to mark something as yes, then mark it as no. Remember that more than one true answer is possible.

Shopping at a Flea Market

1. I went to a great flea market last week and bought a large round metal table.

   ☐ yes ☐ no   a. I went to a market to buy some fleas.

   ☐ yes ☐ no   b. I bought a large table.

   ☐ yes ☐ no   c. The table is made of metal.

2. I had my eye on a small wooden toy ship, but it was too expensive.

   ☐ yes ☐ no   a. I also saw a small toy.

   ☐ yes ☐ no   b. The ship was not made of plastic.

   ☐ yes ☐ no   c. The ship was extremely cheap.

3. My sister told me to get this ugly oil painting, but I decided not to buy it.

   ☐ yes ☐ no   a. My sister wanted me to paint a picture.

   ☐ yes ☐ no   b. My sister recommended that I purchase a painting.

   ☐ yes ☐ no   c. I hated the painting, so I didn't buy it.

4. I told my sister to look at a Spanish language book that I found on one man's table.

   ☐ yes ☐ no   a. I showed my sister a table.

   ☐ yes ☐ no   b. My sister asked me to look at a language book.

   ☐ yes ☐ no   c. The book was on one man's table.

5. She didn't want the language book but picked up a huge coffee table art book instead.

   ☐ yes ☐ no   a. My sister picked up a lot of coffee.

   ☐ yes ☐ no   b. My sister was interested in a coffee table.

   ☐ yes ☐ no   c. The art book was not small.

6. The cashier was a very charming exchange student.

   ☐ yes ☐ no   a. The cashier was very rude to us.

   ☐ yes ☐ no   b. The cashier was from California.

   ☐ yes ☐ no   c. The cashier was a student.

7. We finished our afternoon of shopping with coffee and outstanding desserts at an incredibly nice coffee shop.

☐ yes ☐ no   a. We skipped flea market shopping and went for coffee instead.

☐ yes ☐ no   b. We ate delicious desserts.

☐ yes ☐ no   c. We purchased food and a beverage at the coffee shop.

8. I ate two oatmeal cookies, and my sister got a slice of chocolate walnut pie.

☐ yes ☐ no   a. My cookies had oatmeal in them.

☐ yes ☐ no   b. The walnuts in the pie were chocolate.

☐ yes ☐ no   c. The pie had walnuts in it.

ONE-MINUTE LESSON

The word **too** in front of an adjective (**too expensive**) or adverb (**too quickly**) has a negative meaning. It means that something is not possible or something was not done correctly or well. If you ask someone, "Do you want to go swimming now?" and the person answers, **"It's too late,"** it means the answer is no. The person does not have to say "No, because it's too late." The word **too** often means something is not going to happen.

EXERCISE 11. Speaking Practice: Talking about Grammar

Step 1. Work with a partner.

Step 2. Choose a topic together, and find a website about it. Write the title of your website.

Step 3. Find eight noun phrases that include at least one noun in front of the main noun.

Step 4. Copy your eight noun + noun phrases in the boxes.

Step 5. In your own words, write the meanings of your phrases.

Step 6. As a class, discuss your phrases and meanings with other students.

Title	
Noun + Noun Phrase	**Meaning**
1.	
2.	
3.	
4.	
5.	
6.	
7.	
8.	

EXERCISE 12. Review Test 1: Multiple Choice

Circle the letter of the correct answer. Some are conversations.

1. *Joe:* "What kind of car did you buy?"

   Dan: "I bought an _____ car."

       a. inexpensive two-doors   c. two-doors inexpensive

       b. inexpensive two-door   d. two-door inexpensive

2. My boyfriend bought me a bouquet of a _____ roses today!

       a. dozen red tiny   c. dozen tiny red

       b. red tiny dozen   d. tiny red dozen

3. In my neighborhood, there are several _____.

       a. restaurants pasta   c. pastas restaurants

       b. pasta restaurants   d. restaurants pasta

4. Ryan just built a _____ house.

       a. beautiful two-story   c. beautiful two-stories

       b. two-story beautiful   d. two-stories beautiful

5. "What did you buy Mom for her birthday?"

   "An antique _____."

       a. pots tea   b. teas pot   c. pot tea   d. tea pot

6. I surprised my husband with _____ bicycles for his birthday.

       a. Italian two racing   c. two racing Italian

       b. Italian two racing   d. two Italian racing

7. I'm studying now for tomorrow's _____.

       a. test big vocabulary   c. big test vocabulary

       b. big test vocabulary   d. big vocabulary test

8. On the table was _____ bread.

       a. Cuban fresh Gaston's   c. Gaston's fresh Cuban

       b. fresh Gaston's Cuban   d. Gaston's Cuban fresh

EXERCISE 13. Review Test 2: Production and Evaluation

Part 1.
Read this passage. Circle the words in parentheses that are in the correct order.

My First First-Class Flight

In the summer of 2011, I wasn't sure where to go for my ❶ (vacation summer, summer vacation). I had a few great ❷ (vacations options, options vacations, options vacation, vacation options), but all of them sounded equally good. One possibility was a ❸ (cruise river, river cruise) in Europe. A second possibility was a ❹ (beach vacation, vacation beach, beaches vacation, vacation beaches) at an island resort in southern Thailand. My third ❺ (vacation plan, plan vacation) was a trip to South America, and that is the trip I chose.

My ❻ (fourteen-day adventure, adventure fourteen-days, fourteen-days adventure) began in Buenos Aires, Argentina, and ended in Santiago, Chile. It included a ❼ (ride bike, bike ride) in a suburb of Buenos Aires, ❽ (climbing mountain, mountain climbing, climbing mountains, mountains climbing) in both countries, and a ❾ (farm sheep visit, sheep farm visit) in Chile. I can't believe all of the great places we visited on this amazing trip.

One of my favorite parts of this South American adventure was the flight from Miami to Buenos Aires. The flight was oversold, so the ❿ (agent gate, gate agent) for the airline decided to move me from ⓫ (economy class, class economy) to the first class section of the plane. The ⓬ (service food, food service) was incredible, and I will never forget my flight to South America.

Part 2.

Read this passage. There are eight mistakes. Circle the mistakes, and write the correction above the mistake.

An Anniversary I Won't Forget

Last night my husband and I celebrated our tenth wedding anniversary with a dinner special at a nice restaurant. Our reservation was for 7:30, so I started getting ready around 6. Before leaving our house, I put on a beautiful new dress for this occasion special. Even my husband, who rarely notices clothing, commented on how nice my dress looked. We drove downtown to the restaurant and found a great space parking near the front door. I didn't think I was nervous, but it was a very special evening, so I guess I was a little nervous. My husband ordered a dinner steak, and I ordered spaghetti and meatballs. Everything was going well until our food came. I started eating my spaghetti, but I accidentally dropped a meatball. Unfortunately, the meatball landed on my beautiful dress, and of course it left a stain red from the sauce tomato. I tried hard not to think about how expensive the dress was, but I couldn't stop myself. We had a great dinner, but I'll never forget this anniversary wedding and my dinner meatball.

EXERCISE 14. Reading Practice: Matching Nouns with Their Location

Read these 20 noun + noun phrases. Complete the chart by writing the phrases in the correct column. The grammar from this unit is underlined for you to study, so pay attention to the grammar, especially the first noun.

a <u>world</u> map	<u>fishing</u> pole	a <u>place</u> mat	a <u>steel</u> anchor
a <u>shrimp</u> salad	<u>green</u> tea	a <u>marine</u> radio	a <u>cheese</u> omelet
a <u>golf</u> shirt	<u>running</u> shorts	a <u>leather</u> jacket	a <u>whiteboard</u> marker
<u>tennis</u> shoes	a <u>pencil</u> sharpener	an <u>answer</u> key	a <u>dress</u> rack
an <u>essay</u> exam	a <u>gas</u> tank	a <u>dessert</u> menu	<u>water</u> skis

at a restaurant	in a classroom	at a clothing store	on a boat

EXERCISE 15. Vocabulary Practice: Word Knowledge

Circle the word or phrase that is most closely related to the word or phrase on the left. Use a dictionary to check the meaning of words you do not know.

Vocabulary	Answer Choices	
1. lack	not have	not think
2. a picnic	inside	outside
3. fleas	on your birthday	on your cat
4. a headline	at an office	in a newspaper
5. the square root of 100	10	10,000
6. original	first	last
7. confusing	difficult to understand	easy to understand
8. the peak	low	high
9. a case	a box	a coin
10. a factory	a person	a place
11. insurance	an important thing	an inexpensive thing
12. an expression	animals	words
13. a doughnut	you eat it	you listen to it
14. spill	some cheese	some milk
15. latest	new	old
16. common	never	usual
17. leather	from an animal	from a tree
18. extra	minus 1	plus 1
19. a risk	dangerous	slow
20. translate	languages	meetings
21. an accent	reading	speaking
22. a collar	on a cat's neck	on a cat's tail
23. a hose	numbers	water
24. a recipe	for cooking	for studying
25. a fork	eating	sleeping
26. a register	games	money
27. an anchor	on a plane	on a ship
28. tiny	big	small
29. purchase	buy	sell
30. a pumpkin	you eat it	you play with it
31. keep (doing)	continue (to do)	need (to do)
32. an option	a choice	a plan
33. in a row	Mon., Tues., Wed.	Mon., Wed., Fri.

EXERCISE 16. Vocabulary Practice: Collocations

Fill in each blank with the answer on the right that most naturally completes the phrase on the left. If necessary, use a dictionary to check the meaning of words you do not know.

Vocabulary	Answer Choices	
1. compare A _____ B	for	with
2. _____ cooking	home	house
3. a history _____	book	coin
4. health _____	insurance	language
5. a _____ knife	steak	steaks
6. a 10-year-old _____	child	peak
7. a _____ screen	computer	football
8. he robbed a _____	bank	wallet
9. work _____ a factory	at	on
10. working as a _____	hospital	nurse
11. a shiny _____	buffalo	ring
12. What does that word _____?	mean	pronounce
13. a rice _____	cleaner	cooker
14. a diamond _____	necklace	tie
15. a human _____	brain	lecture
16. a _____ attendant	art	flight
17. _____ glasses	reading	writing
18. in _____ of	front	side
19. climb a _____	flower	tree
20. a _____ movie	war	wars
21. a _____ jacket	pasta	wool
22. _____ for a living	do	make
23. a doughnut _____	car	shop
24. on the corner _____ two streets	of	on
25. eat a _____	cookie	plural
26. a flea _____	market	shop
27. a goldfish _____	bowl	spray
28. a _____ novel	romance	romances
29. worried _____	about	for
30. too _____	delicious	heavy
31. addicted _____ sports	for	to
32. eat _____ but potatoes	nothing	something
33. an oatmeal _____	cookie	exam

EXERCISE 17. Writing Practice

Part 1. Editing Student Writing

Read these sentences about one student's report about an event. Circle the 15 errors. Then write the number of the sentence with the error next to the type of error. (Some sentences may have more than one error.)

_____ a. no subject

_____ b. word order

_____ c. article

_____ d. verb tense

_____ e. preposition

A Beautiful but Dangerous Weather Event
1. On 2008, I went to visit my aunt Sue, who lives in central Kentucky.
2. My trip was at the end of January, so was winter.
3. In my second day there, the weather has turned really bad.
4. All the local weather television reports predicted a record snowfall, and they are correct.
5. Around ten in morning, the snow began to fall.
6. It was first time for me to see snow, and it looked really beautiful.
7. However, the snow does not stop, and there were several accidents of traffic.
8. The snow continues all day, and at times was almost impossible to see anything because the snow was coming down so hard.
9. It keeps snowing for three days, and we had almost twenty inches of snow.
10. My aunt told me that it doesn't snow usually this much.

Part 2. Original Student Writing

Your friend is going to have a new baby in a few months. She drives a very small sports car with two seats, but she has to sell it and buy a minivan. Write sentences or a paragraph telling your friend some of the features of a minivan that are great for a growing family. Practice noun + noun phrases in your writing, and underline them.

Unit 7

Object Pronouns

Discover the Grammar

Read the conversation about an outdoor market, and then answer the three questions.

Line		
1	*Shopper:*	Oh, what a nice old lamp. How much is it?
2	*Owner:*	How much do you want to give me?
3	*Shopper:*	Well . . . I'll say about ten dollars.
4	*Owner:*	Ten dollars? Come on! It's worth much more than that. Look at its
5		beautiful color.
6	*Shopper:*	Well, you asked me what I wanted to give you, and that is exactly
7		what I want to pay. There's a man just down the street who has one
8		just like this, and I'm sure he'll be interested in my price.
9	*Owner:*	Actually, I don't think there's another lamp just like this one. It's
10		unique. And it's an antique, too. A little old lady sold this to me
11		many years ago, and it was hers for years. How about $20?
12	*Shopper:*	Well, I don't know. I really like its shape. Ok, I'll tell you what. I'll
13		give you $15, but that's my final price.
14	*Owner:*	You drive a hard bargain. If you give me $15, then it's yours.

15	*Shopper:*	OK, sure. Here's the money.
16	*Owner:*	Here you go.
17	*Shopper:*	Thanks. Now the lamp is mine. I needed a lamp like this, and now I
18		can cross that off my shopping list.

1. Read the sentences from the conversation again. Who or what do the underlined words refer to? Circle the correct noun.

    a. *How much do you want to give <u>me</u>?*   (the shopper / the owner)

    b. *Look at <u>its</u> beautiful color.*   (the lamp / $10)

    c. *I'm sure <u>he</u> will be interested in my price.*   (the owner / the man down the street)

    d. *I'm sure he will be interested in <u>my</u> price.*   (the shopper / the man down the street)

    e. *. . . it was <u>hers</u> for years.*   (the little old lady / the shopper)

    f. *<u>I</u> do like its shape.*   (the shopper / the owner)

    g. *. . . that's <u>my</u> final price.*   (the shopper / the owner)

    h. *. . . give me $15, and <u>it</u> is yours.*   (the lamp / the price)

    i. *. . . give me $15, and it is <u>yours</u>.*   (the man down the street / the shopper)

2. Find an example of each of these four words in the conversation. All four refer to the same person. Can you explain when we use each of these?

    I   _____

    me   _____

    my   _____

    mine _____

3. What is the difference between *its* and *it's*? Find one example of each.

_____

_____

_____

Grammar Lesson

It is important to understand the difference between subject pronouns and object pronouns. Object pronouns occur after verbs or after prepositions.

Object Pronouns after Verbs

Examples	Subject Pronoun	Object Pronoun
I see Ahmed. Ahmed <u>sees</u> me.	I	me
You called Ana, and Ana <u>called</u> you back.	You	you
He answered the question, and the teacher <u>corrected</u> him.	He	him
She wrote a letter, and the company <u>wrote</u> her back.	She	her
It is a long book. We didn't <u>finish</u> it.	It	it
We won the race. My dad <u>congratulated</u> us.	We	us
They needed help, so Ted and I <u>helped</u> them.	They	them

Object Pronouns after Prepositions

Examples	Subject Pronoun	Object Pronoun
I have 3 new shirts. My mom gave them <u>to</u> me.	I	me
You didn't go to the bank alone. Sam went <u>with</u> you.	You	you
He wrote me an email, and I replied <u>to</u> him.	He	him
She has a birthday today, so I bought a present <u>for</u> her.	She	her
It is a piece of apple pie. Some people eat ice cream <u>with</u> it.	It	it
We painted the house. That job was hard <u>for</u> us.	We	us
They are outside, and bees are swarming <u>around</u> them.	They	them

Rule 1. Use object pronouns after a verb.

Rule 2. Use object pronouns after prepositions. Common prepositions include **at, between, by, for, from, in, near, on, to, under, with, without**.

Rule 3. The object pronoun **them** can refer to people, animals, or things.

Rule 4. If there are two people and the second person is a pronoun, you can omit the first noun to figure out the correct pronoun: *Linda called Nora and [I, me]*: Not correct: *Linda called I.* Correct: *Linda called me.* Therefore, the correct answer is *Linda called Nora and me.*

Rule 5. In any phrase with multiple people that includes I or me, the word I or me <u>always</u> goes last: *She texted John and me. She texted John, Anne, Jessica, and me.*

 BE CAREFUL!

Common Learner Errors	Explanation
1. Marcos called Maria. He called ~~she~~ her at 8:30.	Use object pronouns after verbs.
2. Yesterday was Jana's birthday. We got a very special present for ~~she~~ her.	Use object pronouns after prepositions.
3. My dad made barbecued chicken for ~~me and my sister~~ my sister and me last weekend.	The pronouns I or me always go last when there are multiple people.

EXERCISE 1. Pronouns in Sentences

Read each sentence, and circle the correct pronoun.

1. A: Where is Rio de Janeiro?

   B: (Is, It is, Are, They are) in Brazil.

2. A: Where is Buenos Aires?

   B: (Is, It is, Are, They are) in Argentina.

3. A: Do you like to watch horror movies?

   B: Yes, I love to watch (it, they, them). As a matter of fact, (it, they) are my favorite kind of movie to watch.

4. A: Do you and your sister have the same kind of watch?

   B: Yes, (they, you, we, them) do.

5. A: Have Ali and Tariq ever gone to India?

   B: Yes, (he, they, him, them) have.

6. A: Have you ever eaten sushi?

   B: No, I've never eaten (it, they, them). What does (it, they, them) taste like? Is (it, they, them) very expensive?

7. A: Is a nickel larger than a dime?

   B: Yes, (is, it is, are, they are), but a dime is worth more.

8. A: Did you cook the fish you bought?

   B: Yes, (I, you, it, they) did.

9. A: Do you know the time?

   B: No, I don't. What time (are, are they, is, is it)?

10. A: Why did he buy ten copies of the same book? Did he need (it, them)?

    B: I really don't have any idea why he did (they, them, it), but that is what he did.

Do Online Exercise 7.1. My score: ____ /10. ____ % correct.

EXERCISE 2. Pronouns in Context

Read each sentence, and circle the correct pronoun.

My Great Birthday Cake

Yesterday **❶** (I, me) was very happy because **❷** (it, it's) was my birthday. Yesterday was also my sister's birthday. No, we are not twins. We were born three years apart. My family threw a birthday party for **❸** (we, us). **❹** (We, Us) all went to my aunt's house to celebrate. **❺** (He, She) made a cake for **❻** (us, we) and decorated **❼** (it, them) with colorful icing and candles. The icing decorations included red roses, and our names were written beside **❽** (them, they, we, us). Everyone sang "Happy Birthday" to **❾** (she and I, her and me, I and she, me and her). At the end of the song, **❿** (it, they) was time to blow out the candles. However, **⓫** (they, them) were trick candles, and **⓬** (we, us) needed someone to help **⓭** (we, us). I said to my brother, "**⓮** (We, Us) need

you. Help **⓯** (we, us) blow out the candles." **⓰** (He, Him) agreed, and the three of **⓱** (we, us) blew **⓲** (they, them) out together. Yes, **⓳** (it was, they were) a special day for my sister and **⓴** (I, me).

ONE-MINUTE LESSON

She made a cake for us. The verb **make** uses the word **for** with the person who receives the action of making. Other verbs that use **for** include *get, buy, find,* and *do a favor*. These verbs all have two sentence patterns: *She made a cake* **for** *us* OR *She made us a cake. I got a book* **for** *Joe* OR *I got Joe a book. My uncle did a favor* **for** *me* OR *My uncle did me a favor*.

Grammar Lesson

Reviewing Subject Pronouns, Possessive Adjectives, and Object Pronouns

Subject Pronouns	Possessive Adjectives	Object Pronouns	Examples
I	my _____	me	I am having lunch with my cousin . He made dinner for **me**.
you	your _____	you	Do you have your passport with you now?
He	his _____	him	**He** isn't at his office . I just tried to call **him** there.
she	her _____	her	Did **she** remember to take her umbrella with **her**?
it	its _____	it	What a crazy cat! **It** always chases its tail . Everyone loves **it**.
We	our _____	us	**We** spent our vacation in Asia. My mom went with **us**.
They	their _____	them	**They** love their new car . I see **them** in it all the time.

<u>Rule 1</u>. Possessive adjectives are different from subject pronouns and object pronouns. Possessive adjectives always go in front of a noun. (That noun can be a subject or object.)

<u>Rule 2</u>. Possessive adjectives and their nouns make noun phrases. A noun phrase can be a subject (My **book** is green) or an object (I read my **science book**).

 BE CAREFUL!

Common Learner Errors	Explanation
1. Jonathan is ~~me~~ my oldest brother.	Remember that **me** is an object pronoun and **my** is a possessive adjective.
2. My mother is taking a trip to France. We got a new suitcase for ~~she~~ her.	Remember that **him** and **her** are object pronouns and **he** and **she** are subject pronouns.

EXERCISE 3. Choosing Possessive Words in Context

Circle the correct answers in the story about a graduation present.

Selecting an Important Gift for a Friend

Nichole gave **1** (she, her) friend Roberto a wonderful gift when **2** (he, his) graduated from college. **3** (It, Its) was an MP3 player. When **4** (she, he) bought the gift, the salesperson at the store tried to sell **5** (she, her) one of the new models, but **6** (they, their) all seemed too expensive to **7** (she, her). **8** (She, her) told the salesperson that technology changes quickly, and new models become "old" almost immediately. He said, "True, but all of **9** (us, our) MP3 players are on sale, so you can buy one of **10** (them, their) at a good price." Nichole thought about **11** (it, its) and asked **12** (him, her) to show **13** (him, her) the new models. **14** (They, Their) went to a display, and the salesperson described the selection. The MP3 players were labeled with **15** (they, their) original prices and sale prices, and the sales prices were much cheaper. The salesperson saw **16** (she, her) looking at one of MP3 players, and **17** (he, she) pointed at **18** (it, its) and said, "That's one of **19** (our, us) most popular models." Nichole thought **20** (it, its) was a great bargain. **21** (It, Its) features included a touchscreen and 32 GB memory. Nichole immediately turned to **22** (he, him) and said, "I'll take **23** (them, it)! **24** (It, It's, Is) a gift for a good friend, so wrap **25** (them, they, it) up, please."

Do Online Exercise 7.2. My score: _____ /10. _____ % correct.

EXERCISE 4. Editing: Is It Correct?

If the sentence is correct, put a check mark (✓) on the line. If it is not correct, write X on the line and circle the mistake. Then change the sentence to make it correct. Write the change above the sentence. (*Hint*: There are twelve sentences. Four are correct, but eight have mistakes.)

Last Night's Restaurant Problem

_____ 1. Last night me and my girlfriend had dinner at a restaurant not far from my home.

_____ 2. We both enjoy going there very much because it is a small, friendly place.

_____ 3. We go there often, and the people there know our.

_____ 4. Last night the service was not very good.

_____ 5. We had to wait a long time before a server came to our table.

_____ 6. He was very nice, but he didn't do a very good job.

_____ 7. I ordered chicken with mushrooms, but brought me chicken with cream sauce.

_____ 8. My girlfriend liked his main course a lot.

_____ 9. Unfortunately, the server put the wrong kind of salad dressing on his salad.

_____ 10. We were not happy with the server, but we didn't say anything to he.

_____ 11. We ate just what him brought us.

_____ 12. Because of these problems, we didn't leave a big tip for her.

 Do Online Exercise 7.3. My score: _____ /10. _____ % correct.

EXERCISE 5. Mini-Conversations

Circle the correct words in these eight mini-conversations.

1. A: (I, My) favorite hand gesture is the peace sign. I use (it, them) when people take pictures of (my, me) friends and (I, me).

   B: Yes, I know. I've seen (they, them). (You, Your) do the peace sign in all of (you, your) photos.

2. A: Do (you, your) know when the president is going to speak tonight?

   B: If (I, my) memory is correct, (he, him) is going to speak at 8:30.

3. A: (We, Our) air conditioner is broken. What should (we, our) do?

   B: Call the people at the A/C company, and ask (them, their) what (them, their) rates are.

   A: Actually, I already did that. (It's, Its) going to cost $500 to fix (it, its).

4. A: Is (it, its) ever okay to lie to (you, your) friends?

   B: Not really, but if (they, them) are excited about something and (you're, your) not, then maybe sometimes (you, your) should hide (you, your) true feelings from (they, them) and pretend to be excited.

   A: Well, what about between husband and wife? For example, if the husband just got a new haircut and the wife thinks (it, its) looks terrible, then should (she, her) tell the truth?

   B: Are (you, your) talking about (you, your) husband's new haircut?

   A: Yes, (he, his) hair looks horrible, but (he, his) loves it.

5. A: I've gotten so many speeding tickets that (I, me) had to hire a lawyer. The state wants to take away (me, my) driver's license.

   B: Is the lawyer very expensive?

   A: Yes, (she, her) rates are much more than the actual speeding tickets were, but at least (she, her) is going to help (me, my) keep (me, my) driver's license.

6. A: (You, Your) father is in town this weekend, right? Do (you, your) have any plans?

   B: (We, Our) are going to see a movie tomorrow night. (He, Him) and (I, me) always went to movies together when (I, he) was growing up. It's (we, our) tradition.

7. A: Do (you, your) have to meet with (you, your) boss tomorrow?

   B: Yes, at 11 o'clock. (She, Her) is going to meet with (my, me) team and (I, me).

   A: Good luck, but (you're, your) not going to need (it, its).

8. A: Where did (we, our) park (we, our) car?

   B: Don't ask (me, my). I didn't park (it, them). (You, Your) did.

EXERCISE 6. Sentence Study for Critical Reading

Read the numbered sentences. Then read the three answer choices, and put a check mark (✔) in the yes or no boxes in front of each sentence to show if that answer is true based on the information in the original sentence. If there is not enough information to mark something as yes, then mark it as no. Remember that more than one true answer is possible.

1. My friend Sharon loves the martial artist Jet Li because his action films are in both English and Cantonese.

   ☐ yes ☐ no   a. Jet Li likes my friend.

   ☐ yes ☐ no   b. Jet Li is a martial artist, and people really like her work because it is in two languages.

   ☐ yes ☐ no   c. People like Jet Li's work because his action films are in Japanese and German.

2. She has all of his movies on DVD that he has made during the past 10 years.

   ☐ yes ☐ no   a. She has collected a few of Jet Li's movies.

   ☐ yes ☐ no   b. She has their movies on DVD.

   ☐ yes ☐ no   c. Most of the DVDs were made more than 10 years ago.

3. Jet Li practices a type of martial art that is called Wushu. It got its start in China in the mid-20th century.

   ☐ yes ☐ no   a. Jet Li's martial arts style is Wushu.

   ☐ yes ☐ no   b. Wushu did not begin in Korea.

   ☐ yes ☐ no   c. Jet Li began his work in the mid-20th century.

4. Sharon's son goes to kung fu class three times a week. She doesn't go with him although she really likes martial arts films a lot.

   [yes] [no] a. He likes martial arts films.

   [yes] [no] b. She goes to kung fu class.

   [yes] [no] c. His son goes to kung fu class 3 times a week.

5. Her son loves to practice kung fu, which is also a martial art from China.

   [yes] [no] a. Her son really enjoys kung fu. It is also a martial art.

   [yes] [no] b. His son really enjoys kung fu. It is also from Korea.

   [yes] [no] c. Her son loves to practice kung fu.

6. Last Saturday her son had a tournament at his kung fu school.

   [yes] [no] a. Sharon's son recently had a tournament.

   [yes] [no] b. The tournament was at Sharon's son's middle school.

   [yes] [no] c. The tournament was on Saturday.

7. He competed in three events, and in one event he used his small sword that has a ribbon on its handle.

   [yes] [no] a. Sharon's son competed in more than one event.

   [yes] [no] b. For one event, he used a small sword.

   [yes] [no] c. The small sword has a ribbon on the handle.

8. Sharon took pictures of the two gold medals he won, and one was for his sword competition.

   [yes] [no] a. Sharon's son won two gold medals.

   [yes] [no] b. One of the medals was for his fan competition.

   [yes] [no] c. Sharon took pictures of her gold medals.

ONE-MINUTE LESSON

three times a week We usually say the number of times followed by a quantity of time. For example, we say **three times a week, two times a year, one time a day**. You can say **once** instead of **one time** (*once a day*) or **twice** instead of **two times** (*twice a year*). It is also possible to add the prepositions *in* or *per*, but *per* sounds a little more formal: *twice in a year, twice per year*.

 Do Online Exercise 7.4. My score: ____ /10. ____ % correct.

EXERCISE 7. Speaking Practice: Who Gave It to Me?

The goal of this speaking game is to find out who gave a coin to you. This game practices object pronouns. Each group needs a coin.

Step 1. Work with a group of 4. Each group should sit in a small circle.

Step 2. One student will be the guesser. The other three will be the actors.

Step 3. The guessers will turn away from their groups and cover their eyes for ten seconds.

Step 4. During the ten seconds, one of the three actors will pick up the coin and loudly lay it down on the table or desk behind the guesser.

Step 5. When the teacher says "Go," the guessers have one minute to ask questions to find out who gave the coin to them. Each actor should answer, "No," when asked about the coin. Each actor should also say another actor gave the coin to the guesser. This means that two will tell the truth and one will lie.

Step 6. At the end of one minute, the guessers must make a final guess about who gave the coin to them.

Step 7. Play this game four times so that each student has a chance to be the guesser.

Study this example with a guesser and three students (Maria, Abdul, Lim):

> *Guesser:* Maria, did you give the coin to me?
>
> *Maria:* No, I didn't give it to you. It was Abdul. He gave it to you.
>
> *Guesser:* Abdul, did you give the coin to me?
>
> *Abdul:* No, I didn't give it to you. It was Lim. He gave it to you.
>
> *Guesser:* Lim, did you give the coin to me?
>
> *Lim:* No, I didn't give it to you. It was Maria. She gave it to you.
>
> *Guesser:* Maria, did you give the coin to me?

Continue like this for one minute. Make the actors talk as much as possible by asking as many questions as possible because it is easier to identify the real giver.

Practice subject and object pronouns in sentences like these:

> *Did you give the coin to me?*
> *I didn't give it to you.*
> *He/She gave it to you.*

ONE-MINUTE LESSON

give the coin to me The verb **give** uses the word **to** with the person who receives the action of giving. Other verbs that use **to** include **tell, take, show,** and **lend.** These verbs all have two sentence patterns: *She told the truth to us* OR *She told us the truth. Please take this book to Sue* OR *Please take Sue this book. He showed his new car to us* OR *He showed us his new car. Jason lent $100 to me* OR *Jason lent me $100.*

EXERCISE 8. Review Test 1: Multiple Choice

Circle the letter of the correct answer. Some are conversations.

1. "Is this your coat?"

   "Yes, my mother gave it to ____ last year."

       a. my   b. me   c. I   d. I'm

2. Our teacher told ____ tests were not good.

       a. we that our   c. we that us

       b. us that our   d. us that us

3. "I work at Brooklyn Bank on Green Street."

   "Oh, then you probably know John and Susan. ____ work at that same bank."

       a. They   b. Their   c. Them   d. They're

4. "Where did ____ keys?"

   "I put your keys on the table. Aren't they there now?"

       a. I put your   c. you put my

       b. your put my   d. I put my

5. "Excuse me, I'd like to speak to Mr. Nakano."

   "I'm sorry, but he's not here right now. Do you want to leave a message for ____?"

       a. his   b. he's   c. he   d. him

6. "Hi, Mark and Lee. Why are you guys late?"

   "Well, ____ bus was a little late today."

       a. us   b. our   c. we   d. my

7. Pamela forgot to take ____ when she left the house this morning.

       a. her wallet with she   c. her wallet with her

       b. she wallet with she   d. she's wallet with her

8. "What did Ahmad say about the movie?"

   "He said ____ liked it very much."

       a. his   b. he's   c. him   d. he

EXERCISE 9. Review Test 2: Production and Evaluation

Part 1.
Read this short passage. Choose the correct word to complete the sentence.

Speaking in Public

If ❶ (you, your, you're) have to give a report or a speech in class, ❷ (its, it, it's) can be very scary! Many people say that speaking in public is ❸ (your, we're, their) biggest fear. The best thing to do is to create ❹ (her, his, your) notes ahead of time so that ❺ (your, you, your) are prepared. Also, find some friends to practice in front of so that ❻ (their, they, them) can give you feedback. Remember that ❼ (you, you're, your) speech does not have to be perfect—❽ (our, we; us) make mistakes when ❾ (us, our, we) speak every day. Even though public speaking takes some preparation, ❿ (they, them, it) does not have to be stressful!

Part 2.
Read this short passage. There are six mistakes. Circle the mistakes, and write the correction above the mistake.

When I was 11 years old, my had to give my first public speech. Was terrifying! When I spoke, I grabbed the microphone so hard its almost broke. My knees were shaking, and I thought everyone could see they. My stomach hurt, and I didn't feel good. My speech was good. Everyone applauded. Their thought that I did a good job, and was happy.

EXERCISE 10. Reading Practice: Vacation Shopping

Read this email about a woman on vacation who has bought gifts for her friends. Notice the object pronouns. Then complete the chart on page 208 to match the people with their descriptions. The grammar from this unit is underlined for you.

Hi Marta,

I'm having the best time in Mexico. This vacation is so good for me! I really needed to relax.

Yesterday I went shopping in the market with Jim. I can't believe I bought so many things! First, I got an incredibly beautiful tablecloth and some cloth napkins for us. They weren't cheap, but they were very well made. I'm sure we will enjoy them for many years.

For our friend Jean, I got some silver jewelry, some earrings, and a bracelet. I'm going to give her the earrings when I get home, and I'll save the bracelet and give it to her for her birthday. I'm sure she'll like it.

I wasn't sure what to buy for our friend John. It's so hard to choose things for him! He always gets such nice gifts for us, but then says he doesn't need anything. In the end, I chose a few t-shirts. If he doesn't like them, he doesn't have to wear them, but I wanted to get him something.

Marta, I got a little something for you, too. I won't tell you what it is, but I hope you like it! No, I'm not even going to give you a hint. I'll give it to you when I get back next week. Call me any time after Sunday, OK?

Your friend,

Carole

Put a check mark (✔) in the column with the name of the person or people that each sentence describes. Remember that multiple answers are possible.

	John	Carole	Jim	Jean	Marta
1. Someone bought a gift for him.					
2. Someone bought a gift for her.					
3. She bought a gift for her friends.					
4. She bought a tablecloth.					
5. They are taking their vacation in Mexico.					
6. They are going to receive a gift.					
7. We know what her gift is.					
8. We don't know what her gift is.					
9. We know what his gift is.					
10. Their friend is in a foreign country now.					

EXERCISE 11. Vocabulary Practice: Word Knowledge

Circle the word or phrase that is most closely related to the word or phrase on the left. Use a dictionary to check the meaning of words you do not know.

Vocabulary	Answer Choices	
1. we agree	our ideas are different	our ideas are not different
2. a candle	fire	ice
3. alone	one person	one year
4. congratulate	"Good job!"	"Good luck!"
5. a tip	some bad news	some money
6. unique	regular	special
7. a novel	you read it	you watch it
8. a server	a person	a place
9. a shape	a circle	a stamp
10. fear	afraid	arrive
11. a dime	a coin	a drink
12. cross off	remove	repeat
13. reply	answer	prepare
14. wrap	a gift	a letter
15. knees	arms	legs
16. chase	eat before	run after
17. an antique	new	old
18. swarming	a lot of bees	a lot of keys
19. grab	make	take
20. immediately	right now	right there
21. a wallet	your money	your time
22. icing	you drink it	you eat it
23. a century	100 people	100 years
24. hide	not cook	not see
25. applaud	clap	travel
26. a bracelet	you read it	you wear it
27. salad dressing	you eat it	you wear it
28. a hint	angry words	helpful words
29. a boss	a person	a place
30. jewelry	a ring	a shirt
31. although	and	but
32. a handle	on a medal	on a suitcase
33. rates	prices	beverages

EXERCISE 12. Vocabulary Practice: Collocations

Fill in each blank with the answer on the right that most naturally completes the phrase on the left. If necessary, use a dictionary to check the meaning of words you do not know.

Vocabulary	Answer Choices	
1. a gold _____	fear	medal
2. _____ a message	leave	stay
3. public _____	speaking	working
4. _____ about $20?	How	How much
5. barbecued _____	cheese	chicken
6. _____ you feedback	create	give
7. _____ your wallet	make	take
8. _____ does it taste like?	How	What
9. it seems _____	expensive	very high price
10. _____ now	right	very
11. _____ a hard bargain	carry	drive
12. _____ a tip	leave	stay
13. cross that off my _____	list	name
14. _____ pie	apple	shoe
15. I got a gift _____ you	for	to
16. the same kind v watch	of	for
17. _____ cheaper	more	much
18. an antique _____	baby	doll
19. _____ a party	make	throw
20. enjoy _____	going	to go
21. growing _____	down	up
22. _____ lunch together	have	take
23. Here you _____.	go	say
24. larger _____	than	that
25. it _____ worth a lot	is	has
26. _____ the past 10 years	during	finally
27. _____ a speech	give	number
28. _____ of time	ahead	before
29. _____ of	because	near
30. a _____ gesture	food	hand
31. _____ a nice lamp!	How	What
32. Please do it just _____ this.	between	like
33. interested _____	by	in

EXERCISE 13. Writing Practice

Part 1. Editing Student Writing

Read these sentences about one student's opinion about a new business. Circle the 15 errors. Then write the number of the sentence with the error next to the type of error. (Some sentences may have more than one error.)

_____ a. no subject   _____ d. word order

_____ b. verb tense   _____ e. article

_____ c. singular-plural   _____ f. object pronoun

A Successful Business
1. Vicki and Paul have started a new business last year.
2. They started the small bakery because love to make cakes.
3. They make cakes for all occasion.
4. So far, their business was very successful.
5. Every week they received orders for about forty cake, and they sell it at a good price.
6. People request cakes for many different kind of events.
7. Although most cake are for birthdays, people also order it for graduations and anniversaries.
8. My mother orders a cake special from them the last week for my father's retirement from his company.
9. Everyone commented on how beautiful the cake was.
10. Vicki and Paul work very hard because really want their company to succeed.

Part 2. Original Student Writing

Write sentences or a paragraph about a person that you know who works very hard or a person who is successful at something. Who is the person? What does he or she do? Give specific examples of how hard the person works. Give examples of the person's success. Underline the object pronouns.

Unit 8

Past Progressive Tense

Discover the Grammar

Read the conversation between two friends, and then answer the six questions.

Line	
1	*Kay:* So, Liz, did you have a good time on vacation?
2	*Liz:* Oh, yes! I went to Vancouver, Canada. And guess what? I saw Brad Pitt
3	there!
4	*Kay:* Are you serious? Brad Pitt was in Vancouver? What was he doing there?
5	Was he making a movie?
6	*Liz:* Well, I don't know. No one was filming or acting.
7	*Kay:* So what was he doing?
8	*Liz:* When I saw him, he was shopping.
9	*Kay:* Shopping?
10	*Liz:* Yes, he was with his children, and they were shopping.
11	*Kay:* What were they shopping for? Sports cars? Designer watches?
12	*Liz:* No, they were buying some cheap t-shirts. I was looking at some shoes,
13	and I just looked over, and there he was!
14	*Kay:* And . . . you're sure it was Brad Pitt?

15	*Liz:*	Oh, yes. I was reading a magazine article last week when I went to have
16		my hair cut, so I saw some recent photos of him. The man who was
17		shopping looked exactly the same.
18	*Kay:*	Well, if you're sure.
19	*Liz:*	Oh, I am. It's funny because I was dreaming about him all summer after
20		I saw his last movie. Then I actually got to see him! I'm so lucky!
21	*Kay:*	Yes, you are.

1. Study these five sentences from the conversation. The verbs are made from *was* or *were* + the *–ing* form of the base verb. Write the line number of the examples.

Line	subject + *was/were* + VERB + *–ing*
a. ____	He was shopping
b. ____	They were shopping
c. ____	They were buying
d. ____	I was looking
e. ____	I was reading

2. These verbs describe something that happened _____.
   a. in the past
   b. in the present
   c. in the future

3. These verbs describe something that _____.
   a. started and finished very quickly
   b. took place over a period of time
   c. are still happening now

4. When do you use *was* with this tense? _____
   When do you use *were*? _____

5. This combination of *was/were* + VERB + *–ing* is called past progressive tense. What do you already know about this tense? What other questions do you have?

   _____

   _____

6. When do you think we use simple past tense instead of past progressive tense?

   _____

   _____

   _____

   _____

Grammar Lesson

KEY 3

Past Progressive Tense

Example	subject	*be*	VERB + –ing
I was **watching** TV when you called.	I	was	watching
When the electricity went off, we were **eating** dinner.	we	were	eating
Where was **the thief hiding?**	the thief	was	hiding
Joe was **sitting** here when he got the news.	Joe	was	sitting

<u>Rule 1</u>. In past progressive tense, a verb has two forms: **was VERB + –ing** and **were VERB + –ing**.

<u>Rule 2</u>. We use **was VERB + –ing** with **I, he, she, it; were VERB + –ing** with **you, we,** and **they.**

<u>Rule 3</u>. It is necessary to include a subject (noun or pronoun) before the verb.

<u>Rule 4</u>. Use past progressive tense for an action that was happening when another action interrupted it. In other words, the first action began and was continuing when the second action occurred. Use past continuous for the first or longer action and use simple past for the second action (i.e., the one that interrupts the first): *I was watching TV when you called me.*

<u>Rule 5</u>. Common time expressions for past progressive include *when, while,* and *at that time.* In general, we use **when** for shorter actions and **while** for longer actions.

<u>Rule 6</u>. We can use past progressive with action verbs such as *eat, do,* and *sleep.* We do not use this tense with verbs that do not show an action. Four kinds of non-action verbs that do not usually occur in past progressive tense are *senses (hear, see, smell, feel, sound), emotions (like, love, need, prefer, want), mental state (believe, forget, remember, seem, think),* and *possession (belong, have, own, possess).*

<u>Rule 7</u>. For verbs that end in –e, drop the final –e before adding –ing: *take → taking.*

<u>Rule 8</u>. If a one-syllable verb ends in **consonant + vowel + consonant** (c-v-c), double the final consonant before adding –ing: *cut → cutting* (but *read → reading*).

Rule 9. If a two-syllable verb ends in **consonant + vowel + consonant** (c-v-c), we double the final consonant before adding **–ing** if the pronunciation stress is on the second syllable:

open → *ope__n__ing*	*begin* → *begi__nn__ing*
(o) pen	be (**gin**)
[1st] 2nd	1st [2nd]
because we stress the 1st syllable	because we stress the 2nd syllable

BE CAREFUL!

Common Learner Errors	Explanation
1. We ~~played~~ **were playing** baseball when the storm began.	Don't confuse simple past tense with past progressive tense.
2. While Dan's mom ~~sitting~~ **was sitting** in front of her house, a bird flew into the closed front door.	Use **was** or **were** in the past progressive tense.
3. Dan's family ~~was live~~ **was living** near the baseball field when he began high school.	Remember to use **–ing** with verbs in past progressive tense.

EXERCISE 1. Affirmative Past Progressive

Fill in the blanks with the correct forms of the verbs. Follow the examples.

eat	say	wonder
I _was eating_	I _____	I _____
you _were eating_	you _____	you _____
he _____	he _____	he _____
she _____	she _____	she _____
it _____	it _____	it _____
we _____	we _____	we _____
they _____	they _____	they _____
Jo _____	Jo _____	Jo _____
Jo and I _____	Jo and I _____	Jo and I _____

EXERCISE 2. Comparing Simple Past and Past Progressive

Write the forms of the verbs in the simple past and past progressive tenses. Use the time words in each sentence to help you know whether to use either the simple past or the past progressive tense.

verb	Simple Past Tense	Past Progressive Tense
work	I _____ at Miami Bank from 1997 to 2007.	I _____ at Miami Bank when the name changed from Florida Bank to Miami Bank.
make	The customers _____ deposits at the bank yesterday.	Jill _____ a deposit into her checking account when she found an extra check in her wallet.
walk	Because the bank was so near his office, Joe _____ there.	Joe _____ to the bank yesterday when all of a sudden a storm began.
take	James _____ the bus to the bank because his car was broken.	James _____ money out of his account when the words NO FUNDS appeared in red!
write	Sandra _____ the wrong account number on the form, so she had to fill it out again.	Sandra _____ down her savings account number when she suddenly couldn't remember it.

EXERCISE 3. Which Action Started First?

Each sentence has two verbs. Circle the two verbs, and then put a check mark (✓) by the action that started first. If the two actions started at the same time or if we can't tell which started first, mark the third answer. Follow the example.

1a. I (was calling) my mom when my brother (texted) me.

　　✓ call 　　___ text 　　___ at the same time or we don't know

1b. When my brother (texted) me, I (was calling) my mom.

　　✓ call 　　___ text 　　___ at the same time or we don't know

2a. Bob plugged his cell phone charger into the wall, and the lights went out.

___ go out   ___ plug   ___ at the same time or we don't know

2b. The lights went out when Bob plugged his cell phone charger into the wall.

___ go out   ___ plug   ___ at the same time or we don't know

3a. Pam got mad when Chris dropped her cell phone.

___ drop   ___ get mad   ___ at the same time or we don't know

3b. When Chris dropped her cell phone, Pam got mad.

___ drop   ___ get mad   ___ at the same time or we don't know

4a. While Pam was calling the cell phone company, Chris was cooking dinner.

___ cook   ___ call   ___ at the same time or we don't know

4b. Chris was cooking dinner while Pam was calling the cell phone company.

___ cook   ___ watch   ___ at the same time or we don't know

5a. While I was lifting the laptop, I hurt my wrist.

___ hurt   ___ lift   ___ at the same time or we don't know

5b. I hurt my wrist while I was lifting the laptop.

___ hurt   ___ lift   ___ at the same time or we don't know

6a. My cell phone rang while I was playing a game.

___ play   ___ ring   ___ at the same time or we don't know

6b. While I was playing a game, my cell phone rang.

___ play   ___ ring   ___ at the same time or we don't know

7. What do you notice about the use of a comma in the pairs of sentences?

_____

_____

8. What do you notice about the verb tenses and their order in a sentence?

_____

_____

9. Go to the Internet, and find a sentence that has past progressive tense in it. Copy it here, and share it with your class. Can you understand why the author used past progressive tense?

_____

_____

EXERCISE 4. Simple Past and Past Progressive in Context

Read the conversation about a severe thunderstorm that hit the town yesterday at 6:07 PM and what people were doing when the lights went out. Fill in the blanks with the correct tense of the verbs in the word list. Some verbs are used more than once.

word list	cook	drive	read	sit	walk
	do	put	shop	take	watch

Kevin: "When the storm came, I ❶ _____ at the mall, so I didn't hear the rain at first."

Mindy: "From 6 to 6:30, I always ❷ _____ the local news show, so I ❸ _____ TV when the weather got bad."

Anita: "I know exactly where I was and what I ❹ _____. I ❺ _____ dinner, and we suddenly lost all power. We have an electric stove, so I couldn't finish dinner."

Thomas: "Just when the storm hit, I ❻ _____ a shower. In fact, at first, I didn't hear the heavy rain, but then I realized what was happening."

Brandon: "I ❼ _____ my dog in front of my house. Then the weather turned really bad."

Jackie: "I was in the kitchen. I ❽ _____ away the groceries. I noticed that it was really dark outside, so I knew the weather might get bad. Then all at once, all the lights went out."

Linda: "I ❾ _____ on my porch. I ❿ _____ the paper. I knew it might rain, but I had no idea it was going to be so bad."

Keith: "My cousin and I ⓫ _____ to a restaurant. It started to rain so hard that we couldn't see anything, so we pulled over to the side of the road for a while."

Connecting Grammar and Vocabulary

Verbs like *own* and *seem* that do not show action are not used in past progressive tense. Most verbs are action verbs, so most verbs can be in past progressive tense. This means that there are—in theory—thousands of possible verbs for you to learn, but this is not a good strategy. You should focus on the most commonly used verbs in past progressive tense. Study this list of common verbs for past progressive tense.

10 Frequent Verbs in Past Progressive Tense				
do	live	put	stand	try
get	make	say	think	work

Source: Based on information in the Corpus of Contemporary American English: www.americancorpus.org/

ONE-MINUTE LESSON

The verb **seem** can be difficult for some students. After **seem**, we usually find an adjective: *Jill* **seems nice**. *It* **seems hot** *today. These tomatoes* **seem expensive**, *don't they?* However, you can also use *like* + **adjective** + **noun**: *Jill and Noah* **seem like nice people.**

Do Online Exercise 8.1. My score: _____ /10. _____ % correct.

Grammar Lesson

Past Progressive Tense: Negative

Making a negative statement with past progressive tense is easy. You just follow the same rules for making a negative with the verb *be*, which means you put **not** or **n't** after the form of *be*.

Affirmative	Negative
I was watching TV when you called.	I was **not** watching TV when you called. I **wasn't** watching TV when you called.
At 9, the kids were playing outside.	At 9, the kids were **not** playing outside. At 9, the kids **weren't** playing outside.

<u>Rule 1</u>. We use the word **not** to make a negative sentence with the verb **be** in past progressive: **was not, were not**.

<u>Rule 2</u>. It is possible to use contractions: **wasn't** and **weren't**.

<u>Rule 3</u>. Contractions are common in spoken language and informal writing (such as an email), but they are less common in formal or academic writing.

BE CAREFUL!

Common Learner Errors	Explanation
1. We ~~no were playing~~ were not playing a video game when the electricity went out.	Don't use **no**. Use **not** or the contraction form **n't**.
2. Her call caught me completely by surprise. I ~~didn't expecting~~ wasn't expecting her call.	Don't use **didn't** in past progressive. Use **was not, were not**, or the contraction forms **wasn't** or **weren't**.

EXERCISE 5. Simple Past and Past Progressive Forms

Write the correct forms of these verbs for simple past tense and past progressive tense. If a form is not common, write *not common* in the box. Follow the examples.

	Simple Past		Past Progressive	
	Affirmative	Negative	Affirmative	Negative
1. I/go	I went	I didn't go	I was going	I wasn't going
2. we/like	we liked	we didn't like	not common	not common
3. they/want				
4. it/get				
5. Ana/call				
6. he/put				
7. you/do				
8. it/begin				
9. he/say				
10. she/eat				
11. you/need				
12. I/own				

Do Online Exercise 8.2. My score: ____ /10. ____ % correct.

Grammar Lesson

KEY
3

Past Progressive Tense: Making a Question

To make a question with past progressive, follow the same rules for making any question with the verb *be*. Put the form of *be* before the subject.

Statement	Question
Jen was watching the news at noon.	**Was Jen** watching the news at noon? When **was Jen** watching the news?
You were sleeping when the 11 o'clock news started.	**Were you** sleeping when the 11 o'clock news started? What **were you** doing when the 11 o'clock news started?

Rule 1. It is easy to make a question in past progressive tense. Move **was** or **were** before the subject.

 ### BE CAREFUL!

Common Learner Errors	Explanation
1. Oh, no, I'm sorry! Did I wake you up? ~~Did you~~ **Were you** sleeping?	Use only **was** or **were** in past progressive questions. Do not use **did** with past progressive tense.
2. Where ~~Martin was working~~ **was Martin working** when he bought his first house?	Be sure to move **was** or **were** before the subject in past progressive questions.

 ONE-MINUTE LESSON
If **wake up** has a noun object, you can form the sentence two ways with no difference in meaning: *I will wake up Mark* OR *I will wake Mark up*. However, if you use a pronoun, you must separate the two parts: *I will* **wake** *him* **up** (**wake up him** is never possible). (A verb with two parts such as **wake up** is called **a phrasal verb**. Phrasal verbs are covered in *Clear Grammar 3*.)

EXERCISE 6. Questions in Simple Past and Past Progressive

Make a question from each statement. Decide if the verb in the statement is simple past or past progressive. This will help you write the correct question. Follow the examples.

1. A. Mandy lived in China in 1999.

   Did Mandy live in China in 1999?

   B. Mandy was living in China when you met her.

   Was Mandy living in China when you met her?

2. A. Mandy taught English in the United States before she moved to China.

   _____

   B. Mandy was teaching in the United States before she moved to China.

   _____

3. A. Mandy's family was sad when they heard that she was moving to China.

   _____

   B. Mandy's mom was crying when Mandy said good-bye.

   _____

4. A. Jack was dating Mandy when she moved to China.

   _____

   B. Jack dated Mandy when she lived in the United States.

   _____

5. A. Mandy was packing her suitcases for her move when one of them broke.

   _____

   B. Mandy packed four suitcases to move to China.

   _____

6. A. Mandy was turning off her electricity when she discovered she owed $150 to the electric company.

   _____

   B. Mandy turned off her electricity before she moved to China.

   _____

7. A. Mandy was folding her old coat when she realized she needed a new one.

   _____

   B. Mandy folded her coat and saw a hole in it.

   _____

8. A. Mandy was paying for a new coat when she discovered her credit card didn't work.

   _____

   B. Mandy bought a new coat with cash because her credit card didn't work.

   _____

EXERCISE 7. Editing: Is It Correct?

If the sentence is correct, write a check mark (✓) on the line. If it is not correct, write X on the line and circle the mistake. Then change the sentence to make it correct. Write the change above the sentence. (*Hint*: There are twelve sentences. Four are correct, but eight have mistakes.)

Kathy's New Television

_____ 1. Kathy's family now lives in new, bigger house in a great neighborhood.

_____ 2. They have moved to this new house last year.

_____ 3. Their new house is very larger than their old house.

_____ 4. Kathy was look at her new room and decided that she need a bigger television.

_____ 5. Kathy went online to find a new TV.

_____ 6. When Kathy was shopped online, she found the best price on a great new television.

_____ 7. Once she found this perfect television, she went to the store to buy it.

_____ 8. Unfortunately, while Kathy was hurrying to leave the house, she forgot to measure her new entertainment center for her new television.

_____ 9. Kathy had to drive back home to measure her entertainment center, and then she has to drive back to the store.

_____ 10. She paid for the TV.

_____ 11. The salespeople took the TV to her cars.

_____ 12. Kathy was expecting to take the TV home, but the TV not fit in her car.

Do Online Exercise 8.3. My score: _____ /10. _____ % correct.

EXERCISE 8. Mini-Conversations

Circle the correct words in these eight mini-conversations.

1. A: I saw a new movie last night at the new movie theater.

   B: Oh, really? Did you (like, were liking) it?

2. A: Yes, I did. It had subtitles.

   B: Oh! So they (weren't speaking, not speak) English?

3. A: No. The movie was in Spanish.

   B: I thought that you (were speaking, spoke) Spanish.

4. A: Yes, a little, but not enough to understand a whole movie.

   B: I know what you mean. Sometimes people in the movies (are speaking, speak) too fast to understand everything.

5. A: Didn't you take Spanish classes last semester?

   B: Yes, I (was taking, took) them when I had to withdraw because I got too many hours at my job.

6. A: Oh, I'm sorry. Did you like the class?

   B: Yes! I (loved, was loving) it, but my work schedule was too heavy.

7. A: Well, I hope you can take it again next semester.

   B: Me, too! I (doing, was doing) really well in the class before I had to quit, so I hope to learn even more next time.

8. A: Me, too. Well, I have to go. I'm meeting my friend at the pizza place on 5th Avenue.

   B: Oh, I (was eating, ate) there last week. You'll love it!

Do Online Exercise 8.4. My score: _____ /10. _____ % correct.

EXERCISE 9. Sentence Study for Critical Reading

Read the numbered sentences. Then read the three answer choices, and put a check mark (✔) in the yes or no boxes in front of each sentence to show if that answer is true based on the information in the original sentence. If there is not enough information to mark something as yes, then mark it as no. Remember that more than one true answer is possible.

1. My aunt Pat is my mother's sister. She lives in Detroit, but we live in Denver. She comes to our house about twice a year.

   ☐ yes ☐ no   a. Pat comes to our house in Denver two times a year.

   ☐ yes ☐ no   b. Pat was living in Denver. We were visiting her house two times each year.

   ☐ yes ☐ no   c. My mother has a sister. Her name is Pat.

2. We were taking pictures with Pat in our backyard when lightning struck a big oak tree next to my mother.

   ☐ yes ☐ no   a. We were taking pictures at Pat's house.

   ☐ yes ☐ no   b. Lightning struck the telephone pole in front of the house.

   ☐ yes ☐ no   c. The lightning was hitting the oak tree when we took a picture in my aunt's backyard.

3. I was thinking about visiting my aunt Pat in Detroit when I found a low price on a flight from where I live in Denver.

   ☐ yes ☐ no   a. I visited my aunt Pat in Denver.

   ☐ yes ☐ no   b. I found a low-priced ticket to Detroit.

   ☐ yes ☐ no   c. I was using my computer and found a good flight price.

4. When I was telling my mom about the good price, she decided that she wanted to go with me.

   ☐ yes ☐ no   a. My mother was telling my dad about the good price I found on a flight.

   ☐ yes ☐ no   b. My mother decided to visit my aunt Pat with me.

   ☐ yes ☐ no   c. When she heard about the fare, my mom decided to visit Aunt Pat as well.

5. My dad was thinking about taking a vacation with us, but he has to work.

   ☐ yes ☐ no   a. My dad was working with my aunt Pat in Detroit.

   ☐ yes ☐ no   b. My dad worked with my aunt Pat in Denver.

   ☐ yes ☐ no   c. My dad has to work, so he can't go on vacation with us.

6. I was hoping to visit Comerica Park in Detroit to watch a baseball game, but my aunt reminded me that it's not baseball season.

    ☐ yes ☐ no   a. I was telling my aunt how much I hate baseball.

    ☐ yes ☐ no   b. It's not baseball season, so my aunt reminded me that we can't go see a game when I visit.

    ☐ yes ☐ no   c. My mother was hoping to visit Comerica Park when she goes to Detroit.

7. When I was making my plane reservation to visit my aunt, my computer suddenly turned off.

    ☐ yes ☐ no   a. I bought my ticket online with no problems at all. It was so easy!

    ☐ yes ☐ no   b. When my computer turned off, I was flying to Detroit.

    ☐ yes ☐ no   c. I was frustrated because my computer turned off right when I was making a plane reservation to visit my aunt in Detroit.

8. After I was able to buy my ticket, I remembered that I needed to buy another suitcase!

    ☐ yes ☐ no   a. I wasn't able to purchase a plane ticket because my computer broke.

    ☐ yes ☐ no   b. My suitcase is too small, so I need a new one.

    ☐ yes ☐ no   c. After I bought my ticket, I found the brand-new suitcase that I bought last week.

ONE-MINUTE LESSON

Some expressions use **make,** and some use **do.** You need to memorize the fact that *reservation* goes with the verb **make.** Common expressions with **make** include: **make the bed, make a mistake, make money, make an effort** (to do something). Common expressions with **do** include: **do the dishes, do a favor, do homework, do work.** There is no easy way to know when to use **do** or **make.** You should memorize the most common expressions that you think are useful for your communication in English.

EXERCISE 10. Speaking Practice: What Were You Doing?

The purpose of this speaking activity is to find out what people were doing when another action occurred.

Step 1. Work in groups of three. Choose a time (or important event) that you can all remember well. For example, your group might choose last summer, when a famous singer first sang a very popular song, or 2008.

Step 2. Each person writes four statements about what he or she was doing at that time. For example, you might write *I was living in Canada in 2008* or *I was working at a bank in 2008*. Make three true statements and one false statement. Do not make obviously true or obviously false statements.

Step 3. Take turns reading your four statements. The other students should listen to the speaker's statements and then guess the false statement.

Time: _____

1. _____

   _____

2. _____

   _____

3. _____

   _____

4. _____

   _____

EXERCISE 11. Review Test 1: Multiple Choice

Circle the letter of the correct answer. Some are conversations.

1. "Hey, did you hear the thunder during the rainstorm this afternoon?"

   "No, I didn't. I ____ to some music, and I was using headphones, so I didn't hear anything outside at all."

   a. listened   c. was listen

   b. was listening   d. listening

2. "What ____ to when the storm hit?"

   "The new album by my favorite band."

   a. were you listening   c. listening you

   b. did you listen   d. did you

3. "Cool! Did you get the album at the mall yesterday?"

   "No, my mom ____ our car when I wanted to go to the mall, so I downloaded it instead."

   a. was use   b. was used   c. used   d. was using

4. "Did she have to work in the city yesterday?"

   "No, she ____ her sister who just had surgery."

   a. visited   c. was visit

   b. was visit   d. visiting

5. "First, my mom washed all of her sister's laundry. After that, she ____ lunch for both of them."

   a. made   c. were making

   b. was made   d. was making

6. "After she ate her lunch, her sister felt better and ____ on the sofa."

   a. sitting   b. sat   c. was sat   d. was sit

7. "My mom saw that her sister ____ much better, so she came home that evening."

   a. doing   b. was doing   c. did   d. was did

8. "I am glad that my aunt began to feel better when my mom ____ there."

   a. is   b. has been   c. was   d. is going to be

EXERCISE 12. Review Test 2: Production and Evaluation

Part 1.
Read this short passage. Circle the correct verb tense in the parentheses.

Dr. Brewster Higley ❶ (was born, was being born) on November 30, 1823. He ❷ (was working, works) as a doctor when he wrote the famous American song "Home on the Range." Originally, he ❸ (was writing, wrote) it as a poem in 1872. While someone ❹ (was reading, being read) it to a group of people in 1873, another person decided to write music for the poem and it became a song.

Dr. Higley ❺ (wrote, was writing) "Home on the Range" when he lived in Smith County, Kansas. Kansas lawmakers ❻ (liked, were liking) it so much that they ❼ (were making, made) it the official state song.

Part 2.
Read this short passage. There are six mistakes. Circle the mistakes, and write the correction above the mistake.

I hurt my hand yesterday while I was playing tennis. Did you hearing me yell? I yell very loudly. After I hurt my hand, I left the tennis court. Brad were looking at my hand when he noticed a bright red mark. He was press on the red mark when I finally told him, "Ouch! Stop!" Then Sam came over and looked at my hand, too. While they both was looking at my hand, Sam found a bee stinger! When I was play tennis, I didn't hurt my hand. A bee stung me!

EXERCISE 13. Reading Practice: What Really Happened?

There were three witnesses to a car accident: Melinda, Ed, and José. They spoke about what they saw, but their stories are a little different. Read their stories and then answer the ten questions. The grammar from this unit is underlined for you.

	Ed's Story
	I <u>was walking</u> my dog early one morning when I <u>heard</u> a huge crash. I <u>was wearing</u> an extra jacket because it was cold. When I <u>was running</u> to the cars that crashed, I <u>saw</u> two people inside one of the cars. They <u>weren't wearing</u> any jackets, so I <u>took off</u> my extra jacket and <u>gave</u> it to one of them.
Melinda's Story	**José's Story**
One morning last week, I <u>was talking</u> on my cell phone when I <u>saw</u> a car accident. I <u>was running</u> and <u>talking</u> at the same time because I <u>was calling</u> 911. While we <u>were waiting</u> for the ambulance to arrive, I <u>helped</u> a man put a jacket on one of the passengers.	While I <u>was taking</u> my 5-year-old daughter to school, I <u>saw</u> one car hit another. I <u>was driving</u> slowly when it <u>happened</u>, so I <u>saw</u> the entire thing. When the police <u>arrived</u>, I <u>called</u> my daughter's school to tell them we would be late. When I <u>was talking</u> to the police, the ambulance <u>arrived</u>.

Write the name of the witness or witnesses in each blank.

_____ 1. Who was walking a pet?

_____ 2. Who was talking on a cell phone?

_____ 3. Who was driving with a child?

_____ 4. Who was not alone?

_____ 5. Who was in a vehicle?

_____ 6. Who called 911?

_____ 7. Who saw the car accident happen?

_____ 8. Who put the jacket on one of the car crash victims?

_____ 9. Who ran toward the car accident?

_____ 10. Who talked to the police?

EXERCISE 14. Vocabulary Practice: Word Knowledge

Circle the word or phrase that is most closely related to the word or phrase on the left. Use a dictionary to check the meaning of words you do not know.

Vocabulary	Answer Choices	
1. a magazine	a place	a thing
2. my wrist	near my hand	near my foot
3. funds	people	things
4. dream	when you're moving	when you're sleeping
5. might	perhaps	usually
6. a customer	a person	a thing
7. funny	unhappy	unusual
8. dark	only a little light	only a little money
9. an article	you eat it	you read it
10. to pack	an envelope	a suitcase
11. subtitles	for a book	for a movie
12. remind	not believe	not forget
13. measure	price	size
14. an album	food	music
15. discover	believe	find
16. a poem	a person	a thing
17. quit	begin	stop
18. laundry	clean shoes	dirty clothes
19. notice	buy	see
20. a pet	a cat or a dog	Monday or Tuesday
21. the lights went out	they needed	they stopped
22. famous	people don't know it	people know it
23. a vehicle	you take it off	you travel in it
24. a crash	something bad	something good
25. a victim	a person	a place
26. extra	another	unique
27. entire	whale	whole
28. an ambulance	a person	a thing

EXERCISE 15. Vocabulary Practice: Collocations

Fill in each blank with the answer on the right that most naturally completes the phrase on the left. If necessary, use a dictionary to check the meaning of words you do not know.

Vocabulary	Answer Choices	
1. plug your cell in to the _____	wall	window
2. _____ of a sudden	all	much
3. _____ mad	got	made
4. a savings _____	account	count
5. I dropped my _____	heart	watch
6. I _____ to visit London	enjoy	got
7. my phone _____	rang	sang
8. the _____ went off	education	electricity
9. it _____ me by surprise	brought	caught
10. _____ news	a	the
11. _____ off the electricity	run	turn
12. _____ rain	heavy	thick
13. _____ a game	looking	playing
14. _____ away the groceries	eat	put
15. all at _____	once	one time
16. I was _____ your call	expecting	waiting
17. instead _____	at	of
18. _____ a deposit at the bank	do	make
19. a hole _____ my socks	in	on
20. these _____ don't fit me	books	shoes
21. _____ a vacation	make	take
22. Did you hear _____ bad news?	a	the
23. _____ at all	no	not
24. write _____ a number	down	up
25. fold my _____	shirts	shoes
26. my work schedule is too _____	heavy	large
27. pay for something _____ cash	by	with
28. an oak _____	storm	tree
29. _____ thunder	hear	see
30. _____ lunch	make	put
31. a _____ stung me	bee	mosquito
32. _____ off my jacket	put	take
33. the car hit _____	a road	a tree

EXERCISE 16. Writing Practice

Part 1. Editing Student Writing

Read these sentences about one student's opinion about a teacher. Circle the 15 errors. Then write the number of the sentence with the error next to the type of error. (Some sentences may have more than one error.)

_____ a. no subject	_____ d. word order
_____ b. no –*ing*	_____ e. verb tense
_____ c. singular-plural	_____ f. article

My Patient Teacher
1. I am never on time. I'm sorry to say this, but it is truth.
2. I arrive always late. Is a big problem for me.
3. Yesterday I arrive in class just two minute late. The teacher was stand in front of her desk.
4. She was call the roll. I sat down, and teacher continued with the students' names.
5. My teacher is great. Never she gets angry when I come late.
6. After she called the roll, the teacher gave us pop quiz. Everyone is really surprised.
7. Next the teacher said, "Please turn in your homeworks." Unfortunately, I don't have my homework.
8. When was doing my homework last night, I fall asleep and did not finish it.

Part 2. Original Student Writing

There was a robbery at the grocery store. Three people were shopping at the store. They saw everything. You are the police officer who interviewed these three people after the robbery. Write your summary for each person.

Be sure to practice the grammar in this unit by telling what each person was doing when the robber came in, during the robbery, and when the police arrived. For example, you might write, *The old woman* <u>*was waiting*</u> *in the express lane when the robber came in the front door of the store*. Always underline the grammar point that you have used.

 Unit 9

One and *Other*

Discover the Grammar

Read the advertisement for a pain relief medication, and then answer the four questions.

Line	
1	R U PAIN FREE?
2	Do you get a lot of headaches? If the answer is yes, then we have a remedy
3	for you! Introducing R U PAIN FREE . . . the headache medicine that is
4	different from all the others!
5	We at R U PAIN FREE know that you have taken other headache
6	medicines before, but you're probably not happy with the results. But trust
7	us—this one really works.
8	R U PAIN FREE is special. Other tablets contain chemicals, but
9	R U PAIN FREE uses natural ingredients that will bring you long-lasting
10	relief from headache pain. That's right. Our unique formula includes powerful
11	herbs and other organic ingredients to calm and soothe you.
12	Why spend another day in pain? Try R U PAIN FREE. If you're not happy
13	with the results, we'll give you your money back!

14	You've tried the others; now try R U PAIN FREE, the one with a money-
15	back guarantee.
16	*Call 1-800-Pain-Free for a free sample. If someone in your family also wants*
17	*to try this amazing product, you can ask for another sample with your order.*

1. Underline these words every time they appear in the advertisement: *one*, *other*, *others*, *another*.

2. Look at the two examples of the word *others*. Do they appear before a noun? Yes or no?

   _____

3. From the information here, what is the difference between *another* and *other*?

   _____

   _____

   _____

4. From the information here, what is the purpose of the word *one*?

   _____

   _____

   _____

Grammar Lesson

Pronouns *one* and *it*

	singular		plural
one	Mike: I need a pen to sign this form. Pam: There's a black **one** in the top drawer.	ones	Ana: Do you sell t-shirts here? Jo: Yes, we do. The white **ones** are made of cotton and are on sale, and the colorful **ones** are a little more expensive.
	one = *a pen*		ones = *t-shirts*
it	Ali: Have you seen my cell phone? Tom: No, I don't know where **it** is.	them	Marc: Where are Victor and Ana? Ben: I don't know. I haven't seen **them** today.
	it = *my cell phone*		them = *Victor and Ana*

Rule 1. One and it are pronouns* and can take the place of a noun.

Rule 2. We use one to replace a general noun. If I have a tray of cookies and want to know if you want to eat a cookie, I might hold out the tray of cookies and ask you, "I've just made these cookies. Would you like **one**?" Here we use a pronoun because we do not want to repeat the noun *cookie*. We use one because we are not talking about a specific cookie. (Maybe there are 15 cookies on the plate, and you can take any cookie you would like.)

Rule 3. We use it to replace a specific noun. If we are talking about school, I might ask you, "Are you good at math?" and you might answer, "I like it, but I'm not very good at it." Here, I want to use a pronoun because I don't want to repeat *math* two more times. I use it because I'm talking about *math*, a very specific school subject.

---

*The word one can also be an adjective when it is used at the beginning of a noun phrase: *one reason, one difficult part*.

BE CAREFUL!

Common Learner Errors	Explanation
1. The belts were cheap, so I bought ~~a black and a brown~~ a black one and a brown one.	Use the word **one** or **ones** after a descriptive adjective. Do not use the adjective by itself.
2. I bought cookies for all of you. The ~~smalls~~ small ones are oatmeal, and the ~~bigs~~ big ones are almond.	Descriptive adjectives are never plural.

EXERCISE 1. Using *one* and *ones* in Noun Phrases

Write a new phrase changing the noun to **one** or **ones.** Follow the examples.

1. a blue car   *a blue one*

2. larger houses   *larger ones*

3. new ideas   _____

4. the red shirt   _____

5. the cheap shoes   _____

6. the wealthy people   _____

7. young babies   _____

8. an average grade   _____

9. the best answer   _____

10. the tallest buildings   _____

11. the most expensive watches   _____

12. a really good reason   _____

Do Online Exercise 9.1. My score: _____ /10. _____ % correct.

EXERCISE 2. Scrambled Sentences with *one* and *ones*

Unscramble the sentences. Add commas where needed. Follow the examples.

1. (one / Sue / have / the / ideas / best / good / but / has)

   Tom and Matt _both have good ideas, but Sue has the best one._

   _____

2. (get / a / but / decided / to / cold / I / one / sandwich)

   Lim ordered a hot _____

   _____

3. (depart / $400, / a / there / you / is / one / if / early / cheaper / but)

   I found a flight to New York for _____

   _____

4. (of / opening / every / stores / ones / are / but / lot / new / month)

   Main Street has a _____

   _____

5. (don't / that / I / care for / the / restaurant / but / sweet / ones)

   I like the spicy dishes at _____

   _____

6. (one / better / on / first / than / test / second / the / on / the)

   I think I did _____

   _____

7. (need to / you / your / your / buy / feet / hurt / bigger / shoes / ones)

   If _____

   _____

8. (never / one / colors / buy / for / so / loud / I / orange / sweaters / will / an)

   I don't like _____

   _____

ONE-MINUTE LESSON

After the verb *decide*, you can use **to + verb** or **on + noun**: *For our next event, we decided* **to meet** *in Barcelona. For our next event, we have decided* **on Barcelona.**

EXERCISE 3. *one* or *ones*

Read each sentence, and circle the correct answer.

Leigh's New Job

1. Leigh got a promotion at work. It was the (promotion one, promotion ones, one, ones) she was hoping for.

2. She got a new office. This (new, new one, ones) is on the 9th floor.

3. Her (old, one, old one, old ones) was on the 2nd floor.

4. There are two paintings on the wall in her new office. The smaller (one, ones, large, new) was painted by a famous local artist.

5. She also has a new desk with two wide drawers. The left (one, ones, desk one, desk ones) is where she keeps her receipts.

ONE-MINUTE LESSON
We use **on** with floors in a building. *The new office is* **on** *the 9th floor.* Be sure to use the ordinal number 9th, not the regular number 9.

Do Online Exercise 9.2. My score: _____ /10. _____ % correct.

Grammar Lesson

Pronouns *another, other(s),* and *the other(s)*

General (Indefinite)		
	adjective	**pronoun**
singular	These cookies are great. Can I please have **another** <u>cookie</u>?	These cookies are great. Can I please have **another**?
plural	I ate two cookies. There are still ten **other** <u>cookies</u> in the bag.	I ate two cookies. There are still ten **others** in the bag.

Specific (Definite)		
	adjective	**pronoun**
singular	There were 5 cookies, but I ate 4 of them. I saved **the other** <u>cookie</u> for you.	There were 5 cookies, but I ate 4 of them. I saved **the other** for you.
plural	There were 5 cookies, but I ate 3 of them. I saved **the other** <u>cookies</u> for you.	There were 5 cookies, but I ate 3 of them. I saved **the others** for you.

<u>Rule 1</u>. **Another** can be an adjective or a pronoun. As a pronoun, the word **another** can appear by itself.

<u>Rule 2</u>. **Others** is always a plural pronoun. As a pronoun, **others** does not appear in front of a noun.

<u>Rule 3</u>. **Other** can appear with a singular or plural noun: *my other friend, my other friends.* The word **other** means "additional."

<u>Rule 4</u>. We use **another** to mean "additional," but we use **the other** or **the others** to name the last person or thing in a group. We use **the other** or **the others** to refer to specific nouns.

BE CAREFUL!

Common Learner Errors	Explanation
1. My pen has run out of ink, so I need ~~other~~ another.	Use the word **another** to mean "one more." Do not use the word **other** for this meaning.
2. June and July are hot, but the weather in the ~~others~~ other months is very nice.	Do not use the pronoun **others** in front of a noun. Do not put two plural words together.
3. This author's work is excellent. I wish I could read ~~other~~ another of her books.	Do not use the pronoun **other** by itself. It is never a singular pronoun.

EXERCISE 4. Using Forms of *other* in Sentences

Read each situation, and then circle the correct answer.

1. I have five teachers. One is from New York, and the (other ones, others ones, others teacher) are from Florida.

2. I have (another, other, the other, others, the others) dictionary at home.

3. G-R-E-Y is one of two ways to spell this word. What is (other, another, the other) way?

4. There are (another, other, the other, the others) books on the bottom shelf.

5. The first and last letters in "read" are consonants, but (another, the other, others, the others) are vowels.

6. This is the only difficult test. All the (others, another, other) tests are easy.

7. This is the only difficult test. All the (others, another, other) ones are easy.

8. This is the only difficult test. All the (others, another, other) are easy.

9. I'm really very thirsty. Could I please have (another, other) soft drink?

10. Some people arrived at noon. (Another, Other, Others) came at one.

11. I have two nice shirts. This one is white, and (other, another, the other) one is green.

12. The morning manager at the restaurant is Chris. The night manager is someone else. Chris is very nice, but (another, the other, other) manager is very strict.

13. If you want to talk to me (another, other) time about this situation, just let me know.

14. Some people choose their job based on salary, but (another, other, the other, the others, others) reasons include location, benefits, and schedule.

Do Online Exercise 9.3. My score: ____ /10. ____ % correct.

Connecting Grammar and Vocabulary

When *another* and *other* are adjectives, it is possible to use hundreds or thousands of nouns after them. It is useful for you to learn some of the most common nouns after these two expressions.

Memorize these forms so that you write them or say them easily in English.

12 Words with *Another*	12 Words with *Other*
1. another **one**	1. one other **thing**; several other **things**
2. another **way**	2. in other **words**
3. another **thing**	3. other **people**
4. another **example**	4. that other **one**
5. another **question**	5. one other **question**; several other **questions**
6. another **person**	6. one other **way**; a few other **ways**
7. another **problem**	7. on the other **hand**
8. another **kind**	8. on the other **side**
9. another **time**	9. one other **kind**; several other **kinds**
10. another **sort**	10. the other **place**; a few other **places**
11. another **type**	11. the other **day**
12. another **possibility**	12. one other; several other **parts**

Source: Michigan Corpus of Academic Spoken English: http://quod.lib.umich.edu/m/micase/.

ONE-MINUTE LESSON

in other words Always use **other** in front of a plural noun: **other words, other people, other places**. Never use **others** as an adjective in front of any noun.

EXERCISE 5. *another one* versus *the other*

Write **another one** or **the other one** on each line.

1. Sarah is filling out an application to a university now. She is going to fill out
_____ to a different university tomorrow.

2. Gabriela needs to write two letters. She's going to write one now. Then she's
going to write _____ tomorrow.

3. I'm going to buy two shirts. I'm going to buy one today, and I'm going to buy
_____ tomorrow.

4. John's reading a book now. He wants to read _____
next week.

5. I have three cats. Two of them are black, and _____
is white.

6. I have several watches. I really like them a lot. I think I'm going to buy
_____ next Saturday when I go to the mall.

7. Alexa has four tropical fish. Two are neon blue, and one is neon yellow.
_____ is bright white.

8. I am reading a newspaper now. Tomorrow I'm going to read
_____.

9. She has two sisters. One is short, and _____ is tall.

10. I have two credit cards in my wallet. There is _____ in
my dresser drawer. There are three credit cards all together. Two of them have
low interest rates, and _____ has a high interest rate.

EXERCISE 6. Forms of *other*

Write **another one, the other one, other, others,** or **the others.**

1. I have a diet soda here on the table. I have _____ in my car. The diet soda on the table is cold, so I'm going to open this one. _____ is not cold, so I'm going to put it in the refrigerator for a while and drink it later.

2. Dorothy bought twelve apples at the farmer's market. She ate two of the apples. Now she is going to bake _____ in a pie.

3. We have two pages of homework. I did one page last night, and I'm going to do _____ in a few minutes.

4. Many students come to class on time. A few _____ come late.

5. Five people came to class. One has his book, but _____ don't have their books.

6. Susan has two vacations this summer. She's going on a trip to Spain in June. She's going to go on _____ in August.

7. A few students bring their lunch to school. A few _____ buy their lunch on campus.

8. Many students don't eat breakfast. Many _____ students don't eat lunch.

9. I have two pens. I don't like this pen. I prefer _____.

10. Jimmy has two brothers. One is in Nigeria, and _____ is in Egypt.

11. Four men work here at night. Four _____ work here in the day.

12. The park has many children in it now. One child is flying a kite. _____ is sailing a toy boat. Some _____ are playing football.

Do Online Exercise 9.4. My score: _____ /10. _____ % correct.

EXERCISE 7. Editing: Is It Correct?

If the sentence is correct, put a check mark (✔) on the line. If it is not correct, write X on the line and circle the mistake. Then change the sentence to make it correct. Write the change above the sentence. (*Hint*: There are twelve sentences. Four are correct, but eight have mistakes.)

A Teacher's Teaching Schedule

_____ 1. I have been an English teacher for 10 years. I have taught in three schools. Two were in the U.S., and another one was in Mexico.

_____ 2. I have five classes this semester. Two are grammar classes, two are reading classes, and the other is a listening class.

_____ 3. My listening class is small, but my others classes are pretty big.

_____ 4. My first grammar class is in the morning, but the second one is in the afternoon.

_____ 5. Most of the students in this class speak Spanish, and a few other speak Chinese or Vietnamese. The rest speak French.

_____ 6. In my another class, there are almost 30 people. It's quite big.

_____ 7. Of my two grammar classes, I enjoy teaching the second one more because the students are more serious.

_____ 8. In others words, the students in the second class work harder and come to class more prepared and ready to learn. In addition, they ask me more questions in class.

_____ 9. My two reading classes are similar in many ways. I enjoy teaching them a lot, and I know the students are learning a lot, too.

_____ 10. I enjoy both of my reading classes for many reasons, but the main is that the students prepare for the class so well that it is a true pleasure to teach these two classes.

_____ 11. I have only three kinds of classes—grammar, reading, and speaking—but there are several others kinds at our school.

_____ 12. In other semester in the future, I hope to teach a writing class because I can help students with their grammar in a writing class.

EXERCISE 8. Mini-Conversations

Circle the correct words in these eight mini-conversations.

1. A: Do you want to go shopping at the Riverside Mall downtown?

   B: No, I'd rather go to the Elm Street Mall because it is (another, the one, the other one) that is close to my house.

2. A: What are you shopping for?

   B: Next Sunday is Father's Day. I already got my dad a gift, but I think I can find a better (other one, one, another, other).

3. A: What gift did you get for your dad?

   B: The gift I bought was a necktie.

   A: Yeah, I think you can find (other, one, another, another one) gift. How about some movie tickets?

4. A: No, he doesn't go to the movies often. Do you have any (other, another, other ones) suggestions?

   B: I think your dad would like a golf shirt.

5. A: That's a great idea! He likes (others, other ones, ones) with stripes.

   B: If you want to buy a golf shirt, then we should not go to the mall. Let's go to (another, an other, other) place where they sell a lot of sports stuff.

6. A: We don't need to go to a sports store. They sell golf shirts at a lot of (another one, other, another) places.

   B: That's true. Also, (another, the other, the others) possibility is to buy a hat for your dad. He spends a lot of time in the sun on the golf course.

7. A: It is a good idea, but he won't wear it. He has a lot of hats. He doesn't wear (the others, the other, another), so he won't wear a new one.

   B: Wow, it seems like your dad is picky.

8. A: Yeah, he really is.

   B: Is it so hard to buy a present for (another, the other, the others) members of your family?

EXERCISE 9. Sentence Study for Critical Reading

Read the original sentences. Then read the three answer choices, and put a check mark (✔) in the yes or no boxes in front of each sentence to show if that answer is true based on the information in the original sentence. If there is not enough information to mark something as yes, then mark it as no. Remember that more than one true answer is possible.

1. There are four people in our family, and we have three cars. My sister and I share one. The others belong to my parents.

   ☐ yes ☐ no a. There are two children in the family.

   ☐ yes ☐ no b. Each child has a car.

   ☐ yes ☐ no c. The parents have more than one car.

2. There are a lot of dirty dishes in the kitchen. Some of the dirty dishes are on the counter. The others are in the sink. I hope my roommate cleans the kitchen soon.

   ☐ yes ☐ no a. Most of the dirty dishes are in the sink.

   ☐ yes ☐ no b. There is one person living in the apartment.

   ☐ yes ☐ no c. The dirty dishes are in the sink and on the table.

3. Ten people are waiting for the bus. Here comes the bus, but it is very crowded. Three people will be able to get on. Another bus is coming in fifteen minutes. The others will have to wait.

   ☐ yes ☐ no a. Thirteen people are now on the bus.

   ☐ yes ☐ no b. More than seven people are waiting for the bus.

   ☐ yes ☐ no c. More than seven people cannot get on the bus.

4. Melanie has to write three papers for school. She will write one tonight. She will write another tomorrow. The other paper will have to wait until next week.

   ☐ yes ☐ no a. Melanie will write three papers tonight.

   ☐ yes ☐ no b. Melanie will write two papers next week.

   ☐ yes ☐ no c. Two papers are for Melanie's English classes.

5. My nephew was holding four red balloons. The wind was blowing pretty hard, and one flew away. Then he gave one to his little sister.

   ☐ yes ☐ no a. My niece received a red balloon.

   ☐ yes ☐ no b. The boy now has two balloons.

   ☐ yes ☐ no c. The balloons were the same color.

6. One reason to study is to get a good grade. I think that another reason to study is to learn new things. Other reasons are to make your parents happy and to impress your teacher.

  ☐ yes ☐ no   a. There are exactly three reasons listed.

  ☐ yes ☐ no   b. The second reason is much more important than the third one.

  ☐ yes ☐ no   c. The fifth reason is about your teacher.

7. Many students went to the concert on Friday night. Some students drove their cars. Others rode the subway. The ones who drove were sorry because traffic was so bad. They were late for the concert. The ones who rode the subway were happy.

  ☐ yes ☐ no   a. Most of the students rode the subway to the concert.

  ☐ yes ☐ no   b. Some students were late for the concert.

  ☐ yes ☐ no   c. The students who rode the subway were late.

8. Miami is a famous city in the United States. Another is New York. Others include San Francisco, Chicago, Denver, and Dallas.

  ☐ yes ☐ no   a. Miami and New York are famous U.S. cities.

  ☐ yes ☐ no   b. New York and Miami are the two most famous cities in the United States.

  ☐ yes ☐ no   c. The last four cities are more famous than the first ones.

ONE-MINUTE LESSON

With the word **night**, we use the preposition **at: at night**. However, when we include the name of that day, we use on because we use **on** with days: **on Friday night**.

EXERCISE 10. Speaking Practice: Talking about Grammar

Step 1. Work with a partner. One of you is Student A and is responsible for the A sentences, and the other is Student B and is responsible for the B sentences.

Step 2. Read the pair of sentences. Both A and B have an underlined part. Which one is correct, and which one is wrong?

Step 3. Circle the letter of the wrong sentence. Then write your reason on the line.

Step 4. Compare your answers. Discuss any differences. Can you both explain why you say a sentence is wrong?

1. A. Those sandwiches look delicious. I would like to eat <u>the other one</u>.

   B. I enjoyed my trip to Miami last month. I want to go there <u>another time</u>.

   Reason: _____

2. A. Some people like fish, but <u>others</u> can't stand the smell or taste of it.

   B. There is a book on the desk, and there is <u>other</u> on the sofa.

   Reason: _____

3. A. The teacher was sick, so <u>another</u> one came to our class today.

   B. Please give me <u>other</u> glass of water. I'm so thirsty!

   Reason: _____

4. A. The test had 10 questions. Number 1 was easy, but <u>the another ones</u> were hard.

   B. She has two brothers. One lives in Miami, and <u>the other</u> is in Philadelphia.

   Reason: _____

5. A. For our next vacation, let's go to Paris. <u>Another</u> good place might be London.

   B. <u>Another</u> telephone numbers for the bank are 555-9921 and 555-9922.

   Reason: _____

6. A. A student can only use this computer for one hour if there are <u>other</u> students waiting.

   B. The plate was not clean, so I asked the waitress to bring me <u>other</u> plate.

   Reason: _____

EXERCISE 11. Review Test 1: Multiple Choice

Circle the letter of the correct answer. Some are conversations.

1. "Did you buy a new phone last week?"

   "No, but I'm going to buy _____ today."

       a. it   b. one   c. some   d. other

2. Four men work here in the morning, and four _____ work here in the evening.

       a. ones   b. others   c. others ones   d. the others

3. "One of the students is reading a book."

   "What are _____ doing?"

   "They're reading, too."

       a. the ones   c. the others

       b. the others ones   d. another one

4. I love cats. In fact, I have five of them. Four are black, and _____ is gray.

       a. four   b. it   c. the other   d. another

5. "May I use this green pen?"

   "No, please don't use _____. It's leaking ink."

       a. it   b. another   c. one   d. the other

6. I have a CD here on the table, and I have a few _____ in my car.

       a. another   c. others ones

       b. anothers   d. others

7. "Would you like an apple?"

   "Yes, I'd like _____."

       a. other green   c. a green one

       b. a green   d. other green one

8. There _____ on the table.

       a. is other book   c. is another books

       b. are other books   d. are the other book

EXERCISE 12. Review Test 2: Production and Evaluation

Part 1.

Unscramble the words in parentheses to complete the sentences in this passage about a tourist destination in South America.

Patagonia is a famous region in South America. Patagonia is located in two countries. (one/Chile/is/the/Argentina/other/and/is)

❶ _____ Most of the time, the weather in

Patagonia is mild, (times/but/other/at) **❷** _____,

it can be extremely cold. Many tourists visit Patagonia every year.

(visit/reason/one/ tourists/that) **❸** _____

Patagonia is to see glaciers. Perito Moreno is the most famous glacier, but

(others/356/are/there) **❹** _____.

(to/other/tourists/choose) **❺** _____ go

hiking or horseback riding. (visit/another/to/option/is/tourists/for)

❻ _____ the waterfalls and lakes. If you like

nature, you should visit Patagonia. Patagonia is becoming more popular

with tourists, and now it is getting crowded. In fact, there has been talk

of limiting the number of visitors allowed each year and discussion of

(options/other/protect/to) **❼** _____ the

nature of Patagonia. In any case, (one/Patagonia/place/is)

❽ _____ that all nature-lovers can enjoy.

Part 2.
Read this passage. There are six mistakes. Circle the mistakes, and write the correction above the mistake.

Bookstores can be a popular place to spend time. In the past, bookstores were a place only for shopping. Today, people go to bookstores for many reason. The most popular one have coffee shops inside where you can order your favorite coffee drink or tea. Others have big, comfortable couches where you can sit and study. Other new trend is that some bookstores don't make you buy the book. You can sit in the store and read a book from the shelf. Other reason people visit a bookstore is to meet friends. Some people don't even look at the books in the bookstore. They go to the coffee shop just to meet their friends. Although many people like bookstores, other prefer to buy e-books instead of going to the bookstore. E-books are electronic books. They are different from the other one because you download them on your computer or e-reader. An e-reader can hold hundreds of books. With e-books, you can take your bookstore anywhere.

EXERCISE 13. Reading Practice: Giving Advice

Read this letter from a student to her friend. Then answer the eight questions on page 257. The grammar from this unit is underlined for you.

Dear Maddie,

How are you doing? You're probably busy. I'm very busy these days, too. I'm sorry I haven't kept in touch better, but my life is kind of crazy right now. I have three final exams this semester. <u>One</u> is tomorrow in calculus class. I'm a little worried about it because I just don't understand the subject very well. Some of my classmates understand everything, but <u>others</u> can't understand some of the most basic concepts. I talked to a friend in class about my situation, and he is going to try to help me. If I need more help, I'll ask <u>another</u> classmate.

Then I have <u>another</u> exam on Wednesday for my history class. The class was great, and I really enjoyed it. In fact, of all my classes, this was my favorite one), but I'm scared about the final. There are so many names and dates to remember!

My last exam is biology. You know how much I love science. I'm not worried about this one, but the <u>other</u> two are making me nervous. Oh, well, in <u>another</u> week it will all be over.

Anyway, I don't have any <u>other</u> news . . . it's just study, study, study for me right now. Please write back and let me know how you are. Did Kevin ever call you for <u>another</u> date? I hope so! But if not, don't worry. There are plenty of <u>others</u> out there who are just as nice. Someday you will find the right <u>one</u>. I just know it. ☺

Take care,

Stephanie

1. Which adjectives best describe Stephanie's life now according to her letter?

   a. boring and unexciting

   b. crazy and adventurous

   c. crazy and lots of studying

   d. lots of studying and partying

2. Which test will Stephanie take first?

   a. calculus

   b. chemistry

   c. biology

   d. history

3. How does Stephanie feel about her calculus exam?

   a. It is the easiest one.

   b. It is the simplest one.

   c. It is her favorite one.

   d. It is the most difficult one.

4. What subject is Stephanie's favorite one in school?

   a. math

   b. science

   c. history

   d. English

5. True or False. All the students in Stephanie's calculus class are nervous about the exam tomorrow.

6. True or False. Stephanie is good at remembering names and dates in history.

7. True or False. Stephanie has a very exciting life and doesn't spend a lot of time studying.

8. True or False. Stephanie went on many dates with a boy named Kevin.

EXERCISE 14. Vocabulary Practice: Word Knowledge

Circle the word or phrase that is most closely related to the word or phrase on the left. Use a dictionary to check the meaning of words you do not know.

Vocabulary	Answer Choices	
1. wealthy	a lot of money	a lot of people
2. replace B	boat → oat	boat → goat
3. guarantee	50%	100%
4. average	unique	usual
5. a drawer	like a circle	like a square
6. calm	noisy	quiet
7. almond	you eat it	you make it
8. colorful	bright	dark
9. local	far	near
10. a tablet	medicine	sports
11. I just made this cake.	maybe 10 minutes ago	maybe 10 hours ago
12. amazing	very bad	very good
13. a schedule	coins	hours
14. a manager	a person	a thing
15. used to work	the past	the present
16. an opportunity	a chance	a committee
17. one sort	one kind	one weight
18. I ran out of ink.	I have ink now.	I need ink now.
19. a sink	air	water
20. underneath	above	below
21. in fact	sure	unsure
22. a toy	for children	for drivers
23. a waterfall	a beach	a mountain
24. stripes	circles	lines
25. a remedy	starts a problem	finishes a problem
26. gray	black + white	red + yellow
27. picky	helpful	selective
28. ingredients	to give something	to make something
29. nervous	not calm	not clear
30. traffic	many cars	many hills
31. a balloon	in the air	in the water
32. X is over	we will begin X	we finished X
33. a concept	an idea	an obstacle

EXERCISE 15. Vocabulary Practice: Collocations

Fill in each blank with the answer on the right that most naturally completes the phrase on the left. If necessary, use a dictionary to check the meaning of words you do not know.

Vocabulary	Answer Choices	
1. a tray of _____	cookies	shirts
2. made _____ plastic	in	of
3. I don't _____ for coffee.	care	need
4. _____ a promotion	do	get
5. my _____ hurts	desk	foot
6. a very loud _____	beverage	color
7. Are you good _____ math?	at	to
8. _____ a headache	get	put
9. a spicy _____	coin	dish
10. another _____	one	ones
11. a strict _____	boss	pet
12. _____ the 9th floor	in	on
13. I spent two hours _____.	to run	running
14. _____ medicine	eat	take
15. soft _____ leather	brown	open
16. based _____	about	on
17. a _____ worker	hard	heavy
18. takes the _____ of Y	place	time
19. X is different _____ Y	from	to
20. a credit _____	card	paper
21. a _____ drink	calm	soft
22. _____ home	at	in
23. _____ to	belong	share
24. the _____ sink	bedroom	kitchen
25. a painting _____ the wall	in	on
26. _____ my wallet	in	on
27. _____ a kite	fly	run
28. _____ football	gaming	playing
29. Were you happy _____ the results?	for	with
30. _____ the counter	in	on
31. _____ out of time	put	run
32. I will call you _____ 15 minutes.	after	in
33. _____ the drawer	at	in

EXERCISE 16. Writing Practice

Part 1. Editing Student Writing

Read these sentences about one student's opinion about college. Circle the 15 errors. Then write the number of the sentence with the error next to the type of error. (Some sentences may have more than one error.)

_____ a. no subject   _____ d. word order

_____ b. verb tense   _____ e. article

_____ c. wrong form of *other*   _____ f. preposition

Leaving Home for College
1. In some countries, it is not common for an 18-year-old to leave home, but in U.S., is normal.
2. In America, many high school students are leaving home when they graduate.
3. They choose usually to go to a college in a city that is not near from their home.
4. For example, when I graduated at high school, I went to a university about five hours from home.
5. Of course I have to leave home, so got an apartment.
6. Most university students lived in their own apartments.
7. Some students prefer to live alone, but other like to live with another person.
8. Prefer to have a roommate because living by myself is not a lot of fun.
9. When I come home, I sometimes feel sad because there was no one in the apartment to talk to.
10. Roommates can cook dinners delicious together and talk about their days, so it feels like a family.
11. Roommates can study together, and they can make life better in many others ways.
12. Other reason I prefer to have a roommate is to help share the cost of the apartment.

Part 2. Original Student Writing

Choose a vacation destination. Write sentences or a paragraph about this place and the reasons people go there. Practice *another, the other, other,* or *others*. Underline this vocabulary in your writing.

 Unit 10

Possessive

Discover the Grammar

Read this conversation between a mother and a daughter, and then answer the two questions.

Line		
1	*Mother:*	Kayla, I want your help cleaning up the living room. There's stuff all
2		over the table here.
3	*Daughter:*	Well, it isn't mine!
4	*Mother:*	Oh? Isn't this your cell phone?
5	*Daughter:*	No, mine isn't all scratched up like that. That's Jeff's.
6	*Mother:*	Oh, so it is. OK, please take it to his room later then. And what
7		about this wallet? Isn't this yours?
8	*Daughter:*	No, I don't have a wallet like that.
9	*Mother:*	Well, whose is it, then?
10	*Daughter:*	It looks like Dad's. Look inside.
11	*Mother:*	Oh, yes, you're right. It's his. OK. I'll take care of it, but this book
12		isn't his. *One Chance for All Her Life*. That must be yours.

13	*Daughter:*	Yes, all right, that's mine.
14	*Mother:*	And look at all these papers! Whose papers are these?
15	*Daughter:*	Um, mom? They're yours. Yours and Dad's.
16	*Mother:*	Oh . . . you're right. They're ours. Sorry!

1. Find these sentences in the conversation. Write the line number where they are located in the parentheses. Then read them again. Who or what is each under-lined word referring to? Circle the correct answer.

(   ) a. Well, it isn't <u>mine</u>! (mother's / Kayla's)

(   ) b. OK, please take it to <u>his</u> room later then. (Jeff's / Dad's)

(   ) c. But this book isn't <u>his</u>. (Jeff's / Dad's)

(   ) d. That must be <u>yours</u>. (Jeff's / Kayla's)

(   ) e. <u>Yours</u> and Dad's. (Mother's / Kayla's)

(   ) f. They're <u>ours</u>. (Mother's and Kayla's / Mother's and Dad's)

2. Circle the meaning (A or B) that you think means the same as the first sentence.

Sentences	Meaning A	Meaning B
a. That's my sister's.	That's hers.	That's theirs.
b. That's my sisters'.	That's hers.	That's theirs.
c. That belongs to me.	It's mine.	It's ours.
d. Those are my brother's.	They're theirs.	They're his.
e. Those are my brother's.	They belong to him.	They belong to them.
f. That book belongs to Joe.	It is his.	It is theirs.
g. This belongs to you.	It's mine.	It's yours.
h. It's my parents'.	It's yours.	It's theirs.

Grammar Lesson

Possessive

Possessive Nouns	
's or s'	of
The book belongs to Joe. It is **Joe's book**.	This book has a long title. **The title of this book** is long.
The books belong to Joe. They are **Joe's books**.	The bookshelf has strong legs. **The legs of the bookshelf** are strong.
The books belong to the boy. They are **the boy's books**.	I liked the story. The ending was good. I liked **the ending of the story**.
The books belong to the boys. They are **the boys' books**.	What great books! The publisher is located in London. **The publisher of the books** is in London.

Rule 1. 's shows possession for people: *Bob's car, the man's name, the girls' toys*

Rule 2. 's is also used with some time words: *today's newspaper, tomorrow's weather*

Spelling Rule 3. We can use 's or just ' to show possession.

If the noun is singular, add 's: The boy → The boy's name.

If the noun already ends in s, add just ': The boys → The boys' names.

If a proper noun ends in s, you can add ' or 's: James → James' OR James's sweater.

(A proper noun is the name of a person, place, or thing: *James, Boston, Pepsi*.)

Rule 4. of is used with things: the name of the hotel, the color of this car.

Rule 5. 's or of can be used with animals, but we often use 's with a pet: my cat's name OR the name of my cat.

Rule 6. 's or of can be used with words that mean groups of people, such as a city or a country: *the city's problems* OR *the problems of a city*.

Rule 7. Use **whose** to ask about the owner of something. It is not necessary to use a noun after **whose** if the reference is clear.

 Two people are pointing to a dog:

> A: *Oh, no! There's a big dog by the door! I'm afraid of dogs!*
>
> B: **Whose** *is it? Is it Mr. Miller's dog? Is it a stray dog?*

Rule 8. It is possible to have two possessives next to each other: **These are Ann's daughter's books.**

 ## BE CAREFUL!

Common Learner Errors	Explanation
1. The ~~plan of the president~~ president's plan will create new jobs.	Do not use **of** with people. Instead, use 's or '.
2. ~~Lauras phone number~~ Laura's phone number starts with 7, not 6.	Be sure to use an apostrophe with –s for possession.
3. The two ~~girl's~~ girls' cameras are identical.	Use 's with a singular noun and just ' after a plural noun.
4. ~~This movie's ending~~ The ending of this movie is very surprising.	Use **of** with a possessive of things. Do not use 's for things.
5. ~~For who is this~~ Whose book is this?	Use **whose** to ask about the owner of something.

 ONE-MINUTE LESSON
Don't confuse **whose** and **who's**. The word **whose** is for possession, but the word **who's** is a contraction for *who is* or *who has*. **Whose** *book is that?* **Who's** *your boss now?* (= *who is*) **Who's** *eaten at that restaurant before?* (= *who has*).

EXERCISE 1. Possessive Forms

Circle the letter of the correct possessive form. Follow the example.

Things You Might Find at a School

1. (a.) the principal's office
   b. the office of the principal

2. a. the pencil sharpener's handle
   b. the handle of the pencil sharpener

3. a. the computer's color
   b. the color of the computer

4. a. the table's legs
   b. the legs of the table

5. a. the teacher's car
   b. the car of the teacher

6. a. the girls' books
   b. the books of the girls

7. a. today's student newspaper
   b. the student newspaper of today

8. a. the desk's color
   b. the color of the desk

9. a. Frank's dictionary
   b. the dictionary of Frank

10. a. the students' test papers
    b. the test papers of the students

Do Online Exercise 10.1. My score: _____ /10. _____ % correct.

EXERCISE 2. Possessive Forms

Write the correct possessive form. Follow the examples.

Sentence	Topic
1. Kevin has a car.	Kevin's car
2. The box has a cover.	the cover of the box
3. The child has a toy.	_____
4. Scott has a pencil.	_____
5. The woman has a ring.	_____
6. I bought this newspaper today.	_____
7. The pencil has a point.	_____
8. The car belongs to Tim.	_____
9. The story has a beginning.	_____
10. Mr. Smith has a tie.	_____
11. The homework is for tomorrow.	_____
12. This city has a problem.	_____
13. Ned owns a house.	_____
14. The secretary does work.	_____
15. Andrea has a hobby.	_____

Do Online Exercise 10.2. My score: ____ /10. ____ % correct.

EXERCISE 3. Possessive Forms in Sentences

Combine the two sentences. Write the correct possessive form. Follow the example.

1. Carol owns a house. It is large.

   Carol's house is large.
   _____

2. Carol also has a large car. It is green.

   _____

3. The blue car is in the driveway. Carol's son owns the car.

   _____

4. Carol has a pool. It is square.

   _____

5. The science books are on the desk by the door. They belong to Carol's sister.

   _____

6. The coins are very old. The coins belong to Carol's husband, Mike.

   _____

7. Mike has a new office. It is at the corner of Park Street and Maple Avenue.

   _____

8. This city's problem is traffic. It is the main problem.

   _____

EXERCISE 4. Possessive Forms in Context

Read the paragraph about a family dinner. Circle the correct possessive forms.

The Family Dinner

My boyfriend's family had a big dinner at ❶ (the house of his grandmother,

his grandmother's house) last Sunday. My boyfriend was really excited about

seeing his nephews. "Wow!" he exclaimed when he saw ❷ (his sister's oldest son,

the oldest son of his sister). "❸ (Jimmy's hair, The hair of Jimmy) has really

grown!" His sister laughed and said, "I know! And would you look at

❹ (the clothes of Johnny, Johnny's clothes)—they are getting too small because

he's growing so much!" ❺ (The mother of my boyfriend, My boyfriend's

mother) was so happy to see all of the children together. She made sure that

her camera was working well, and then she took pictures of everyone. She was

also glad that ❻ (the dining room table of her brother, her brother's dining

room table) was big enough for the whole family!

ONE-MINUTE LESSON
The word **take** has many different meanings, but one usage is to **take a photo of someone.** Remember to use **take** (not *make*) with *photo, picture, pic, shot,* or any other word that means "photo." If you want to tell who is in the photo, use the preposition **of.** Some tourists might ask you, **"Can you take a picture of us?"**

Do Online Exercise 10.3. My score: _____ /10. _____ % correct.

Grammar Lesson

Possessive Pronouns

Possessive Pronouns		
Subject Pronouns	Possessive Pronouns	Examples
I → mine		You have your book, and **I have mine.**
you → yours		I have my book, and **you have yours.**
he → his		I have my book, and **he has his.**
she → hers		I have my book, and **she has hers.**
we → ours		They have their books, and **we have ours.**
they → theirs		We have our books, and **they have theirs.**

Rule 1. Possessive pronouns are used in place of possessive adjectives and nouns. For example, **mine** can take the place of **my book** or **my books**.

Rule 2. **Mine** is the only possessive pronoun that does not end in –s.

Rule 3. There is no difference in English between singular or plural with possessive pronouns. For example, **hers** can mean **her book** or **her books**.

EXERCISE 5. Practicing Possessive Forms

Fill in the chart with the correct questions and answers about possession. Follow the example.

	Question	Answer 1	Answer 2
1. book/Joe	Whose book is it?	It is Joe's book. It is Joe's.	It's his book. It's his.
2. keys/Mark (Your name is Keith.)			
3. fault/Keith			
4. toys/my sisters			
5. toys/my sister			
6. toys/my children			
7. toys/my kids			
8. coat/Lee			
9. hat/Mr. Hamm			
10. recipe/Mrs. Lim			

EXERCISE 6. Editing: Is It Correct?

If the sentence is correct, put a check mark (✓) on the line. If it is not correct, write X on the line and circle the mistake. Then change the sentence to make it correct. Write the change above the sentence. (*Hint:* There are eight sentences. Two are correct, but six have mistakes.)

The Broken Vacuum

_____ 1. The plug on my old vacuum broke last week, and the hose was about to break, too.

_____ 2. Two of my favorites store's had sales on vacuums, so I bought a new one.

_____ 3. After I brought the vacuum home, I noticed it's attachment brush was missing.

_____ 4. I checked the boxes contents, but there was no brush!

_____ 5. I called the store's customer service number, and they asked me to bring in the vacuum and the box it came in.

_____ 6. I went to put everything back in the box, but I couldn't find the vacuums filter.

_____ 7. I finally found the filter and put the box in the car. As I closed the car's trunk, I crushed the box.

_____ 8. Luckily, the stores return policy didn't include boxes!

Do Online Exercise 10.4. My score: _____ /10. _____ % correct.

EXERCISE 7. Mini-Conversations

Circle the correct words in these eight mini-conversations.

1. A: (Your, You're) pizza looks good.

   B: Yes, it's very delicious! (Mine, My) friend said I should order it.

2. A: What are the ingredients in this (pizza, pizza's)?

   B: It's got fresh tomatoes, onions, mushrooms, and green peppers.

3. A: Oh, so (your, you're) a vegetarian?

   B: No, why do you ask?

4. A: Because there is no meat on (your, you're) pizza!

   B: Oh, you're right! Actually, my friend is a vegetarian, so he never orders meat on (his, he's) pizza.

5. A: So what is (your, you're) favorite kind of pizza?

   B: I like (my, mine) pizza with goat cheese and lots of garlic.

6. A: Garlic?

   B: Yes, (its, it's) the best! You should try it!

7. A: I like (my, mine) with onions and pineapple.

   B: Pineapple? Isn't that too sweet for a pizza?

8. A: Not for me! I love it.

   B: Ok, well maybe the next time you order it, I will try a slice of (your, yours).

EXERCISE 8. Sentence Study for Critical Reading

Read the original sentences. Then read the three answer choices, and put a check mark (✓) in the yes or no boxes in front of each sentence to show if that answer is true based on the information in the original sentence. If there is not enough information to mark something as yes, then mark it as no. Remember that more than one true answer is possible.

1. Sharon's pet bird's name is Crackers.

   ☐ yes ☐ no   a. Sharon has a pet bird.

   ☐ yes ☐ no   b. The bird doesn't have a name.

   ☐ yes ☐ no   c. It is named Crackers.

2. There's a bird that lives outside in our garden.

   ☐ yes ☐ no   a. There is a bird that lives inside.

   ☐ yes ☐ no   b. The bird lives in the garden.

   ☐ yes ☐ no   c. The garden belongs to our neighbor.

3. There is a picture of a bird in the gold frame that sits on Mark's desk.

   ☐ yes ☐ no   a. There is a picture of a child in the frame.

   ☐ yes ☐ no   b. The frame is gold.

   ☐ yes ☐ no   c. The frame sits on a desk that belongs to Mark.

4. The bird's cage in the living room broke.

   ☐ yes ☐ no   a. The cage broke.

   ☐ yes ☐ no   b. The living room has a cage in it.

   ☐ yes ☐ no   c. The cage was on the patio.

5. The bird's main pastime is looking at itself in the mirror in the corner of the cage.

   ☐ yes ☐ no   a. There is a mirror in the cage.

   ☐ yes ☐ no   b. In the past, the mirror was in the center of the cage.

   ☐ yes ☐ no   c. The bird can see itself.

6. The bird's seeds are all over the floor under its cage.

   ☐ yes ☐ no   a. There are seeds all over the floor under the cage.

   ☐ yes ☐ no   b. The cage has several birds in it.

   ☐ yes ☐ no   c. The cage is messy because there are so many birds in it.

7. Mark put his newspaper on the bottom of the bird's cage.

    ☐ yes ☐ no a. The newspaper belongs to Mark's mother.

    ☐ yes ☐ no b. Mark put the newspaper on the bottom of the cage.

    ☐ yes ☐ no c. The bird sleeps on the newspaper.

8. Mark's cat is watching the bird in its cage.

    ☐ yes ☐ no a. The cat was watching the bird when it flew out of its cage.

    ☐ yes ☐ no b. The cat belongs to Mark.

    ☐ yes ☐ no c. The bird suddenly flew out of its cage.

EXERCISE 9. Speaking Practice: Family Tree

Student A

Step 1. Work with a partner. Student A works on this page. Student B works on page 276.

Step 2. Your family tree is missing some of the information, but your partner has this information. Take turns asking questions to complete this chart.

    <u>Examples:</u> Who is Theo's wife? OR What is Theo's wife's name?

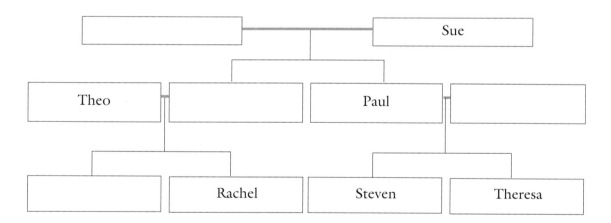

EXERCISE 9. Speaking Practice: Family Tree

Student B

Step 1. Work with a partner. Student B works on this page. Student A works on page 275.

Step 2. Your family tree is missing some of the information, but your partner has this information. Take turns asking questions to complete this chart.

<u>Examples</u>: Who is Carl's wife? OR What is Carl's wife's name?

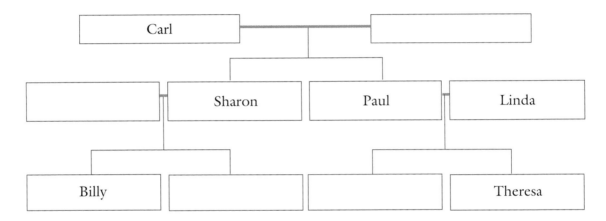

Write six sentences about the people on the tree. Write three true statements and three false statements. Write true or false on the line. Take turns reading your statements in pairs or small groups. The other students have to say whether your statements are true or false. Follow the examples.

False	A.	Rachel is Paul's wife.
True	B.	Linda's husband's name is Paul.
_____	1.	_____
_____	2.	_____
_____	3.	_____
_____	4.	_____
_____	5.	_____
_____	6.	_____

EXERCISE 10. Review Test 1: Multiple Choice

Circle the letter of the correct answer. Some are conversations.

1. "Did you buy the table?"

   "No, I didn't. ____ were not strong enough."
      a. The legs the table   c. The table's legs
      b. The legs of the table   d. The table of the legs

2. These are not my books. These are ____.
      a. the books of Henry   c. Henry's books
      b. Henry's the books   d. the books of Henry's

3. "What are you reading?"

   "I'm reading ____."
      a. the newspaper of today   c. the newspaper's today
      b. today the newspaper's   d. today's newspaper

4. "Who is that boy in the green sweater?"

   "____ is Vic Richards. He's new."
      a. The boy's name   c. The name of the boy
      b. The name's boy   d. The boy of the name

5. Donna suggested, "Let's buy this cake! It looks delicious!"

   Her brother agreed and then asked the bakery cashier, "Excuse me, what is
   ____?"
      a. the price of this cake   c. the price's cake
      b. the cake of this price   d. the cake's price

6. "Of all the students in our class, who speaks English the best?"

   "I think ____ is the best."
      a. the English of Carrine   c. Carrine's English
      b. the Carrine's English   d. the English's Carrine

7. "Which house is yours?"

   "That one over there. The white house on the corner. That's ____."
      a. mine house   b. mine   c. my house's   d. my

8. "____?"

   "It's Claudia's."
      a. Whose is that car   c. Who is that car
      b. Whose car is that   d. Who that car is

REVIEW **EXERCISE 11. Review Test 2: Production and Evaluation**

Part 1.

Read this passage. Fill in the blanks with the correct possesive form using the words in parentheses.

This is Luke Walker. He is standing in front of his house. You can see his car in front of his house. The man next to Luke is his father. Luke's father's name is Len.

Do you like (Luke/house) ❶ _____? It is about five years old. (Luke/house) ❷ _____ is not very old, so the house is still in good condition.

What do you think about (Luke/house/the color) ❸ _____ _____? Do you like it? Luke painted his house white because it's a good color for a house. Do you agree?

What do you think about (the size/the house) ❹ _____ _____? The house is not very big, but it was not very expensive. (the price/the house) ❺ _____ was very good. He only paid $125,000.

Part 2.

Read each sentence carefully. Look at the underlined part. If the underlined part is correct, circle the word *correct*. If it is wrong, circle the word *wrong*. Then write the correction above.

correct	wrong	1. <u>The class of Paula and Jan</u> is not very big.
correct	wrong	2. What's <u>this cake's price</u>?
correct	wrong	3. Is your name on <u>the front of the envelope</u>?
correct	wrong	4. <u>Tomorrow's homework</u> is not very difficult.
correct	wrong	5. Do you know <u>this ice cream's name</u>?
correct	wrong	6. <u>The boys' books</u> are on the table.
correct	wrong	7. When is <u>the last day of Larry</u> at the office?

EXERCISE 12. Reading Practice: A Newspaper Report

Read this article about a horse show. Fill in the chart, and answer the six questions. The grammar from this chapter is underlined for you.

Katy and Summer Starr Win At Last!

High school show jumper Katy Morris and her horse Summer Starr finally won a jumping competition last weekend at the County Fair. We say "finally" because Katy and Summer Starr have had bad luck all year.

First, <u>Katy's horse</u> had a problem with her back leg. "<u>Summer Starr's left hind leg</u> hit <u>the top of a jump</u> during practice," explains Katy, "and she got a little cut. It wasn't too serious, but I couldn't exercise her for a few weeks. We had to miss <u>the first show of the season</u>."

Then, <u>a piece of Starr's saddle</u> suddenly broke while Katy was riding, right before the next show. "I needed a saddle! Fortunately, <u>a friend of mine named Ben</u> lent me <u>his</u>," says Katy, "but it didn't really fit Summer Starr, and we didn't do very well in the competition."

Next, while driving to a show, <u>her parents' car</u> had a flat tire, and they couldn't fix it in time and missed the show.

Summer Starr is <u>Katy's first horse</u>. "I used to ride <u>my sisters' horses</u>," she says, "but it's much better to have a horse that is just <u>mine</u>." Katy is on her <u>high school's riding team</u> and competes in many

different types of events. However, jumping is a favorite of <u>hers</u>.

After watching her friends win ribbons all year, Katy and Summer Starr finally got <u>theirs</u> on Friday. They hope their good luck will continue through <u>this summer's shows</u> as well.

	Question	Answer 1	Answer 2
1. horse/Katy	Whose horse is it?	It is Katy's horse. It is Katy's.	It's her horse. It's hers.
2. saddle/Ben			
3. ribbon/Katy and Summer Starr			
4. horses/my sister			
5. car/parents			
6. saddle/Summer Starr			

EXERCISE 13. Vocabulary Practice: Word Knowledge

Circle the word or phrase that is most closely related to the word or phrase on the left. Use a dictionary to check the meaning of words you do not know.

Vocabulary	Answer Choices	
1. a handle	a person	a thing
2. a hobby	you do it at work	you do it outside work
3. nephews	boys	girls
4. stuff	places	things
5. a cover	above	below
6. an owner	a person	a place
7. glad	happy	large
8. X is missing	we have X	we don't have X
9. a vegetarian	a person	a thing
10. a competition	to find the very best	to have a big party
11. it belongs to me	it's mine	it's not mine
12. a recipe	for buying something	for cooking something
13. a cage	for a bird	for a bus
14. square	3 sides	4 sides
15. the ingredients	a building	a pizza
16. publish	apples	books
17. a patio	a house	a trip
18. attach	alone	together
19. an envelope	for a letter	for a present
20. the driveway	a bank	a house
21. a murder	someone is dead	someone is rich
22. a tie	for a man	for a baby
23. to jump	go down	go up
24. scratched	damaged	improved
25. enough	statement	sufficient
26. agree	a different idea	a similar idea
27. seeds	from a grape	from a stone
28. to notice	to permit	to see
29. toys	children	weather
30. exclaim	say loudly	say softly
31. suddenly	you expected it	you didn't expect it
32. a team	a group of people	a group of things
33. a wallet	for friends	for money

EXERCISE 14. Vocabulary Practice: Collocations

Fill in each blank with the answer on the right that most naturally completes the phrase on the left. If necessary, use a dictionary to check the meaning of words you do not know.

Vocabulary	Answer Choices	
1. I'm afraid _____ spiders.	from	of
2. _____ the corner of Main and Elm	at	in
3. _____ happy	so	too
4. the _____ policy	enter	return
5. all _____ the table	again	over
6. enough _____	cheap	money
7. is _____ in	located	location
8. _____ the batteries	check	review
9. I'm reading _____.	the paper of today	today's paper
10. take care _____ something	for	of
11. the trunk of a _____	car	house
12. a _____ sharpener	pencil	window
13. I'm _____ about going there	excited	interested
14. a vacuum _____	cleaner	washer
15. a _____ frame	clock	picture
16. in _____ of	place	time
17. have a sale _____ shirts	of	on
18. it's _____ there	owner	over
19. _____ good condition	in	on
20. my _____ family	all	whole
21. _____ a car	now	own
22. a slice of _____	pants	pizza
23. all _____	the year	year
24. a _____ saddle	horse's	turkey's
25. _____ a picture	make	take
26. _____ my opinion	in	on
27. _____ the summer	through	while
28. _____ about this?	What	Why
29. while _____	drive	driving
30. _____ my brothers and sisters	all	whole
31. a dining room _____	dinner	table
32. a flat _____	motor	tire
33. _____ a competition	put	win

EXERCISE 15. Writing Practice

Part 1. Editing Student Writing

Read these sentences about one student's opinion about a law. Circle the 15 errors. Then write the number of the sentence with the error next to the type of error. (Some sentences may have more than one error.)

_____ a. preposition (*at, on, in*)   _____ d. possessive

_____ b. article   _____ e. verb tense

_____ c. singular-plural

Traffic Fines
1. Do you know that you have to wear seat belt when you are on a car?
2. The police can stop you if you're not wearing you're seat belt.
3. The police can give you a ticket for not wearing your seat belts, and then you must pay fine.
4. The cost of the fine was usually between $50 and $100.
5. When you received a ticket, you may receive points on you license.
6. When you have too many point, you may lose your driver's license.
7. Have you ever gotten traffic ticket?
8. When you got a ticket, why were you getting one?
9. A few year ago, I got the ticket because I was speeding.
10. I have gotten this ticket on August 2011.

Part 2. Original Student Writing

Write a paragraph about a rule or law in your city, town, state, country, school, or organization that you disagree with. Who made the rule? What or whom does the law help? Why do some people think that it is necessary? When you are finished writing, underline all of the possessives in your paragraph.

Comparatives and Superlatives of Adjectives

Discover the Grammar

Read this conversation between two people who are discussing the difficulty of deciding on a destination for a trip. Then answer the six questions.

Line	
1	*Amy:* Did you finally choose a vacation destination?
2	*Ed:* No, Michael and I still can't agree on a destination.
3	*Amy:* Really? The last time you and I talked, you were trying to choose
4	between Ecuador and Japan.
5	*Ed:* That's right. We just can't figure out which one to choose.
6	*Amy:* Which do you prefer?
7	*Ed:* Well, I really want to go to Ecuador because it has a lot of older history. I
8	also like it because the airfare is cheaper. Flying to Japan is a lot more
9	expensive.
10	*Amy:* And what does Michael say?

11	*Ed:*	Well, he wants us to go to Japan because he is into architecture, and he
12		says Japan's architecture is newer and therefore more interesting to him.
13	*Amy:*	Well, I like to travel a lot, and one of my main reasons for visiting a place
14		is to try the local food. What do you guys think about Japanese and
15		Ecuadorean food? I mean, I know something about Japanese food, but I
16		have no idea what food in Ecuador is like.
17	*Ed:*	Michael loves Japanese food. In fact, he's practically addicted to sushi.
18		For him, there's nothing more delicious than sushi.
19	*Amy:*	OK, so that's Michael's opinion. What do you know about Ecuadorean
20		food? What's it like?
21	*Ed:*	Well, it's certainly spicier than Japanese food. I don't mean that it's hot. I
22		just mean they cook with many different kinds of spices. A typical meal
23		might include beef, fried green bananas, and some salad.
24	*Amy:*	Well, to be honest, both types of food sound good to me. By the way, I
25		heard it's hot there. Is that true?
26	*Ed:*	At this time of year, it will be sunnier in Ecuador than in Japan.
27	*Amy:*	Is it also more humid? It's tropical, right?
28	*Ed:*	Yes, on the coast it will be wetter, but it will be very nice up in the
29		mountains.
30	*Amy:*	So now what?
31	*Ed:*	Well, we don't know where we're going to go. We have to make a
32		decision very soon. I think we might just flip a coin.
33	*Amy:*	You know you need to decide soon. If you wait too long, airfares are
34		going to get higher.
35	*Ed:*	I agree. I keep reading about both places, and neither place sounds more
36		beautiful than the other. I mean, they both sound like great places, so our
37		decision seems more difficult than ever.

1. In Lines 7 to 34, find and underline seven adjectives that consist of a simple adjective and the letters *–er*.

2. Complete the chart. In the left column, write your seven *–er* words from the conversation. In the right column, write the root or base form of the word. Follow the example.

–er adjective	root adjective
1. older	old
2.	
3.	
4.	
5.	
6.	
7.	

3. In Lines 7 to 37, find and underline five phrases that contain the word *more* and the word that comes immediately after. (Each phrase consists of only two words.)

4. Complete the chart. In the left column, write the two-word phrase that begins with *more* from the conversation. In the right column, write the root word of the phrase. Follow the example.

more + adjective phrase	root adjective
1. more expensive	expensive
2.	
3.	
4.	
5.	
6.	

5. We use *–er* or *more* for comparison of two people or things. Why do you think we use *–er* with some words and *more* with others?

_____

_____

_____

_____

6. Now use your answer from Question 5 to write the comparative forms of these adjectives. (These words are not in the conversation.)

a. important _____

b. tall _____

c. beautiful _____

d. difficult _____

e. easy _____

f. dangerous _____

g. big _____

h. salty _____

i. hard _____

j. comfortable _____

Grammar Lesson

Comparative of Adjectives

–er	I think Japanese is harder **than** English.
more	I think Japanese is **more** difficult **than** English.

<u>Rule 1</u>. Use **more** or **–er** when comparing two things or people.

<u>Rule 2</u>. Use **–er** with adjectives that have **one syllable**: tall → taller, cheap → cheaper.

<u>Rule 3</u>. Use **–er** with adjectives that have **two syllables and end in –y**. Remember to change the –y to an –i: crazy → crazier, easy → easier.

<u>Rule 4</u>. Use **more** with all other adjectives, including adjectives that have **two syllables** (not ending in –y) or more: dangerous → **more** dangerous, recent → **more** recent.

<u>Rule 5</u>. A few forms are irregular, so remember these: good → **better**, bad → **worse**, far → **farther/further**.

<u>Rule 6</u>. Comparative sentences usually use the word **than** for the second person or thing: Cairo is bigger **than** Abu Dhabi.

<u>Spelling Rule 7</u>. Double the final consonant in a one-syllable adjective that ends in **consonant-vowel-consonant** (c-v-c): red → redder.

 ## BE CAREFUL!

Common Learner Errors	Explanation
1. I am ~~more busy~~ busier in the morning than in the afternoon.	Don't use **more** with short adjectives.
2. This color is ~~more darker~~ darker than that one.	Don't use two comparatives.
3. Katya is taller ~~that~~ **than** her sister Olga.	Use **than** with comparative forms.
4. My office desk is ~~biger~~ **bigger** than my home desk.	Remember to double the final consonant in one-syllable adjectives that end in consonant-vowel-consonant (c-v-c).

Connecting Grammar and Vocabulary

English has thousands of adjectives, but you need to learn the most frequent comparative adjectives with *–er* and *more*.

40 Frequent Comparative Adjectives in English	
20 Frequent *–er* Comparative Adjectives	**20 Frequent *more* Comparative Adjectives**
1. **better** food	1. a **more accurate** answer
2. a **bigger** apartment	2. a **more comfortable** chair
3. **cheaper** prices	3. a **more common** animal
4. a **closer** school	4. a **more complex** situation
5. a **darker** color	5. a **more complicated** situation
6. an **earlier** class	6. a **more dangerous** place
7. an **easier** job	7. a **more difficult** job
8. a **faster** way	8. a **more effective** method
9. a **greater** risk	9. a **more efficient** person
10. a **harder** class	10. a **more expensive** house
11. **higher** prices	11. a **more important** event
12. a **larger** company	12. **more interested** students
13. a **later** flight	13. a **more interesting** class
14. a **longer** vacation	14. a **more likely** result
15. a **lower** temperature	15. a **more popular** destination
16. an **older** man	16. a **more powerful** bomb
17. a **smaller** table	17. a **more recent** problem
18. **stronger** medicine	18. a **more serious** person
19. **worse** weather	19. a **more significant** date
20. a **younger** teacher	20. a **more successful** business owner

Sources: Corpus of Contemporary American English, *Longman Grammar of Spoken and Written English*, Michigan Corpus of Spoken Academic English

Do Online Exercise 11.1. My score: ____ /10. ____ % correct.

EXERCISE 1. Comparative Forms of Adjectives

Write the correct comparative form of the adjectives.

1. happy_____

2. comfortable_____

3. old _____

4. interested _____

5. early _____

6. cheap _____

7. effective _____

8. serious_____

9. light _____

10. important_____

11. common_____

12. big _____

13. good _____

14. difficult_____

15. great_____

16. easy _____

EXERCISE 2. Using Comparative Adjectives in Context

Fill in the blank with the correct comparative form of the adjective in parentheses.

International Facts

1. (big) Colombia is _____ than Paraguay.

2. (rainy) Japan has a _____ climate than Saudi Arabia.

3. (cheap) Venezuela has _____ gasoline than the United King-dom.

4. (low) Costa Rica has a _____ altitude than Peru.

5. (small) Morocco is big, but it is _____ than Egypt.

6. (spicy) Malaysia has _____ cuisine than Vietnam.

7. (famous) Thailand's beaches are _____ than South Korea's beaches.

8. (short) Canada's summers are _____ than Ecuador's summers.

9. (far) The Seychelles are _____ from Tanzania than the Comoros.

10. (colorful) Some say that Australia's coral reefs are _____ than the coral reefs in the Bahamas.

Grammar Lesson

Superlative of Adjectives

| the _____ –est | I think Japanese is the hardest language in the world. |
| the most _____ | I think Japanese is the most difficult language in the world. |

Rule 1. Use the most or the –est when comparing three or more things or people.

Rule 2. Use the –est with adjectives that have one syllable: tall → the tallest, cheap → the cheapest.

Rule 3. Use the –est with adjectives that have two syllables and end in –y. Remember to change the –y to an –i: (crazy → the craziest, easy → the easiest.

Rule 4. Use the most with all other adjectives, including adjectives that have two syllables (not ending in –y) or more: dangerous → the most dangerous, recent → the most recent.

Rule 5. A few forms are irregular, so remember these: good → the best, bad → the worst, far → the farthest/the furthest.

Rule 6. Superlative sentences sometimes use the words in or of to name the group or category. We usually use of with a plural word and in with a group word: Russia is the largest of all the countries in the world.

Spelling Rule 7. Double the final consonant in a one-syllable adjective that ends in consonant-vowel-consonant (c-v-c): red → the reddest.

BE CAREFUL!

Common Learner Errors	Explanation
1. Marina is the ~~most busy~~ busiest person that I know.	Don't use most with short adjectives.
2. The ~~most darkest~~ darkest room in our office has only one window.	Don't use double superlatives.
3. Katya is the tallest person ~~from~~ in my class.	It is common to use of or in with superlatives.
4. My office desk is the ~~bigest~~ biggest in our office.	Remember to double the final consonant in one-syllable adjectives that end in consonant-vowel-consonant (c-v-c).

Connecting Grammar and Vocabulary

English has thousands of adjectives, but you need to learn the most frequent superlative adjectives with –**est** and **most**.

40 Frequent Superlative Adjectives in English	
20 Frequent –*est* **Superlative Adjectives**	**20 Frequent** *most* **Superlative Adjectives**
1. the **best** day	1. the **most** beautiful picture
2. the **biggest** cat	2. the **most** common name
3. the **closest** house	3. the **most** controversial news
4. the **earliest** date	4. the **most** dangerous person
5. the **fastest** runner	5. the **most** difficult test
6. the **finest** silk	6. the **most** effective teacher
7. the **greatest** athlete	7. the **most** exciting movie
8. the **hardest** test	8. the **most** expensive restaurant
9. the **highest** mountain	9. the **most** famous singer
10. the **hottest** day	10. the **most** important class
11. the **largest** lake	11. the **most** influential president
12. the **latest** news	12. the **most** interesting conversation
13. the **longest** river	13. the **most** likely winner
14. the **lowest** temperature	14. the **most** obvious answer
15. the **nearest** bus stop	15. the **most** popular girl
16. the **newest** dress	16. the **most** powerful speech
17. the **oldest** sister	17. the **most** recent episode
18. the **smallest** book	18. the **most** serious illness
19. the **strongest** man	19. the **most** significant event
20. the **youngest** brother	20. the **most** successful student

Source: Corpus of Contemporary American English: www.americancorpus.org/

EXERCISE 3. Superlative Forms of Adjectives

Write the correct superlative form of the adjectives.

1. amazing _____

2. controversial _____

3. good _____

4. obvious _____

5. early _____

6. sweet _____

7. wealthy _____

8. safe _____

9. close _____

10. valuable _____

11. common _____

12. early _____

13. important _____

14. likely _____

15. far _____

ONE-MINUTE LESSON
Whether you use **–est** or **most** for the superlative, remember to use **the: the best, the tallest, the cheapest, the most expensive, the most important, the most amazing.**

Do Online Exercise 11.2. My score: ____ /10. ____ % correct.

EXERCISE 4. Using Superlative Adjectives in Context

Fill in the blank with the correct superlative form of the adjective in parentheses.

Ideas for Reducing Expenses and Saving Money

1. (common) One of _____ concerns of people today is saving money.

2. (obvious) _____ way to save money is to cook at home and not eat at a restaurant.

3. (tough) Buying coffee from a coffee shop every morning also wastes a lot of money, but it is one of _____ habits to break.

4. (effective) Using coupons is perhaps _____ way to save money at the grocery store.

5. (cheap) Coupons can really help you get _____ price for the items you buy.

6. (smart, efficient) _____ and _____ shoppers use coupons to get a lot of all their groceries for free!

7. (early) In addition, when you travel, you can sometimes save money by reserving your plane ticket and hotel at _____ possible time.

8. (good) Becoming a member of a frequent flyer program is one of _____ ways to save money on future travel because you can earn points for free trips for family members and friends.

9. (economical) Instead of driving big cars that guzzle gas, many people are buying hybrid cars because they are _____ vehicles available.

10. (expensive) To help my budget, I shop online because I can almost always find _____ brands at discount prices there.

11. (big) Saving a little money every day now could help you be able to make _____ investment of your life down the road.

12. (important) Yes, for many people, buying a house is _____ investment they will ever make. How about you? How will you spend all the money you save?

EXERCISE 5. Comparative and Superlative Forms

Complete the chart with the missing forms.

Adjective	Comparative	Superlative
1. interesting		
2. serious		
3. sweet		
4. simple		
5. famous		
6. long		
7. valuable		
8. controversial		
9. quick		
10. funny		
11. significant		
12. far		

Do Online Exercise 11.3. My score: _____ /10. _____ % correct.

EXERCISE 6. Editing: Is It Correct?

If the sentence is correct, put a check mark (✓) on the line. If it is not correct, write X on the line and circle the mistake. Then change the sentence to make it correct. Write the change above the sentence. (*Hint:* There are twelve sentences. Four are correct, but eight have mistakes.)

Annabelle's First Apartment

_____ 1. Annabelle got her first job as an English teacher in Tokyo. Her new apartment is more small than her old apartment in Canada.

_____ 2. Tokyo is one of the most expensive city in the world, so the apartments are very expensive.

_____ 3. However, Annabelle likes her new apartment because she has a great view of the city from her window.

_____ 4. The view is amazing during the day. However, it is amazinger at night when she can see Tokyo Tower.

_____ 5. Annabelle's new neighbor is a very nice old woman. Annabelle thinks she is the nice person she has ever met.

_____ 6. This apartment has the shortest commute to Annabelle's school. It only takes Annabelle 15 minutes to walk to work.

_____ 7. In Canada, Annabelle had to drive for 20 minutes to get to a grocery store, but her new apartment is more closer to several stores.

_____ 8. In fact, the closest grocery store is only five minutes on foot.

_____ 9. Her new apartment isn't perfect. There is only one elevator, so during the busiest times of the day, she sometimes has to walk up ten flights of stairs.

_____ 10. The most striking different between her new apartment and old apartment is that she doesn't wear shoes inside her new one.

_____ 11. Annabelle has just put up new curtains. The new curtains are more dark than the old ones.

_____ 12. Of all the places she has ever lived, Annabelle thinks this apartment may be the best places.

EXERCISE 7. Mini-Conversations

Circle the correct words in these eight mini-conversations.

1. A: How many siblings does Carl have?

   B: He has two sisters, Minnie and Frannie. Carl is the (oldest, older), and Minnie is (the oldest, older) than Frannie.

2. A: Of all the places you visited in Europe, what was your favorite vacation there?

   B: That's an easy question. By far, my trip to the countryside in Holland was (the best, better). I saw (the most beautiful, the more beautiful) tulips. I know that Amsterdam is (the most popular, a more popular) destination than the country-side, but I really liked the open spaces and nature in the countryside.

3. A: I would never go skydiving!

   B: Why? It looks like so much fun.

   A: No, it doesn't! It looks like (the most dangerous, more dangerous) thing a person can do.

   B: Really? Could you think it's (most dangerous, more dangerous) than swimming with sharks? That's what my cousin did in Australia last year.

4. A: I thought you were going to the airport in the morning.

   B: I was, but I changed to a (latest, later) flight.

5. A: Oh, you look awful! Did you catch a cold?

   B: Yes, I did. I took two aspirin in the morning, and then I went to the doctor later to get some (strongest, stronger) medicine.

6. A: How did your parents like your new boyfriend? Did they like him (the best, better) than your last boyfriend?

   B: No. My parents want me to find (the most serious, a more serious) person.

7. A: In America, a girl's 16th birthday is the most important. We call it a "Sweet Sixteen." How about in Mexico?

   B: Actually, the 15th birthday is (the most important, a more important) event than the 16th birthday. We call it a *quinceañera*.

8. A: I can't believe it's raining today! I was so excited to go to the beach. Do you want to go tomorrow instead?

   B: Actually, I think tomorrow will be (worse, more worse) weather than today. Maybe we should just reschedule for next week.

EXERCISE 8. Sentence Study for Critical Reading

Read the original sentences. Then read the three answer choices, and put a check mark (✓) in the yes or no boxes in front of each sentence to show if that answer is true based on the information in the original sentence. If there is not enough information to mark something as yes, then mark it as no. Remember that more than one true answer is possible.

1. Rugby is one of the most popular sports in England. It is also one of the most popular sports in Australia and New Zealand.

   ☐ yes ☐ no   a. Rugby is a popular sport in England.

   ☐ yes ☐ no   b. Rugby is more popular in Australia than New Zealand.

   ☐ yes ☐ no   c. Rugby is popular in England, Australia, and New Zealand.

2. This sport began in 1823 when a student at Rugby School in England was playing soccer. He picked up the ball and ran with it, which is not allowed in soccer. This action became popular, and the game of rugby was born.

   ☐ yes ☐ no   a. Rugby comes from soccer.

   ☐ yes ☐ no   b. In both sports, you can pick up the ball with your hands.

   ☐ yes ☐ no   c. Rugby is less than two centuries old.

3. In the United Kingdom, rugby is called rugger, and in New Zealand, it is called footy.

   ☐ yes ☐ no   a. Both countries call the game rugger and footy.

   ☐ yes ☐ no   b. Footy is a term that is used in New Zealand.

   ☐ yes ☐ no   c. The term *footy* is more popular than the term *rugger.*

4. Rugby might seem dangerous because the players don't wear helmets or pads like American football players. However, both rugby players and American football players can have serious injuries.

   ☐ yes ☐ no   a. Rugby is more dangerous than American football.

   ☐ yes ☐ no   b. Rugby players and football players wear different types of helmets.

   ☐ yes ☐ no   c. American football players think that rugby is more dangerous than their sport.

5. There are two groups of rugby teams. They are the Rugby League and the Rugby Union. The Rugby League has fewer rules than the Rugby Union.

   ☐ **yes** ☐ **no**   a. The Rugby Union has more rules than the Rugby League.

   ☐ **yes** ☐ **no**   b. The Rugby League has more rules than the Rugby Union.

   ☐ **yes** ☐ **no**   c. The Rugby League is in Australia, but the Rugby Union is in New Zealand.

6. A regular rugby game has 15 players. However, in rugby sevens, there are only 7 players. Therefore, rugby sevens has fewer players.

   ☐ **yes** ☐ **no**   a. Rugby sevens has between 7 and 14 players.

   ☐ **yes** ☐ **no**   b. Teams in regular rugby are bigger than in rugby 7s.

   ☐ **yes** ☐ **no**   c. In a regular rugby game, there will be 16 players on the field.

7. Rugby was an Olympic sport until 1924, but then it was not included for the rest of the twentieth century. In 2009, the Olympics committee voted to include rugby again.

   ☐ **yes** ☐ **no**   a. Rugby was played in the Olympics in 1924.

   ☐ **yes** ☐ **no**   b. Rugby was played in the Olympics in 1976.

   ☐ **yes** ☐ **no**   c. Rugby was played in the Olympics in 2008.

8. In the twentieth century, rugby was an Olympic sport only four times (1900, 1908, 1920, 1924). France won the first gold medal, Australasia* won the second one, and the U.S. won the others.

   ☐ **yes** ☐ **no**   a. France won more gold medals in rugby than Italy or Canada.

   ☐ **yes** ☐ **no**   b. In the twentieth century, the U.S. won the most gold medals in rugby.

   ☐ **yes** ☐ **no**   c. Australasia won two gold medals in rugby.

🕐 **ONE-MINUTE LESSON**
Whether you use –er or **more** for the comparative, remember to use **than: fewer than, smaller than, bigger than, more important than, more expensive than, more interesting than.**

🖱 **Do Online Exercise 11.4. My score: _____ /10. _____ % correct.**

---

*A name for combined Australia/New Zealand teams in the early 1900s.

EXERCISE 9. Speaking Practice: Using Consumer Reviews to Find the Best Product

Step 1. Work in pairs. Choose one of the categories. Choose three different brands or titles to compare. Write the names or titles.

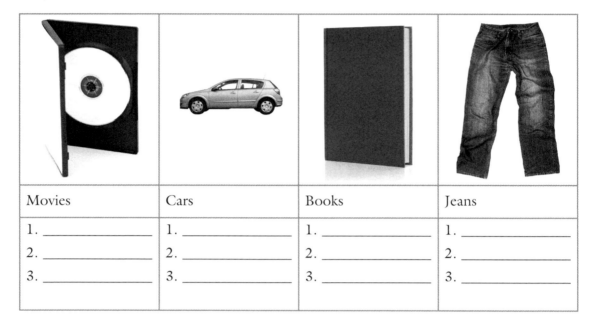

Movies	Cars	Books	Jeans
1. _____	1. _____	1. _____	1. _____
2. _____	2. _____	2. _____	2. _____
3. _____	3. _____	3. _____	3. _____

Step 2. Discuss the brand names or titles that you chose. Make comparisons that you can agree on. If you like, make a poster to illustrate your brands or titles. Follow the examples.

Movies

Movie X is more exciting than Movie Y.

Movie Z is the most exciting of the three.

Movie Y is longer than Movie X or Movie Z.

The music in Movie Z is better than the music in Movie Y.

Step 3. Present your comparisons to the class. Recommend one or more of the choices.

Cars

People who care about the environment should buy the SuperBug. It gets the best mileage.

People who want a sports car should buy the Turbo. It's the fastest and the most fashionable.

People with a lot of children should buy the VanWagon. It's the largest.

EXERCISE 10. Review Test 1: Multiple Choice

Circle the letter of the correct answer. Some are conversations.

1. A: "None of the boys wants to work."

   B: "That is true, but Paul and Joseph are certainly ____."

       a. more lazy   c. the most lazy

       b. lazy   d. the laziest

2. Chris is the ____ student in the class.

       a. better   c. best

       b. better than   d. most good

3. Peter didn't eat breakfast today, so of course he is ____ than we are.

       a. more hungry   c. hungry

       b. hungrier   d. the hungriest

4. I'm not sure how tall Sue is, but I think she is ____ her sister.

       a. taller from   c. taller than

       b. tall from   d. tall than

5. A: "Let's buy this cake."

   B: "Good idea. It looks much ____ than the other one."

       a. fresher and deliciouser   c. more fresh and deliciouser

       b. fresher and more delicious   d. more fresh and more delicious

6. I like your cell phone better than mine because yours is more ____.

       a. better   c. strong

       b. cheap   d. modern

7. If you look at this map, it's clear that Brazil is ____ than Argentina.

       a. bigger   c. the biggest

       b. more big   d. big

8. I don't want to buy this desk because it's too ____.

       a. heaviest   c. heavier

       b. the heaviest   d. heavy

EXERCISE 11. Review Test 2: Production and Evaluation

Part 1.
Read this passage. Circle the correct answer in the parentheses.

Next year three friends and I are going to take a trip together. That was an easy decision, but now we face a ❶ (more hard, harder) decision. We have to choose a place. Our three choices are Hawaii, Russia, and Argentina. The ticket to Hawaii is expensive, but the ticket to Argentina is ❷ (expensiver, more expensive) than the ticket to Hawaii. However, the ticket to Russia is by far ❸ (more expensive, the most expensive) of all three.

Argentina has good weather in the summer, but I think the weather in Russia in the summer is ❹ (gooder, better). Some people in our group think that the weather in Hawaii is ❺ (better, the best) of all three places.

What are we going to do? I think that Russia is ❻ (nicer, more nice) than Hawaii, but some other people don't agree. Greg thinks that Argentina is ❼ (interestinger, more interesting) than Hawaii, but he wants to visit Russia, too. We knew this was going to be a ❽ (difficult, more difficult, difficulties) decision to make, but we have to reach a decision soon.

Part 2.

Read this passage. There are six mistakes. Circle the mistakes, and write the correction above the mistake.

Three weeks ago, I saw a movie called *Victory*. It was very interesting. However, last night I saw another movie that I also enjoyed. The title of this second movie is *Behind the Wall*. I think this movie was most interesting than *Victory*. Both movies are about a war in the early 1900s, but *Behind the Wall* was more better.

Some people don't want to see *Behind the Wall* because it is so longer. At first, I thought *Victory* was a long movie. It is 90 minutes long, but *Behind the Wall* is longer from *Victory*. At 2 hours and 50 minutes, *Behind the Wall* is in fact almost twice as long as *Victory*.

To be honest, I also enjoyed *Behind the Wall* because I found it more easy to understand. The actors in the second movie acted more well. Some parts of *Behind the Wall* were difficult for me to watch, but this was not true with *Victory*.

ONE-MINUTE LESSON
Use **the** with a period of time such as **the early 1900s**. It can also be a decade (**the** *1990s*), a century (**the** *20ᵗʰ century*), or a named period (**the** *Renaissance,* **the** *Great Depression*).

EXERCISE 12. Reading Practice: Choosing a Vacation Destination

Read this travel brochure. Notice the comparatives and superlatives. Then answer the six questions on this page and page 305. The grammar from this unit is underlined for you.

Come to Florida for your next vacation! Florida, where the sun is <u>warmer</u> and the water is <u>bluer</u> and the nights are <u>more romantic</u> than anywhere else!

In Florida, you can enjoy fine dining in any of our restaurants. The seafood here is <u>the most delicious</u> found anywhere along the southeastern coast. Because of Florida's vibrant mix of ethnic populations, the restaurant choices are <u>more varied</u> and <u>more interesting</u> than what you can find in many other states—and also <u>more delicious</u>! In fact, Florida's many hotels and resorts attract some of <u>the best</u> chefs in the United States.

There are plenty of things to do in Florida. Rent a car while you're here. Among all the southern states, car rental rates in Florida are <u>the lowest</u>. Take a ride on a boat and see the dolphins. Beaches in the other states are <u>more crowded</u> than here in Florida. The sunsets are <u>more beautiful</u> from its shores than any place else you have ever been. Florida's theme parks and amusement parks are <u>the most famous</u> in the world. Your children will enjoy <u>the most exciting</u> vacation they've ever taken because there are so many fun things to do at every park.

Send in the postcard on the back of this brochure, and we'll send you more information. Call us, and you'll receive the information even <u>faster</u>. Then you can start packing <u>sooner</u> for your Florida getaway vacation.

Call 1-888-FLORIDA today!

1. According to the travel brochure, why are there many different kinds of restaurants in Florida?

   a. The hot weather is good for growing many different types of vegetables.

   b. Florida has an Atlantic coast and a Gulf coast, so there are more kinds of seafood.

   c. There are many different people from many different countries in Florida.

   d. Different hotels have different menus for their guests.

2. What does the brochure say about the cost of renting a car in Florida?

   a. It is very cheap.

   b. It is very expensive.

   c. It is similar to the prices in other southern states.

   d. Florida is not the cheapest, but it is very cheap.

3. Which is NOT a reason from the brochure to visit Florida's beaches?

   a. The beaches in Florida are less crowded.

   b. The beaches in Florida have beautiful sunsets.

   c. The beaches in Florida have bluer water.

   d. You can see dolphins in Florida.

4. Why will children enjoy the theme parks and amusement parks?

   a. There are so many things to do.

   b. They are less crowded than other theme parks.

   c. They have dolphins for children to pet.

   d. The people at the parks are the friendliest.

5. According to the brochure, which adjective describes the people of Florida?

   a. exciting

   b. friendly

   c. famous

   d. None of these.

6. What is one way to get more information about Florida?

   a. Send a postcard.

   b. Write an email.

   c. Call one of the Florida parks.

   d. Read the brochure.

7. Work in groups of four. Imagine your family has to decide between a vacation in Florida or another state. Choose a different state. Then compare why your family might visit Florida instead of the other state (or vice-versa). Write some of your reasons here. Use comparatives and superlatives in your discussion.

EXERCISE 13. Vocabulary Practice: Word Knowledge

Circle the word or phrase that is most closely related to the word or phrase on the left. Use a dictionary to check the meaning of words you do not know.

Vocabulary	Answer Choices	
1. a destination	a person	a place
2. worse	very bad	very good
3. complex	very difficult	very important
4. temperature	destination	weather
5. likely	probable	recent
6. cuisine	food	maps
7. complicated	hard	nice
8. common	many people do it	almost nobody does it
9. latest	easiest	newest
10. an injury	earn your salary	hurt your body
11. we're into shopping	every day	right now
12. recent	in the future	in the past
13. climate	calendar	weather
14. successful	bad results	good results
15. an event	a person	a thing
16. controversial	people agree	people disagree
17. tough	difficult	smart
18. commute	persuade	travel
19. local	from a nearby place	with many new people
20. significant	important	unusual
21. wealthy	a lot of money	a lot of time
22. groceries	you buy them	you drop them
23. a brochure	you read it	you turn it
24. down the road	at the bottom	in the future
25. a fare	money	time
26. typical	unique	usual
27. altitude	land	water
28. figure out	know, understand	say, speak
29. obvious	easy to make	easy to see
30. beaches	flying	swimming
31. efficient	it makes you smarter	it uses time well
32. risky	dangerous	important
33. humid	dry	wet

EXERCISE 14. Vocabulary Practice: Collocations

Fill in each blank with the answer on the right that most naturally completes the phrase on the left. If necessary, use a dictionary to check the meaning of words you do not know.

Vocabulary	Answer Choices	
1. my reason _____ doing that	for	of
2. is taller _____	from	than
3. plenty _____ reasons	of	with
4. keep _____	to work	working
5. among _____	this state	these states
6. to _____ honest	be	do
7. even _____	fast	faster
8. difficult _____ to understand	for me	to me
9. agree _____ a price	on	with
10. an effective _____	method	situation
11. a _____ bomb	high	powerful
12. a dark _____	account	color
13. _____ a decision	make	take
14. a controversial _____	cloud	speech
15. a wealthy _____	number	woman
16. reserve a _____	friend	ticket
17. _____ rather	I'd	I've
18. a _____ risk	faster	greater
19. _____ as long as	once	twice
20. a comfortable _____	boss	sofa
21. _____ more expensive	much	very
22. a crowded _____	person	place
23. is more dangerous _____	than	that
24. a _____ of stairs	flight	trip
25. flip a _____	button	coin
26. she's _____ to coffee	addicted	controversial
27. an efficient _____	toy	way
28. a significant _____	problem	temperature
29. according _____	for	to
30. invest your _____	food	money
31. a closer _____	place	disease
32. I'd rather _____	go	going
33. What _____ the food like?	does	is

EXERCISE 15. Writing Practice

Part 1. Editing Student Writing
Read these sentences about one student's opinion about a current topic. Circle the 15 errors. Then write the number of the sentence with the error next to the type of error. (Some sentences may have more than one error.)

_____ a. comparative and superlative   _____ d. verb tense

_____ b. *other/another/others*   _____ e. article

_____ c. no verb

Buying Something Valuable in an Online Auction
1. I recently took part in online auction for four tickets to Paris.
2. I like buying things online, and I take part in online auctions all time.
3. The reason I'm so excited about this auction for trip to Paris is that I won the tickets!
4. Yes, my price was the higher, so the seller was selling the tickets to me.
5. A ticket to Paris not cheap. In fact, a trip to Paris is usually around $1,800 per person.
6. My first price was $400 per ticket, but the seller did not agree to that price because it was too lower.
7. Other prices have been higher than mine. For example, there were many people with bids between $600 and $800.
8. Each day the trip prices got more higher. I didn't want to wait other day.
9. The deadline was midnight last night. At 11:55 PM, I offer $1,100 per ticket.
10. I have to admit that $1,100 is more that I wanted to pay.
11. I decided to offer this price because I really wanted to go to Paris or other place in Europe.
12. I incredibly surprised to find out this morning that the seller accepted my offer, so now the tickets were mine!

Part 2. Original Student Writing

Imagine that you and some friends are at a restaurant and want to order dessert. Write a dialogue or a paragraph in which you discuss three or more options for dessert. Give specific reasons to explain why each dessert is better or worse than the other. Use comparatives and superlatives in your writing. Underline examples of this grammar in your writing.

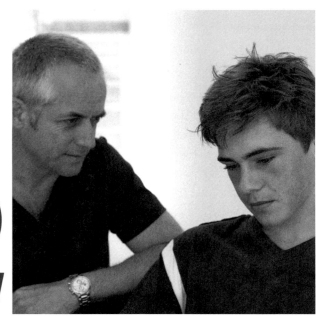

Unit 12

Modals

Discover the Grammar

Read the conversation between a father and his son, and then answer the five questions.

Line	
1	*Son:* Dad, <u>may</u> I use the car tonight?
2	*Father:* Why do you need my car?
3	*Son:* I told my date that I <u>would</u> pick her up about 7:00.
4	*Father:* If you already told her that you <u>would</u> pick her up at 7:00, you <u>must</u> think
5	that I'm going to say yes. What <u>would</u> you do if I needed the car tonight?
6	*Son:* Um, well, I <u>could</u> ask one of my friends if we <u>could</u> go out with them,
7	or we <u>could</u> take the bus.
8	*Father:* Well, I guess you <u>should</u> try one of those options then because I have
9	to go in to the office at 6:30. Now, I <u>might</u> <u>not</u> have to work tomor-
10	row night, so you <u>might</u> be able to use the car then.
11	*Son:* Thanks, Dad, but I <u>may</u> <u>not</u> have a date tomorrow night.
12	*Father:* I see. Well, in that case, don't forget you <u>have to</u> clean the garage!
13	*Son:* I won't forget. Now, I<u>'d better</u> call my friend to see if we <u>can</u> go with
14	him.

1. Study these sentences from the conversation. Circle the correct meanings of the sentence. <u>Hint</u>: Study the underlined words.

   a. I told my date that I <u>would</u> pick her up at 7:00.
      (it's not planned / it is planned)

   b. . . . you <u>must</u> think that I'm going to say yes.
      (you think it's true / you don't think it's true)

   c. . . . or we <u>could</u> take the bus.
      (it's definite / it's possible)

   d. I <u>might</u> <u>not</u> have to work tomorrow night. . . .
      (I definitely will not / Possibly I will not)

   e. . . . I<u>'d better</u> call my friend. . . .
      (it's very important / it's a pretty good idea)

2. Look at the underlined words in the conversation again. Circle the verbs that follow them. What forms are the verbs after the underlined words? Do they have usual verb endings such as −s, −ed, or −ing? Do they use to (infinitives)?

   _____

   _____

3. Which two of the underlined words are really easy for you to understand? What does each mean?

   _____

   _____

4. Which two of the underlined words are not so easy for you to understand? Why are they difficult?

   _____

   _____

5. These underlined words are called modals. Modals are a type of verb. Have you ever heard of modals? What do you know about modals? What questions do you have about modals?

   _____

   _____

   _____

   _____

Grammar Lesson

Modals

Modals are a special group of verbs. Modals change the meaning of a sentence by giving a special "flavor" or "direction" to the main verb in the sentence. (See Appendix D for a list of modals with meanings or Appendix E for a list of meanings with modals.)

Modals	Examples
can	Can you speak a foreign language?
could	Could you tell me where the bank is?
may	May I sit here?
might	It might rain tomorrow.
must	To apply for a license, applicants must be at least sixteen years old.
shall	The landlord shall provide the tenant with two sets of keys.
should	You should go to the doctor soon. You don't look well.
will	Flight 292 will arrive at noon.
would	Would you read this letter and give me your opinion?
had better	I had better take a nap, or I'll never stay awake in class tonight.
would rather	We would rather take a bus there than drive.

Here are some special phrases with similar meanings to modals. These expressions use to before their main verbs.

Phrasal Modals	Examples
have to	We have to study tonight for the big test tomorrow.
have got to	We have got to study tonight for the big test tomorrow.
ought to	If you are tired, you ought to take a nap.
be able to	Sue likes French movies because she is able to speak French.
be going to	I'm going to take you to the clinic now.

Rule 1. Modals are found between the subject and the main verb.

<u>Sue and Lim</u> can <u>play</u> tennis very well.
　　　　S　　　　　　V

Rule 2. Modals have multiple meanings. For example, **may means permission (May I sit here?)** or possibility (**It may rain tomorrow.**). (The meanings will be discussed in the rest of this unit.)

Rule 3. Modals are a type of verb. Unlike verbs, however, they never have any special verb endings such as –s, –ed, or –ing.

Rule 4. We do not use the word to between a modal and its main verb. (However, it is common between two verbs: **I want to go. I need to study.**)

Rule 5. To form a question, you simply move the modal before the subject: **You can play the piano well. → Can you play the piano well?**

Rule 6. To form a negative, you simply add **not** after the modal. In many cases, a contraction is not only possible but actually preferred: **You can go. → You can't go.**

BE CAREFUL!

Common Learner Errors	Explanation
1. In Argentina, it is a law that all citizens ~~must to vote~~ must vote.	Do not use **to** after a modal.
2. The sky is cloudy, so it might ~~raining~~ rain later today.	The verb after a modal has no endings (**–s, –ed, –ing**).
3. Michelle lived in China for ten years, so she ~~can speaks~~ can speak Mandarin well.	Do not add any endings (**–s, –ed, –ing**) to verbs following modals.
4. ~~Do you can lend~~ Can you lend me $100?	To make questions with modals, do not use **do, does,** or **did.**
5. We ~~don't should~~ should not arrive before noon.	For negatives, do not use **don't, doesn't,** or **didn't** with modals.

ONE-MINUTE LESSON
The modal **shall** is not common in general English. You may see **shall** in legal documents, especially contracts. In addition, you may hear it as a question meaning a very polite suggestion with *I* or *we*: **Shall** *I sit here?* **Shall** *we leave now?*

EXERCISE 1. Identifying Modals and Similar Phrases

Circle the modals and similar phrases in these sentences.

Things You Might Hear in a Supermarket

1. "Could you tell me where the canned beans are?"

2. "In some stores, customers have to bag their own groceries."

3. "Would you like paper or plastic?"

4. "I might buy a chocolate cake for dessert tonight if it's on sale."

5. "These peppers don't look fresh to me. They should be bright green."

6. "If you're going to make hamburgers for everyone, you have to buy more meat than that."

7. "These shrimp are really cheap. At this great price, I might get 20 pounds and freeze them for later."

8. "I know you can cook seafood well, but are you able to cook chicken, too?"

9. "Our local apple trees are not producing fruit yet, so these apples must be from out of state."

10. "I know you love bread, so I want to tell you about this new brand they are selling here. You really ought to try it. It's absolutely delicious."

11. "May I have one pound of provolone cheese, please?"

12. "Yes, I'm pretty sure you ought to be able to buy fresh artichokes there."

13. "I would rather have the larger size, please."

14. "We'd better hurry up and check out because the store is going to close soon!"

Do Online Exercise 12.1. My score: _____ /10. _____ % correct.

EXERCISE 2. Scrambled Sentences with Modals

Unscramble the words to write a correct sentence.

Packing for a Vacation

1. Hey, Gabriela! (going / you / can / tell / me / you / where / on / are / vacation?) I forgot!

   _____

2. Oh, we are going to France. You've gone to France several times, so (tell / you / must / take / me / what / to) !

   _____

3. (walking / good / take / You / shoes / should).

   _____

4. (think / we're / do / Oh, / walking / do / to / of / you / going / a / walking / lot)?

   _____

5. Yes, definitely! (a / lot / take / want / You / also / may / of / to / sweaters).

   _____

6. (sweaters / have / take / to / do / Why / we)?

   _____

7. (at / it / year / Because / cool / can / really / time / get / this / of).

   _____

8. Thanks, Jeanette. (pack / would / too / rather / sweaters / I / than / cold / be / many)!

   _____

EXERCISE 3. Modals and *to*

Add **to** where it is needed. Write an X if **to** is not needed.

Comments People Make about Food

1. If you like tuna fish, we can _____ make tuna sandwiches for lunch.

2. People who are on a diet ought _____ eat salad without oily dressings.

3. The doctor said, "You'd better _____ stop eating fried foods now."

4. What are you going to have? I think I might _____ have the beef stew.

5. To make jambalaya, you have _____ have shrimp and rice.

6. What should we _____ serve at the birthday dinner? We could _____ make two pasta dishes, and one could _____ have meat and the other could _____ be vegetarian.

7. People who can't _____ eat much salt should not _____ eat potato chips.

8. If you guys want _____ have a snack, I'll _____ make some popcorn. How does that sound?

9. People who have food allergies must _____ be very careful about what they eat.

10. What's the cheapest restaurant that we can _____ find in this area?

Do Online Exercise 12.2. My score: _____ /10. _____ % correct.

Grammar Lesson

Using *Might*

KEY
13

might	possibility	A one-way ticket **might** cost more than $400. = It is possible that a one-way ticket costs more than $400.
	negative	**might not**

EXERCISE 4. Meanings of Modals

Read the situations and the three answers. Which of the answers might be true? In some cases, more than one answer might be possible. Write the letters of the correct answers on the line. Study the example. Be ready to explain your answer choices.

Example:

_a, c_   Jack has a small vegetable garden. He worked in the garden from 2 to 6. It was a very hot day. It's 6:15 now.

    a. Jack might be very tired.

    b. Jack might be very rich.

    c. Jack might have tomatoes in his garden.

Explanation: If Jack worked in the hot sun for four hours, it is possible that (a) he is very tired. Jack has a vegetable garden, so (c) is also possible because many people who have vegetable gardens have tomatoes. However, (b) is probably not correct here. We have no reason to think that Jack is a rich person.

_____   1. Jill is going to go on vacation on Saturday. She finishes work at 5. Today is Friday, and the time now is 7.

    a. Jill might be at the office.

    b. Jill might be at home.

    c. Jill might be on an airplane.

_____   2. Linda likes sweets. She is at the store right now.

    a. She might buy a cake.

    b. She might buy a steak.

    c. She might be a child.

_____   3. Sami speaks Arabic. He is from northern Africa.

    a. Sami might be from Saudi Arabia.

    b. Sami might be from Morocco.

    c. Sami might be from Kuwait.

_____ 4. Victor lives in a large city in Canada.

    a. He might live in Toronto.

    b. He might speak French.

    c. He might ride a bus to work.

_____ 5. Peter has a Japanese car.

    a. His car might be a Honda.

    b. His car might be a Toyota.

    c. His car might be a Mercedes.

_____ 6. Judy loves to work with children.

    a. She might be a school teacher.

    b. She might be a vacuum repair technician.

    c. She might be a museum volunteer.

_____ 7. Joe went to school for 16 years.

    a. He might be a high school teacher.

    b. He might be a pediatric specialist.

    c. He might be a heart surgeon.

_____ 8. Kristy loves animals and works with them every day.

    a. She might be a zoo trainer.

    b. She might be a college professor.

    c. She might be a veterinarian.

_____ 9. Steve is at the gym six days per week.

    a. He might be a personal trainer.

    b. He might be a part of the cleaning services staff.

    c. He might be a television newscaster.

_____ 10. Jessica is up driving in her car at 4:00 every morning.

    a. She might be a newspaper delivery woman.

    b. She might be a pilot.

    c. She might be a police officer.

Grammar Lesson

Using *May*

may	1. possibility	A one-way ticket **may** cost over $400. = It is possible that a one-way ticket costs over $400.
	2. permission	**May** I sit here?= Is it OK if I sit here?
	negative	**may not** (no contraction)

EXERCISE 5. Practicing *may* in Sentences

Match the situation on the left with the possible reason or cause on the right by drawing a line between the two that go together best.

Group 1

1. I can't go with you to the movie tonight   because the teacher may give a pop test.

2. Don't touch that spider   if I'm not feeling tired.

3. I stayed up late to study   because I may have to work tomorrow.

4. I may go to Rick's party tonight   because it may be poisonous.

Group 2

5. I don't think we can play tennis today   if this headache doesn't stop soon.

6. I may go to the doctor later   because I don't like my boss.

7. I am studying French   because it may rain.

8. I may quit my job soon   because I may get a job in France.

EXERCISE 6. Practicing Writing Sentences with *may*

Unscramble the words to make a permission sentence or question with **may.** Write your answer on the line. Pay attention to punctuation (**.** or **?**). Follow the example.

1. [?] / help / may / you / I

   A: ___May I help you?_____

   B: Yes, I'd like a hamburger, French fries, and a large soft drink.

2. [.] books / if / three / you / you / card / may / library / have / out / a / check

   A: Hi, I'm a new student here, and I'd like to check out some books.

   B: _____

3. [?] / take / we / photographs / may / here

   A: _____

   B: Yes, but don't use a flash.

4. [?] / I / your / use / telephone / to / may / my / mom / call

   A: _____

   B: Sure. Go ahead. It's on the table near the television.

5. [.] / send / an / to / computer / email / you / my / may / her / use

   A: I need to get in touch with my professor right away.

   B: _____

6. [?] / here / sit / may / I

   A: _____

   B: Sure. No one's sitting there.

7. [?] / see / we / may / map / your

   A: _____

   B: Yes, but I need it back when you are finished looking at it.

8. [?] / I / may / borrow / your / phone

   A: _____

   B: OK, but the signal is not good here.

9. [.] / not / you / may / eat / reservation / without / a / there

   A: Are we allowed to eat dinner in the new dining hall?

   B: Yes, but _____.

10. [!] / heavy / want / may / to / very / you / jacket / take / a

    A: Is it a good idea to go to Iceland in December?

    B: Sure, but _____

ONE-MINUTE LESSON
After the word **finish,** we often put a noun: **I finished dinner at 8.** However, if you want to include an action word associated with that noun, you must add **–ing** to the verb: **I finished eating dinner at 8.**

Grammar Lesson

Using *Can*

can	1. ability	She **can** speak several languages fluently. = She **is able to** speak several languages fluently.
	2. permission	**Can** I sit here? (informal) = Is it OK if I sit here?
	negative	cannot, can't

EXERCISE 7. Sentences with *Can*

Complete the sentences with the correct forms. If the blank is in the first sentence, use **be able to** and if the blank is in the second sentence, use **can.** Follow the example.

1. John isn't able to write Arabic.

   = John _____*can't write*_____ Arabic.

2. They _____ email.

   = They can't send email.

3. Ken and Sam are able to speak French well.

   = Ken and Sam _____ French well.

4. Most people are able to cook spaghetti, but they _____ bread.

   = Most people _____ spaghetti, but they can't bake bread.

5. Nadia's only twelve, so of course she is not able to drive a car yet.

   = Nadia's only twelve, so of course she _____ a car yet.

6. The flowers _____ here because there is not enough sunlight.

   = The flowers can't grow here because there isn't enough sunlight.

7. Many people are able to drive an automatic car, but they can't drive a manual car.

   = Most people _____ an automatic car, but they _____ a manual car.

8. I'm very short, so I'm not able to reach the top shelf in the kitchen.

   = I'm very short, so I _____ the top shelf in the kitchen.

9. He hasn't graduated from college yet, so he _____ medicine yet.

   = He hasn't graduated from college yet, so he can't practice medicine yet.

10. We _____ him because his phone isn't working.

    = We can't reach him because his phone isn't working.

EXERCISE 8. Speaking Practice: What Can You Do?

Work with a partner.

Step 1. The left column is your list. There are 18 actions. Put a check mark (✔) by five of the actions. Do not let anyone see your list. You can choose actions that you really can do, or you can choose actions that you cannot do. You do not have to tell the truth.

Step 2. Work with a partner. Take turns trying to guess each other's list. Student A begins by asking about any of the actions. For example, "Can you bake a pineapple cake?" If Student B has a check mark by that action, then Student B says "Yes, I can," and it is still Student A's turn to ask questions. When Student B says "No, I can't" to a question, then it is Student B's turn to ask a question.

Step 3. The winner is the first student to guess all five of his or her partner's actions.

Your List	*Your Partner's List*
_____ play tennis	_____ play tennis
_____ speak French	_____ speak French
_____ fly on a plane	_____ fly on a plane
_____ run 100 meters in 10 seconds	_____ run 100 meters in 10 seconds
_____ drive a race car	_____ drive a race car
_____ ski down a really high mountain	_____ ski down a really high mountain
_____ understand science well	_____ understand science well
_____ sing high and low notes	_____ sing high and low notes
_____ say the alphabet backward	_____ say the alphabet backward
_____ bake a pineapple cake	_____ bake a pineapple cake
_____ eat really spicy food	_____ eat really spicy food
_____ read Japanese	_____ read Japanese
_____ add and subtract quickly	_____ add and subtract quickly
_____ operate a computer	_____ operate a computer
_____ rollerblade	_____ rollerblade
_____ write with your left hand	_____ write with your left hand
_____ drink coffee without milk or sugar	_____ drink coffee without milk or sugar
_____ cook rice	_____ cook rice

EXERCISE 9. Conversations with *can* and *may*

This exercise has eight small conversations in it. Some dialogues use *can* or *may* to ask permission, and others use *can* to express ability. Read Speaker A's comment on the left and then find what Speaker 2 probably says in response. Write the letter of Speaker B's response on the lines on the left. Follow the example.

Speaker A

___d___ 1. Can Michael drive?

_____ 2. Can Michael drive your car?

_____ 3. May I sit here?

_____ 4. Hey, can you go with us to the beach tomorrow?

_____ 5. Excuse me. May I use this telephone?

_____ 6. Can you operate this computer? It looks kind of hard.

_____ 7. Can I borrow twenty dollars until the day after tomorrow?

_____ 8. Can elementary school students have cell phones at school?

Speaker B

a: No way! My insurance only covers me.

b: I know it looks hard, but actually, it's pretty easy. Let me show you.

c: Actually, I'm saving this seat for my friend. Sorry.

d: Yes, he can. He has a license. He knows how to drive well.

e: I'm really sorry, but I'm broke.

f: No, my father said that I have to stay home to help clean the house.

g: A long time ago schools made rules against that. Young children don't have any need for them.

h: Let me ask my supervisor. If she says no, there is another one down the hall.

Do Online Exercise 12.3. My score: _____ /10. _____ % correct.

Grammar Lesson

Using *Could*

KEY
13

could	1. polite request	**Could** you tell me where the bank is? = Please tell me where the bank is.
	2. past ability	When I was a child, I **could** run much faster. = When I was a child, I was able to run much faster. <u>Note:</u> Do not use **could** to express past ability in the affirmative for a specific event. *At the house this morning, I* ~~could~~ *withdraw $200.* Use *was able to.* In the negative, both are possible.
	3. suggestion	You **could** fly to New York. It's not so expensive now. = I suggest flying to New York.
	4. conditional	If I had a million dollars, I **could** travel anywhere. = I don't have a million dollars, but if I received the money, the money would allow me to travel anywhere.
	5. possibility	Mark **could** be at work now, but I'm not sure. = It is possible that Mark is at work now, but I don't know.
	negative	**could not, couldn't**

ONE-MINUTE LESSON
When the word **stop** tells the name of the action that you finished or ended, you must add **–ing** to that word: **He can't stop running**.

EXERCISE 10. *Could* = Polite Request

Part 1.

Unscramble the words to make a request with *could*. Write your new question on the line. Pay attention to punctuation [?]. Follow the example.

a. [?] me museum the of location you please tell the could

   Could you please tell me the location of the museum?

b. [?] salad and please glass of could you a me a iced tea bring

   _____

c. [?] in front of you this bag during takeoff put you under the seat could please

   _____

d. [?] could again please word you explain that

   _____

e. [?] change you give could please dollar for a me

   _____

f. [?] please watch could price tell me you the of this

   _____

g. [?] window you open could please the

   _____

Part 2.

Match the polite requests in Part 1 to the responses in Part 2 by writing the letter of the request by the number of the response. The first one has been done for you.

1. __f__   OK, let me see. The sale price for this month only is $49.95.

2. _____   Sure. Would you like lemon with your tea?

3. _____   I already tried, but I can't. I think it's stuck.

4. _____   OK. A dilemma is a kind of problem. It's a situation when you don't really know what to do. For example, if you like your current job a lot, but another company offers you more money, do you change jobs? Part of you wants to stay, and part of you wants to leave. This is a dilemma. Is that clear now?

5. _____   I already have another bag there. Could you put this in the overhead compartment?

6. _____   Go to the corner and turn left. Go two blocks. It will be on your right.

7. _____   Sure. Would you like four quarters?

EXERCISE 11. Sentences Practicing *can* and *could*

Underline the correct modal in each sentence.

1. When I was in junior high school, I (can't, couldn't) drive a car.

2. People who live in Paris (could, can) see the Eiffel Tower every day.

3. Zachary practices basketball every day, so he (can, could) play very well.

4. When I was little, I (could, can) spend time with my grandparents every day.

5. In college, I (can, could) stay up very late, but now it's very difficult!

6. After many years of practice and lessons, I (could, can) now speak French.

7. My pet bird is very talented! He (can, could) open a box to get a treat inside.

8. When I was in high school, I (could, can) sing in front of people. Now I'm too scared!

9. Brittany (can, could) cook an amazing lasagna, so we should ask her to come over and make one for us!

10. Justin (could, can) run very long distances in college, but when he hurt his knee, he had to stop running.

Do Online Exercise 12.4. My score: _____ /10. _____ % correct.

EXERCISE 12. Expressing Past Ability

Correct or wrong? Read each sentence carefully. Look at the underlined part. If the underlined part is correct, circle the word *correct*. If it is wrong, circle the word *wrong*. Then write the correction above the mistake.

correct   wrong   1. *A:* Did you ever find your German-English dictionary?

B: Yes, I <u>found</u> it.

correct   wrong   2. *A:* Did you ever find your German-English dictionary?

B: Yes, I <u>could find</u> it.

correct   wrong   3. *A:* Did you ever find your German-English dictionary?

B: No, I <u>wasn't able to find</u> it.

correct   wrong   4. *A:* Did you ever find your German-English dictionary?

B: No, I <u>couldn't find</u> it.

correct   wrong   5. *A:* Did you talk to Martha last night?

B: No. I called and called, but I <u>couldn't reach</u> her.

correct   wrong   6. *A:* Did you talk to Martha last night?

B: Yes, finally I <u>could talk</u> to her at 11:30.

correct   wrong   7. *A:* Did you pass your driving test yesterday?

B: No, I <u>wasn't able to pass</u> it. I might try again next week.

correct   wrong   8. *A:* Were you able to get your driver's license yesterday?

B: No, I <u>couldn't get</u> it. I have to try again.

correct   wrong   9. *A:* How was Mr. Crawford's speech at the meeting?

B: It was great. He <u>could give</u> a really wonderful speech!

correct   wrong   10. *A:* Where is Carolyn?

B: Finally she <u>could get</u> her visa for Russia, so she's at the travel agency now making flight and hotel reservations.

EXERCISE 13. Speaking Practice: *could* for Suggestions

Read these situations, and then write a suggestion for the person using **could.** When you have finished, discuss your possible answers in small groups. Who has the most interesting suggestion? The best suggestion? The funniest suggestion? Follow the example.

1. *Problem:* "I don't know what to do. My friend gave me a new CD, but I already have this same CD. On the one she gave me, she wrote "Happy Birthday" with a black pen, so I can't return this CD to the store."

    Suggestion: ___You could sell your first CD at a used CD store.___

2. *Problem:* "My son is not doing so well in school. He was a very good student, but recently his grades haven't been very good. I don't want to put a lot of pressure on him. Any suggestions?"

    Suggestion: _____

    _____

3. *Problem:* "I have a big test next Monday, but I don't really understand the material that is going to be on the test. I have tried to read the book, but I just don't understand it."

    Suggestion: _____

    _____

4. *Problem:* "It's my cousin's birthday, but I don't know what to get her. I like her a lot, and I want to get a very special gift for her, but I just don't have any ideas for a present. The last time I saw my cousin in person was back in 1989, so I don't really know her very well."

    Suggestion: _____

    _____

5. *Problem:* "I need some change to make a phone call. I have a one-dollar bill but no coins. What are my possibilities?"

    Suggestion: _____

    _____

6. *Problem:* "There is a big dinner party tomorrow night at a good friend's house. I'm sure she will serve meat for the main course, and some of the vegetable dishes may have bacon in them. I'm a vegetarian. I don't know what to do."

    Suggestion: _____

    _____

Grammar Lesson

Using *Will*

will	1. future	According to the report, the rain will be heavy. = The report says the heavy rain is coming.
	2. polite request	Will you explain this grammar point to me again? = Please explain this grammar point to me again.
	negative	will not, won't

<u>Note</u>: We normally use *be going to* for a previously planned trip: *What are you going to do tomorrow? I'm going to visit my aunt.* We usually use *will* for spontaneous decisions: *Ok, I'll call you when I arrive in Miami because I don't want you to worry.* We can use either *will* or *be going to* for predictions (such as weather).

EXERCISE 14. *will* and *be going to*

Fill in the blanks in these conversations with **will** or **be going to**. Sometimes both are possible.

1. A: What _____ do next Saturday?

   B: Hmmm, I don't know. Why?

2. A: Oh, no! No one brought ice. That's the end of this party!

   B: Don't worry. Listen. I have an idea. I have a car, so I _____ go to the store to get some ice.

3. A: Do you think Luke _____ get that job in Boston?

   B: I don't know. I hope he gets it.

4. A: Jen, I _____ go to the post office. Do you have anything to be mailed?

   B: No, but thanks for asking.

5. A: Erin, can you take me to the bank now? I need to cash this check.

   B: Sure. I _____ drive you there.

6. A: Why do you have that suitcase with you?

   B: Because I _____ fly to Los Angeles when school finishes today.

7. A: Wow, this box is heavy!

   B: Don't lift that by yourself. I _____ help you with it.

8. A: I saw Doug this morning. He has his driving test today.

   B: Yes, I saw him, too. He was a little nervous, but I think he _____ pass the test this time!

9. A: Excuse me.

   B: Yes, I _____ be with you in a minute. Let me make one more phone call, OK?

10. A: Man, it's so hot in here! Could you please open that window?

   B: Sure. I _____ do it.

EXERCISE 15. Requests with *will* and a Reason

Draw a line to connect the **will** requests with the correct explanations. Follow the example.

1. Will you pass me the salt?	I can't answer it by myself.
2. Will you tell me the time?	I wonder if it needs more salt.
3. Will you help me with this question?	I can't reach it.
4. Will you taste this soup?	I forgot my watch today.
5. Will you turn up the volume?	I'd like to call you.
6. Will you open your books to page 200?	Time is up.
7. Will you be home later?	I can't hear it very well.
8. Will you please pass in your papers?	Today's class is about the map on that page.

Do Online Exercise 12.5. My score: ____ /10. ____ % correct.

EXERCISE 16. Original Requests with *will*

Complete each request with the words **Will you please** and a question mark, and then add a good reason. Your reason should end with a period.

1. ___Will you please___ turn up the radio?

   I'd really like to hear the morning traffic report. _____

2. _____ help me pick up this box

   _____

3. _____ get me some ice

   _____

4. _____ hand me that book

   _____

5. _____ turn off the light in the living room

   _____

6. _____ eat lunch with me today

   _____

7. _____ get me a new pen

   _____

8. _____ feed my fish while I'm on vacation

   _____

Grammar Lesson

Using *Would*

would	(1) offering, inviting	**Would** you like some tea? = Do you want some tea?
	(2) polite request	**Would** you read this letter and give me your opinion? = Please agree to read this letter and give me your opinion.
	(3) conditional	If you received a hundred dollars from your father, what **would** you do? = You have not received a hundred dollars from your father, but if that happens, what is your plan?
	negative	**would not, wouldn't**

KEY
13

EXERCISE 17. *want* and *would like*

Complete the sentences with the correct forms. If the blank is in the first sentence, use **want,** and if the blank is in the second sentence use **would like.**

1. (want)   <u>Do</u> you <u>want</u>
   to play tennis this evening?

   (would like) <u>Would</u> you <u>like</u>
   to play tennis this evening?

2. (want)   I _____ some coffee
   with cream.

   (would like) I _____ some coffee with cream.

3. (want)   They _____ some help with the homework.

   (would like) They _____ some help with the homework.

4. (want)   _____ you _____ to watch TV with us?

   (would like) _____ you _____ to watch TV with us?

5. (want)   Why _____ you _____ to stay at that hotel? It's
   not very good.

   (would like) Why _____ you _____ to stay at that hotel? It's
   not very good.

6. (want)   _____ you _____ a sandwich? We have several
   different kinds of meat.

   (would like) _____ you _____ a sandwich? We have several
   different kinds of meat.

7. (want)   I _____ another sandwich, please. They're really great!

   (would like) I _____ another sandwich, please. They're really great!

8. (want)   _____ the teacher _____ us to type our reports?

   (would like) _____ the teacher _____ us to type our reports?

EXERCISE 18. Speaking Practice: Making Requests with *would*

Read the description of the people in the conversation. Then write two possible requests with **would** for each person. Follow the example. When you finish, compare your answers with other students.

1. A dentist is speaking to a patient.

   Would you please sit here?

   Would you open your mouth wide and say "Ah"?

2. A teacher is talking to the students in his or her class.

   _____

   _____

3. A customer is talking to a taxi driver.

   _____

   _____

4. Debra is speaking to her friend Julia. Julia is at the front door of Debra's house. Julia is visiting Debra.

   _____

   _____

5. Paul and Ben are making plans for the weekend. Saturday is Ben's birthday.

   _____

   _____

6. Mary and Adam are in the same English class. They have a huge test on Monday. Mary is worried about her grade on the test.

   _____

   _____

7. Stephan is interested in taking karate classes. He is visiting the school, and he has questions about the price and when the classes meet.

   _____

   _____

8. Carlos needs to take the TOEFL® exam. He wants to buy the best study guide, but he is not sure which one to purchase. His friend Omaida just took the exam last month.

   _____

   _____

9. Maddie and Gregg are sitting in the family room together. Maddie is too warm.

_____

_____

10. Robin hurt her ankle and is resting on the sofa. She is thirsty, and Brad is walking by the room.

_____

_____

Grammar Lesson

Using *Should* and *Ought To*

KEY
13

should/ ought to	1. advising, suggesting	I like both shirts, but I think you **should** get the red one. = I think it's a good idea for you to get the red shirt. <u>Note</u>: It is common to say *I think* before you use *should* because it sounds nicer.
	2. expectation	We **should** have 52 cards, but there are only 50. = I expect us to have 52 cards, but we don't.
	negative	**should not, shouldn't** **ought not to (no contraction)**

EXERCISE 19. Using *should* to Give Advice

Read the situations, and write a sentence in which you give some advice to the person with a problem. Follow the example. (Remember that we usually say *I think* when we use *should*.)

1. Irene works very hard. She is often very tired because she works so much. She never takes a vacation, and she always stays at the office very long hours. What do you think about her situation?

   I think she should take a vacation as soon as possible.

2. Mr. Findley is a math teacher. Two of his students were cheating on the last test. Gina gave some answers to Peter. What do you think Mr. Findley should do?

   _____

3. Laura has a job offer in a much larger city, but she prefers small towns. The new job pays almost triple her current salary for the same amount of work. What do you think Laura should do?

_____

4. Officer Johnston stopped a driver for speeding. The driver said that the reason he was speeding was that he was late for a very important meeting. What do you think Officer Johnston should do?

_____

5. Ryan is supposed to give a speech on Tuesday night for his class, but his favorite band is playing that night. He really wants to go to the concert, but if he reschedules his speech he will have to ask a classmate to change days with him. What do you think Ryan should do?

_____

6. Sandra has made plans to go out for her best friend's birthday, but her brother is coming into town that evening and wants to visit her. She has arranged some fun activities for her friend, but she does not want to disappoint her brother. What do you think Sandra should do?

_____

7. Terrell needs to go to campus to buy a book, which will only take a few minutes. There is no student parking available near the bookstore, but there are plenty of faculty/staff parking spaces open. What do you think Terrell should do?

_____

8. Brooke took pictures of her friends and her grandparents at her birthday party, and she gave away all of her prints to her friends. Her grandmother called her and asked for some pictures of the party, but she doesn't have any left. What do you think Brooke should do?

_____

9. Jay accepted an unpaid internship at a law firm for the summer, but he now has an opportunity to travel to Italy and stay for free with his cousins. What do you think Jay should do?

_____

10. Jackie is my best friend, and she just started going out with Danny, a person that I don't like very much. Jackie keeps asking me what I think of Danny. I know she's going to ask me about him, so what should I say? I care for her and want her to be happy.

_____

EXERCISE 20. Using *should* and *ought to*

Read these strange or unusual situations. Tell what the problem is by writing how the situation should be. Use **should** or **ought to.** (They have the same meaning.)

1. A: I just called Jill, but she wasn't home.

   B: That's strange. It's 8:30, so she _should be home now. (OR ought to be home now.)_

   _____.

2. A: This spaghetti is still hard.

   B: That's strange. I cooked it for fifteen minutes, so _____

   _____.

3. A: Oh, no. This check is wrong.

   B: What do you mean?

   A: It's only for one week of work, but I worked for two weeks, so_____

   _____.

4. A: Hey, this box of crayons has only nine crayons.

   B: Wow, you're right. One is missing. The box _____

   _____.

5. A: I think the teacher made a mistake with my grade.

   B: What do you mean?

   A: Well, the test has one hundred questions, and I missed nineteen, but the teacher wrote seventy-one on my test.

   B: Yeah, that's wrong. Your score _____

   _____.

6. A: Can you believe this weather? I can't believe how hot it is!

   B: The weather forecaster on TV said that the weather is warmer than usual now.

   A: I heard that, too. Today's high temperature will be 92 degrees, but this is extremely unusual for this area of Canada for September.

   B: Yeah, the weather _____

   _____.

Do Online Exercise 12.6. My score: _____ /10. _____ % correct.

7. *A:* I think we're out of dishwashing detergent.

    B: What? I just bought three bottles last week! They were on sale.

    A: Really? I just looked under the sink for more. The only one I can see is almost empty.

    B: I can't believe that! There _____

    _____.

8. *A:* What's this?

    B: It's a late notice on the electric bill. Didn't you pay it?

    A: Yes, I mailed a check over a week ago for the full amount.

    B: Well, if it's been over a week, the check_____

    _____.

Grammar Lesson

 Using *Must* and *Have To*

must / have to	1. obligation, necessity	You **must** be at least sixteen to apply for a license. = You **have to** be at least sixteen to apply for a license. <u>Note:</u> **Must** is more formal and is more common in writing. **Have to** is more common in speaking and is often pronounced as *hafta*.
	2. conclusion	The new music store is huge. They **must** have thousands of CDs there. = I conclude that they have thousands of CDs there.
	negative	**must not, mustn't; do not have to, don't have to**
<u>Note:</u> *must* and *have to* have the same meaning, but the negatives are different. *You must not go = Do not go!* *You don't have to go = You can go, but it is not necessary or required.*		

EXERCISE 21. Using *must* in Formal Situations

Draw lines to connect the part of the sentence in the middle column to the correct phrase that comes before it and the correct phrase that comes after it.

1. Canadians must   turn off their computers   in order to travel to Egypt.

2. Job applicants must   register for classes   by the day before the semester begins.

3. All passengers must   get a visa   before the plane can take off.

4. New students must   get a vaccination   by August 27.

5. All first graders must   sign their applications   against measles.

EXERCISE 22. Using *have to* in Informal Situations

Draw lines to connect the part of the sentence in the middle column to the correct phrase that comes before it and the correct phrase that comes after it.

1. The teacher has to   eat vegetables and fruit   before we can go to the movies.

2. I have to   finish this homework   because they are getting old.

3. Children have to   read that book twice   because she has an important meeting.

4. We have to   help my parents   so they can be healthy and strong.

5. You have to   end class a little early   in order to understand its message.

EXERCISE 23. Speaking Practice: Things I Have to Do

Read each situation. Then make a list of five things you have to do in that situation. When you finish, compare your answers with a partner. Choose the best three answers that you and your partner can think of.

Situation A. You are going to take a vacation in London. The month is November. You are going to be there for a week. You don't know anyone there. This is your first trip to London. What are five things that you have to do?

I _____ .

I _____ .

I _____ .

I _____ .

I _____ .

Situation B. You are going to have a dinner at your house. You want to invite about 15 people. What are five things that you have to do?

I _____ .

I _____ .

I _____ .

I _____ .

I _____ .

Situation C. You are moving from your current place (house or apartment) to a new place. It is not very far (only about fifteen minutes by car). You want to move out on Friday and move in on Monday. What are five things that you have to do?

I _____ .

I _____ .

I _____ .

I _____ .

I _____ .

EXERCISE 24. Using *must* for Conclusions

Read the sentences, and then write a logical conclusion. Follow the example.

1. *Clue 1:* The new student's name is Pierre Rousseau.

   Clue 2: He speaks English with a French accent.

   Question: What can you guess about Pierre's nationality?

   He must be French.

2. *Clue 1:* Jack got up very early this morning. Then he worked at the office from 7:30 to 3:30.

   Clue 2: He helped his neighbor paint her house from 4:30 to 5:45.

   Question: Jack told you yesterday that he might want to play tennis tonight. Jack just called to tell you that he cannot play tonight. Why do you think he can't play?

   _____

3. *Clue 1:* Dan accidentally broke a vase at my house last night.

   Clue 2: Dan just came to my house, and he has a small gift about fifteen inches high and twelve inches wide. The box is not very heavy.

   Question: What do you think is in the box?

   _____

4. *Clue 1:* Brenda had a big exam yesterday in chemistry, which is her worst class.

   Clue 2: She found out today that she got a 96 (out of 100) on the exam.

   Question: How do you think Brenda feels right now?

   _____

5. *Clue 1:* Keith told you that his new Nissan car is parked in front of the school.

   Clue 2: There are only two Japanese cars in the parking lot. The red one is a Toyota, and the blue one is a Nissan.

   Question: What can you guess about the color of Keith's new car?

   _____

6. *Clue 1:* Your friend Frankie announced his engagement to Suzanne last month.

   Clue 2: You received a beautiful, large, engraved envelope from Frankie and Suzanne.

   Question: What can you guess about the contents of the envelope?

   _____

7. *Clue 1:*   Your next-door neighbor's son jumped too hard on their large sofa and broke it.

   Clue 2:   A store delivery truck arrived and is parked in front of their house.

   Question: What can you guess about the contents of the delivery truck?

   _____

8. *Clue 1:*   Felix is flying to Milwaukee sometime today.

   Clue 2:   You just tried calling Felix, but his cell phone goes directly to voicemail.

   Question: What can you guess about where Felix is right now?

   _____

Grammar Lesson

Using *Had Better*

KEY
13

had better	very strong advice or warning	You'd better leave now, or you'll miss the bus. = If you don't leave now, you will miss the bus.
	negative	had better not (no contraction)

ONE-MINUTE LESSON

Be careful with the modal **had better.** It is used from a person of higher power to a person of lower power. Parents can use this phrase with their children, but never vice versa! *Parent: You'***d better*** finish doing your homework now!*

Do Online Exercise 12.7. My score: _____ /10. _____ % correct.

EXERCISE 25. Practicing *had better*

Draw lines to match Sentences 1–6 with Sentences a–f to make six mini-conversations.

1. I don't have to show you my license. Why are you bothering me?

2. Do you think two chickens will be enough? Henry and Abby can really eat a lot.

3. OK, I'll see you at the party tonight, and I'll have ten bags of ice with me.

4. I wrote this paper myself.

5. This steak is cooked. Look. If you cut it, there is no pink part.

6. I don't want to eat any more.

a. You'd better clean your plate, or you can't have any dessert.

b. I know that you didn't write this. These are not your own words. You'd better tell me the truth, or I'll give you an F for sure.

c. Sir, you had better show me your license now. You were speeding. You were going 50 miles per hour, but the speed limit here is only 30.

d. I don't want to argue. You'd better bring me another steak, or I'll ask to speak to the manager.

e. You're right. We'd better cook three chickens just to make sure we have enough food. Those two like to eat a lot!

f. OK, you'd better not forget, and you'd better not be late. We can't start the party without that ice!

EXERCISE 26. Editing: Is It Correct?

If the sentence is correct, put a check mark (✓) on the line. If it is not correct, write X on the line, and circle the mistake. Then change the sentence to make it correct. Write the change above the sentence. (*Hint:* There are eight sentences. Two are correct, but six have mistakes.)

_____ 1. I really love my car, but I should to have a bigger one.

_____ 2. Tom was late, so he not could call his girlfriend.

_____ 3. Children in this country must go to school until they are 16 years old.

_____ 4. In the United States, we no one can drive on the left side of the street.

_____ 5. You must be quiet! We shouldn't wake the baby!

_____ 6. That could be the most ridiculous thing I've ever heard. You can be joking!

_____ 7. Terri left two hours ago, so she can be here by now. It shouldn't take her this long to get here.

_____ 8. The doctor says I should to lose weight. I have to do it for my health.

EXERCISE 27. Mini-Conversations

Circle the correct words in these eight mini-conversations.

1. A: Barbara hasn't eaten all day. She (must, can) be so hungry!

   B: OK, I'll ask her if she (would rather, should) have a sandwich or a salad.

2. A: Brett doesn't know if he (ought to, is going to) take three or four classes this summer.

   B: Well, I think he (should, might) take only three. Don't you think four is too many?

3. A: (Must, Would) you have lunch with me today?

   B: Yes, I think I (would rather, can). I'm free all day!

4. A: My grandfather is 91 years old. I don't think he (should, shall) drive.

   B: You (will, ought to) take him for a driving test if you're worried.

5. A: Have you seen my new shoes? I (wouldn't, can't) find them anywhere!

   B: If you can't find them, maybe you (should, shall) put them away in the closet next time.

6. A: Ugh! This box is too heavy. I (couldn't, can't) lift it!

   B: OK, don't worry! I (will, had better) help you with that.

7. A: I (must, am going to) go to the store later. Do you need anything?

   B: Yes, I do. I (will, am going to) make a list for you.

8. A: (Can, Will) I smoke in here?

   B: No way! This is a hospital, and you (haven't got to, can't) smoke in a hospital in the United States.

Do Online Exercise 12.8. My score: _____ /10. _____ % correct.

EXERCISE 28. Sentence Study for Critical Reading

Read the original sentences. Then read the three answer choices, and put a check mark (✓) in the yes or no boxes in front of each sentence to show if that answer is true based on the information in the original sentence. If there is not enough information to mark something as yes, then mark it as no. Remember that more than one true answer is possible.

1. Sean's broken leg has healed, so he's happy that the cast is off and he can go swimming again.

   ☐ yes ☐ no a. Sean had to wear a cast on his arm because he broke it.

   ☐ yes ☐ no b. His doctor told him that it was OK to get the cast wet.

   ☐ yes ☐ no c. He is happy because the cast is off and he can swim now.

2. I've got an exam during my planned vacation, so I need to take it early.

   ☐ yes ☐ no a. I am going on vacation in three months.

   ☐ yes ☐ no b. I have to take an exam next week.

   ☐ yes ☐ no c. I would like to take my exam when I return from vacation.

3. Since Rich is out of practice on the piano, we suggested that he take lessons again.

   ☐ yes ☐ no a. Rich could play the piano better before.

   ☐ yes ☐ no b. He can play very well now.

   ☐ yes ☐ no c. He ought to take violin lessons.

4. Since you and Jen had a class together last semester, she'll know who you are because she talks to everyone!

   ☐ yes ☐ no a. Jen is quiet, and she isn't able to talk to anybody.

   ☐ yes ☐ no b. She had a class with you last semester.

   ☐ yes ☐ no c. She shouldn't recognize you when she sees you.

5. Since it's Saturday, I assume that the mail carrier will try to get his route completed early.

   ☐ yes ☐ no a. The mail carrier may be here early today.

   ☐ yes ☐ no b. It's Saturday, so he had better not finish his route early.

   ☐ yes ☐ no c. He could come late, though.

6. I missed your dinner party because I had to work late last night.

    ☐ yes ☐ no   a. I will go to your dinner party tonight.

    ☐ yes ☐ no   b. I didn't have to work.

    ☐ yes ☐ no   c. I wasn't able to leave work to attend your party.

7. Since the project is too big, try breaking it up into smaller sections, asking for an extension, or getting someone to help you.

    ☐ yes ☐ no   a. If I were you, I would break the project into smaller sections.

    ☐ yes ☐ no   b. You might ask for an extension on the deadline.

    ☐ yes ☐ no   c. You shouldn't try to get someone to help you.

8. A plane ticket for my vacation to Quebec this year is too expensive, and it's too long of a drive, so I guess my other option is to take the train.

    ☐ yes ☐ no   a. For my vacation this year, I may go to Quebec.

    ☐ yes ☐ no   b. I might have enough money for a plane ticket, so I won't drive instead.

    ☐ yes ☐ no   c. I might go to Quebec by train.

EXERCISE 29. Review Test 1: Multiple Choice

Circle the letter of the correct answer.

1. Where _____ you like to go tomorrow?

    a. may   c. had better

    b. would   d. can

2. The servant at the dinner party said, "Sir, _____ take your coat?"

    a. would I   c. may I

    b. am I able to   d. am I going to

3. I don't understand this word. _____ you explain it to me, please?

    a. Might   c. Will

    b. Should   d. May

4. Your temperature is 99.7. I think you _____ take some aspirin.

    a. should   c. are going to

    b. would   d. will

5. I turned the air conditioner on twenty minutes ago, but it's still hot in here. It _____ be cool in here already.

    a. has to   c. ought to

    b. is going to   d. would

6. My car broke down. I have my cell phone, so I _____ call the car repair shop right now, or I'll be here forever.

    a. must   c. shall

    b. had better   d. would

7. I bought all this paint because I _____ paint my house tomorrow.

    a. will   c. am going to

    b. must   d. would

8. There are many things that we _____ do on Saturday. One idea is to go to the beach. Another possibility is to visit the local art museum. You are my guest, so just tell me what you would like to do.

    a. are going to   c. would

    b. must   d. could

EXERCISE 30. Review Test 2: Production and Evaluation

Part 1.
Read this short passage. Circle the correct modal in the parentheses.

When you give people constructive feedback, you ❶ (should, shouldn't) use a soft tone. You ❷ (may, can't) want to use words like *perhaps* and *maybe* when you give suggestions. What I ❸ (could, would) do is start with a positive item, and then show them a mistake. You ❹ (might, should) want to tell them how to correct the mistake. You ❺ (must, could) also suggest that they find the mistake on their own. If you ❻ (are going to, had better) show them the mistake, you ❼ (have to, shall) use encouraging words. Smiling and being positive ❽ (had better, will) give them confidence in their own work.

Part 2.
Read this short passage. There are five mistakes. Circle the mistakes, and write the correction above the mistake.

I have a huge Spanish exam tomorrow, so I'm going to ask my best friend Staci to help me study for it. Staci is really good at languages. She should be able to help me with the irregular verbs that might appears on the exam. There are other students in the class that I could asked, but Staci is the best person because she is able explain things really well. I haven't called her yet to ask her to help me, so I'd better to call her soon before someone else asks her for help. I'm sure that with Staci's help, I will doing much better on the exam.

EXERCISE 31. Reading Practice: Going to the Doctor

Read this list of recommendations about going to the doctor. Then answer the three questions on page 351. The grammar from this unit is underlined for you.

When you're not feeling well, do you go to the doctor right away? That can get very expensive. Consider these alternatives to paying high medical bills.

First, decide if you really need to go. Of course, if you have a serious problem, you had better get help. However, if you just have a cold, you may get better just as fast if you stay in bed for a day and rest. Think carefully about how you're feeling and see if you could wait a day before going to the doctor. In the meantime, you should eat healthy food and get plenty of rest.

Second, if you must go to the doctor, ask your doctor if you could buy generic drugs. You can find these cheaper medications at your nearest pharmacy. If you forget to ask your doctor, you could also ask the pharmacist if there are any cheaper generic drugs that work just as well as the brand name ones. Of course, you must ask the pharmacist if there are any dangerous side effects to any drugs, brand name or generics, that you take.

Important: Remember that you must not ever use a friend's medications. Only take medications that a doctor has prescribed to you. You can read a lot of useful information on the Internet, but you shouldn't believe everything that you read. Remember that anyone can post something on a personal web page; they don't have to be experts and they don't have to back up their opinions with research. For serious medical conditions, you should consult a trained professional only.

1. What are the author's three recommendations?

    _____

    _____

    _____

2. Do you agree that these three things are very important to do? Why or why not?

    _____

    _____

    _____

3. Have you ever done these things? Why or why not?

    _____

    _____

    _____

    _____

    _____

    _____

    _____

    _____

EXERCISE 32. Vocabulary Practice: Word Knowledge

Circle the word or phrase that is most closely related to the word or phrase on the left. Use a dictionary to check the meaning of words you do not know.

Vocabulary	Answer Choices	
1. a dessert	a place	a thing
2. a customer	at a bank	at a hospital
3. shrimp	you draw it	you eat it
4. a landlord	a person	a thing
5. hurry up	do carefully	go quickly
6. might	absolutely	perhaps
7. a citizen	an animal	a person
8. a flavor	taste	touch
9. check out	at the airport	at the supermarket
10. an applicant	a person	a thing
11. it's stuck	it can't move	it can't talk
12. bake	bread	salad
13. a dilemma	a meeting	a problem
14. bacon	fruit	meat
15. turn off	start	stop
16. I guess	I think	I would like
17. a dentist	your skin	your teeth
18. give a speech	to a friend	to a group
19. disappoint	negative	positive
20. a snack	a kind of animal	a kind of food
21. to reach (my mom)	speak (with her)	travel (with her)
22. speeding	very fast	very slow
23. May I use yours?	Can I use it?	Should I use it?
24. a spider	four legs	eight legs
25. add	clouds	numbers
26. lift	pick up	turn up
27. your opinion	what you purchase	what you think
28. a garage	a car	a pet
29. fluently	a little	well
30. hand me a thing	buy it for me	pass it to me
31. a divorce	end a marriage	start a marriage
32. a firm	a person	a place
33. the takeoff	going down	going up

EXERCISE 33. Vocabulary Practice: Collocations

Fill in each blank with the answer on the right that most naturally completes the phrase on the left. If necessary, use a dictionary to check the meaning of words you do not know.

Vocabulary	Answer Choices	
1. _____ sale	in	on
2. _____ a nap	do	take
3. an _____ tree	apple	apples
4. I'll _____ you up at 7.	pick	take
5. _____ sure	cute	pretty
6. bright _____	gray	yellow
7. _____ a date	have	take
8. it might rain _____	later	yesterday
9. one pound _____ cheese	from	of
10. in that _____	case	time
11. to _____ your groceries	bag	pack
12. _____ up	hurry	rapid
13. I _____ better leave now.	have	had
14. _____ awake	come	stay
15. study _____ a test	for	to
16. this _____ of bread	brand	product
17. apply _____ a license	for	to
18. a one-way _____	person	ticket
19. _____ in touch with someone	get	turn
20. it's kind of _____	cloudy	weather
21. _____ an email	make	send
22. she's _____ work	at	in
23. a poisonous _____	snake	wheel
24. she is _____ a diet	in	on
25. spend _____	information	time
26. the weather _____ cold	got	put
27. don't eat _____ foods	fried	frying
28. _____ ahead	go	say
29. _____ rather	could	would
30. _____ this area	in	on
31. several _____	time	times
32. quit a _____	job	trip
33. go on _____	vacation	work

EXERCISE 34. Writing Practice

Part 1. Editing Student Writing

Read these sentences about a couple's wedding plans. Circle the 15 errors. Then write the number of the sentence with the error next to the type of error. (Some sentences may have more than one error.)

_____ a. modal

_____ b. preposition

_____ c. verb tense

_____ d. word order

_____ e. article

_____ f. possessive

Ben and Haley's Wedding
1.   The last May, Ben and Haley decided to get married.
2.   To get married, they first had to get a license marriage.
3.   To get their license, they went for City Hall.
4.   When they got there, they have to speak to special clerk.
5.   The clerk said, "If you want to get this kind of license, you need your birth certificate. The rule on this is clear. You may have all your papers."
6.   Haley had hers, but Ben didn't have him.
7.   Haley got angry to Ben.
8.   Haley said, "Ben, I have reminded you yesterday that you should to bring your documents."
9.   Haley and Ben drove home for get his documents.
10. They returned to same office again and spoke to the manager officer.
11. Haley asked, "Where should we to sign our names?"
12. The clerk got the license for Ben and Haley, so they were finally able to have them wedding.

Part 2. Original Student Writing

You have traveled abroad a few times, but your friend is going to Europe (or another distant country) for the first time. Write sentences or a paragraph offering suggestions on what to pack, places to visit, or items your friend should buy for his or her spring trip. Practice modals in your writing, and underline them.

Appendix A: Parts of Speech

Category	Definition	Examples
noun	a name of a person, place, or thing	*Maria, a store, a book*
verb	shows action or state of being	*eat, take, is*
pronoun	takes the place of a noun	*he, him*
adjective	describes a noun or pronoun	*good, delicious, green*
preposition	shows relationships	*in, with, for*
conjunction	connects	*and, because, if*
adverb	describes verbs, adjectives, or other adverbs	*quickly, very, extremely*
interjection	expresses strong emotion	*Wow! Oh! No!*

Appendix B: Verb Tenses

Tense	Example
simple present	*I* drive *to my office every day.*
simple past	*I* lived *in an apartment in 2009.*
simple future	*I* will help *you with that job.*
present progressive	*I* am reading *these verbs right now.*
past progressive	*I* was watching *TV during the storm last night.*
future progressive	*I* will be flying *to Japan at midnight tonight.*
present perfect	*I* have been *here since 9 AM today.*
past perfect	*I* had been *in France twice before.*
future perfect	*I* will have finished *this work by midnight.*
present perfect progressive	*I* have been living *in Sacramento for two years.*
past perfect progressive	*I* had been reading *all night.*
future perfect progressive	*I* will have been working *here for thirty years.*

Appendix C: 60 Irregular Verbs

All verbs in English have three basic forms: **present, past,** and **past participle**. The past and past participle forms of **regular verbs** use *–ed*. (These two forms are the same.)

Present	*Past*	*Past Participle*
play	played	played
work	worked	worked
react	reacted	reacted

The past and past participle forms of **irregular verbs** are different. Common endings for the past participle forms of irregular verbs include *–en, –ne,* or *–n*, but there are many possibilities. For some verbs, the irregular forms are the same for both past and past participle forms.

Present	*Past*	*Past Participle*
see	saw	seen
go	went	gone
wear	wore	worn
put	put	put

English has thousands of verbs, but only a small number are irregular. Students must memorize the irregular forms that are most commonly used.

Present	Past	Past Participle	Present	Past	Past Participle
1. be	was/were	been	31. leave	left	left
2. become	became	become	32. lend	lent	lent
3. begin	began	begun	33. let	let	let
4. break	broke	broken	34. lose	lost	lost
5. bring	brought	brought	35. make	made	made
6. build	built	built	36. meet	met	met
7. buy	bought	bought	37. put	put	put
8. catch	caught	caught	38. read	read	read
9. choose	chose	chosen	39. ride	rode	ridden
10. come	came	come	40. run	ran	run
11. cost	cost	cost	41. say	said	said
12. cut	cut	cut	42. see	saw	seen
13. drink	drank	drunk	43. sell	sold	sold
14. drive	drove	driven	44. send	sent	sent
15. do	did	done	45. show	showed	shown
16. eat	ate	eaten	46. sing	sang	sung
17. fall	fell	fallen	47. sit	sat	sat
18. feel	felt	felt	48. sleep	slept	slept
19. find	found	found	49. speak	spoke	spoken
20. fly	flew	flown	50. spend	spent	spent
21. forget	forgot	forgotten	51. steal	stole	stolen
22. freeze	froze	frozen	52. swim	swam	swum
23. get	got	gotten	53. take	took	taken
24. give	gave	given	54. teach	taught	taught
25. go	went	gone	55. tell	told	told
26. have	had	had	56. think	thought	thought
27. hit	hit	hit	57. understand	understood	understood
28. hold	held	held	58. wear	wore	worn
29. keep	kept	kept	59. win	won	won
30. know	knew	known	60. write	wrote	written

Appendix D: Modals and Meanings

Organizing by Modal: Modals and Multiple Meanings		
Modal	**Meanings**	**Examples**
might	possibility	*A one-way ticket might cost more than $400.*
may	(1) possibility	*A one-way ticket may cost more than $400.*
	(2) permission	*May I sit here?*
can	(1) ability	*She can speak several languages fluently.*
	(2) permission	*Can I sit here? (informal)*
could	(1) polite request	*Could you tell me where the bank is?*
	(2) past ability	*When I was a child, I could run much faster.*
	(3) suggestion	*You could fly to New York. It's not so expensive now.*
	(4) conditional	*If I had a million dollars, I could travel anywhere.*
	(5) possibility	*Mark could be at work now, but I'm not sure.*
will	(1) future	*According to the report, the rain will be heavy.*
	(2) polite request	*Will you explain this grammar point to me again?*
would	(1) offering, inviting	*Would you like some tea?*
	(2) polite request	*Would you read this letter and give me your opinion?*
	(3) conditional	*If you received a hundred dollars from your father, what would you do?*
should / ought to	(1) advising, suggesting	*I like both shirts, but I think you should get the red one.*
	(2) expectation	*We ought to have 52 cards, but there are only 50.*
must	(1) obligation, necessity	*The rule book says that applicants must be at least 16 years old to apply for a license.*
	(2) conclusion	*The new library is huge. There must be thousands of books in it.*
had better	strong advice or warning	*You'd better leave now, or you'll miss the bus.*

Appendix E: Meanings with Modals

Organizing by Meaning: Modals and Multiple Meanings		
Meanings	**Models**	**Examples**
request	can	*Can you tell me where the bank is?*
	could	*Could you tell me where the bank is?*
	would	*Would you read this letter and give me your opinion?*
	may	*May I have your full name?*
	might	*Might I offer you some tea? (formal)*
permission	can	*Can I sit here? (informal)*
	could	*Could I sit here?*
	would	*Would you mind if I sit here?*
	may	*May I sit here?*
necessity	must, have to	*The rule book says that applicants must be at least 16 years old to apply for a license.*
possibility	may, might, could	*A one-way ticket may cost more than $400. (50% chance)*
	should, ought to	*A one-way ticket should cost more than $400. (better chance)*
	must	*A one-way ticket must cost more than $400. (almost certain)*
	will	*A one-way ticket will cost more than $400. (definite)*
advisability	should, ought to	*I like both shirts, but I think you should get the red one.*
	had better	*You'd better leave now, or you'll miss the bus.*
expectation	should, ought to	*We should have 52 cards, but there are only 50.*
conclusion	must	*The new library is huge. There must be thousands of books in it.*